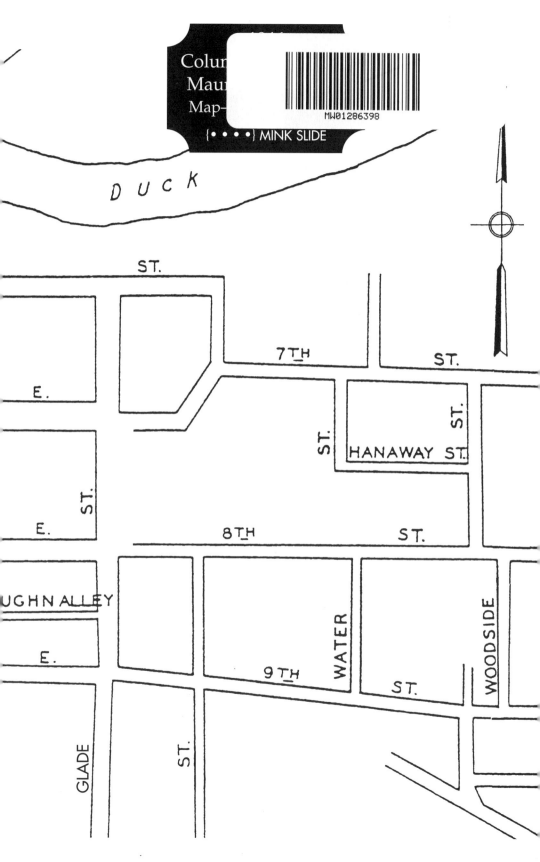

Colu...
Mau...
Map—

{• • • •} MINK SLIDE

MW01286398

DUCK

ST.

7TH   ST.

E.

HANAWAY ST.

ST.   ST.

E. ST.

E.   8TH   ST.

UGHN ALLEY

WATER

WOODSIDE

E.

9TH   ST.

GLADE

ST.

No More Social Lynchings

Robert N. Skard, M.D.

No More Social Lynchings

Robert W. Ikard

HILLSBORO PRESS
Franklin, Tennessee

TENNESSEE HERITAGE LIBRARY
Bicentennial Collection

Printed in the United States of America

01   00   99   98   97   5   4   3   2   1

Library of Congress Catalog Card Number: 97–68416

ISBN: 1–57736–031–1

Cover by Bozeman Design

HILLSBORO PRESS
an imprint of
PROVIDENCE HOUSE PUBLISHERS
238 Seaboard Lane • Franklin, Tennessee 37067
800-321-5692

To my parents,
Mr. and Mrs. Robert Edwin Ikard,
who always took pride and pleasure in
Columbia, Maury County, Tennessee, and
contributed mightily to this, their hometown.

Contents

Preface   ix
1. Dimple of the Universe   1
2. More Than an Argument over a "Small Debt"   11
3. A Walk into Darkness   27
4. The THP Bull in a Racial China Shop   37
5. Big (and Strange) Fish in a Little Pond   51
6. Federal Grand Jury   63
7. The Trial in Tennessee   79
8. One More Time   105
9. A Hemi-Century Perspective   115
Epilogue   131
Abbreviations   143
Notes   145
Bibliography   169
Index   175

Preface

During my years of specialty postgraduate work and practicing surgery, I had studied history for pleasure and to expand my intellectual perspective. Despite extensive reading and modest publication, I correctly saw myself as a rank amateur historian. I sought to modestly rectify that status by taking history courses at Belmont University in Nashville, Tennessee.

In seeking a subject for such a course in the summer of 1995, I decided to study an event vaguely remembered from my childhood, the 1946 "race riot" in Columbia, Tennessee. The only image I recalled was that of an olive-clad soldier walking beside me on the sidewalk of the main drag of West Seventh Street within one block of the imposing grey, three-story, domed courthouse. He carried a rifle and seemed to be a powerful military man to a curious, unsophisticated eight-year-old lad. My parents raised me in a disciplined home to honor them, the Presbyterian Church, and the United States. I therefore felt (in addition to a delicious hint of danger) awe and obeisance for this authority figure who represented everything that was right about my nation. After all, this was just after the great World War II, and everyone respected our boys who had rescued the world from Hitler and Tojo.

I had not the vaguest idea that others in my town might see such soldiers as oppressors or that the reason for their domestic deployment was a harbinger of postwar riots and several decades of national racial realignment. Those pending troubles were inapparent even after 1946. Recurrent experiences reminded me of the discriminatory, illogical fact of legal segregation. There was the derision of teenage boys' laughter as I mistakenly drank from the "colored" fountain, only feet away from the "white" one in the McClellan's five-and-dime store. Much more uncomfortable was the dictum against allowing blacks to eat ice cream or drink soda pop at the drugstore fountain on the square where I worked when twelve years old.

I had "slept out" with the children of black tenants on the property where we too rented and, in high school, enjoyed playground basketball with blacks. However, no blacks were in my school. My parents said segregation must end. My father, in particular, said that if I went away to school (presumably north), I would certainly meet interesting, intelligent, and ambitious black students. Still, I was untroubled by local conditions and apparently accepted Columbia common wisdom that "they just aren't ready" for integration and full citizenship.

I graduated from high school a decade after the riot and enjoyed the stimulation of family and friends interested in current affairs. Yet, I could recall no conversation in depth about this stark disruption of local calm. Townsfolk rarely discussed it, but when they did, they inevitably used hushed, rushed voices.[1] Twenty years after the event, the local daily newspaper's reminiscence column remembered the riot date, February 25, 1946, with squibs on a hospital circle meeting, the Maury County Garden Club, and a meeting of the Women's Society of the Williamsport Methodist Church.[2] In addition to learning *just what happened*, I also hoped to discover the reasons for this continually cursory local treatment—whether fear, embarrassment, or lack of knowledge about the riot and its import.

I found much more information than could be used in the summer project. Inevitable side stories to the main event became intriguing and important to me. Most of the participants from a half-century ago were dead, and many of those still alive had poor recall or hesitated to discuss their roles or perspectives. Such challenges served as impetuses, not frustrations, to a search for the truth about the mysterious riot that had riven my town.

Some semantical choices deserve explanation. Many blacks and critics of authorities' management of the Columbia affair object to its being called a "riot." They interpret that offensive action such as an invasion or wanton destruction must occur before a fracas can be called a "riot." I cannot, however, find a dictionary that defines the word that way. *Riot* has become the prevalent historic designation, which seems accurate enough and will be used herein.

In this era of heightened sensitivity, a word about racial vocabulary is appropriate. My parents insisted their children respect and be courteous to societal segments and individuals. A key feature of that necessary politeness was to avoid demeaning designations. The prevalent "nigger" was absolutely forbidden. "Colored" was acceptable but the precise "Negro" preferred. It was understandable if the southern tongue occasionally lapsed into "nigra." However, that laziness of diction could never segue for us to the prohibited epithet. Similarly, writing the term was inexcusable.

All materials reviewed for this work are naturally replete with contemporaneous designations—*darkie, boy, girl*, etc. Some of these will be used in the narration to convey a sense of the time and an accurate representation of my sources, both personal and archival. My final arbiters in this jargon matter were the many black citizens I came to know during the research. The majority had no particular labeling preferences and liked the balanced *black* and *white*. Most shared the author's disdain for the multisyllabic, divisive *African American*. I have used the terms with which they were most comfortable.

East Eighth Street in Columbia was called "Mink Slide" by most blacks and all whites. Many blacks came with time to consider this a derogatory, undignified term—yet another bit of Negro jargon that colorfully defined their separate but secondary status. I understand that judgment of the name but will use the designation—for separateness was the cause of the riot. Besides, it is a clever term, and I accept it as having no negative racial connotations.

I have acquired considerable information from trial records, newspapers, and personal interviews. I encountered the historian's inevitable challenge of finding the truth from contradictory stories, as participants' veracity ranged from dead solid, verifiable truth through dissimulation and obfuscation to (euphemistically) prevarication. The initial comment about memories isn't judgmental. A scientific fact—after fifty years, memories fail. This problem is relevant to historians and explains many of the contradictions I encountered. In correlating resultant opinions, versions, and accounts, I always sought corroboration. When confirmation of fact was unavailable, I tried to be as objective as possible.

I am incapable of providing a comprehensive social or historical analysis of the riot. I will only give cursory placement and analysis of the situation and some of its nationally important participants in the Civil Rights movement. Instead, I seek to tell the story fully and accurately before all of its participants are gone. This is a narrative, and professional social scientists may use the recorded truth as they will.[3]

There may be criticism of bias because this story is told by a local son. That potential distortion though seems outweighed by my zeal to honestly understand my home county and its people—including their strengths and weaknesses, successes and failures, truths and falsehoods—in relation to the pivotal 1946 disturbance. I will not anachronistically apply current standards. This is a story about those folks in that time.

CHAPTER ONE

Dimple of the Universe

FIRST CENTURY

The author and historian John Trotwood Moore lived in Columbia, Tennessee, during the late nineteenth and early twentieth centuries. During that time, he coined the phrase "Dimple of the Universe" in reference to the Middle Tennessee or Nashville basin, the geologic remnant of a huge prehistoric lake. The rim of that basin was the watershed of the Cumberland and Tennessee Rivers.

From general usage, "The Dimple" was co-optated by Maury County as its own proud designation. The county was blessed with natural riches: good water from the serpentine Duck River, a temperate climate (mean annual temperature, 59.3° F), more than fifty inches of rain per year, and fertile soil, especially rich in limestone and phosphate. The terrain, rolling hills with an elevation of five hundred to one thousand feet, was covered with plentiful timber. "If ever there was a second Eden formed for man, here it was." All of Giles and portions of Bedford, Hickman, Lawrence, Lewis, and Marshall Counties were later created from Maury, leaving a residual area of 614 square miles.[1]

Cherokee, Chickasaw, and Shawnee Indians had long hunted the benign and bountiful region. In the late eighteenth century, settlers came from the Carolinas and Virginia to claim land grants awarded for Revolutionary War service. The inevitable struggle between natives and the predominantly Protestant, Scots-Irish immigrants officially ended to

1

the detriment of the Indians with treaties signed at Tellico (1805) and Washington (1806). The Tennessee State Legislature chartered Maury County, named for prominent Williamson Countian Abram Maury, in November 1807.

By similar enactment, the legislature incorporated the growing village of Columbia in November 1817. The town was laid out on a hill south of the Duck River, into which drainage flowed. Columbia's aggressive early leaders recognized the town's considerable potential and proposed it as Tennessee's permanent capital. Unfortunately their bid lost out to Nashville.[2]

Early in Maury County history, one of its sons achieved the highest national prominence. James K. Polk took his secondary education and first practiced law in the county before serving as a U.S. congressman and Tennessee governor and becoming the eleventh president of the United States in 1844. He retired to Tennessee after an honorable and productive term as chief executive. His last trip to Columbia was in April 1849, two months before his death.[3]

Middle Tennessee did not have huge plantations nor a reliance on a single cash crop, a situation characteristic of the Deep South. In Maury County, non-slave owners were slightly in the white majority, and the average inventory of slaves among the better agricultural counties in Middle Tennessee was twelve. Only 5 percent of slaveholders had thirty or more slaves. Still, there were more than twelve thousand slaves in Maury County, and several farmers owned more than a hundred. Some farm operations, most less than one thousand acres, were large enough to support self-sufficient plantations on which some of the most beautiful mansions in the South were built.[4]

By 1860, Maury County had a strong, agriculture-based economy featuring diverse crops. Cereals, particularly corn, grew well in the mineral rich soil. Important secondary crops included tobacco, cotton, and vegetables. As in the Lexington, Kentucky, basin to which the county was often compared, the ability to grow bluegrass made livestock production profitable. After Davidson County, it had the most valuable land in Middle Tennessee.[5]

Along with the rest of the western two grand divisions of Tennessee, Maury County came down foursquare for the Confederates in the Civil War. On June 8, 1861, the electorate voted 2,731 to 58 for secession. Judge William Turner estimated the county contributed around twenty-one companies to the war, including the Maury and Bigby Grays. Though no major battles were fought in the county, opposing armies continually marched through it and frequently used Columbia for headquarters throughout the war.

Two native Maury combatants left historic Civil War footprints. Brigadier General Gideon Pillow, a political-officer, amply demonstrated the South's unpreparedness and spotty generalship with his role in the first major Confederate loss, the debacle at Fort Donelson. Sam Watkins was from the other end of the command chain. This literate, feisty, enlisted man wrote perhaps the archetypal account of an infantryman's perspective of war in his memoir, "*CO. AYTCH,*" *Maury Grays, First Tennessee Regiment.*[6]

INTO THE MODERN ERA

Recovery from the war was well underway by 1876. Economic security was tenuous, however, and unlike prior to the war, wives had to participate in the economy more directly. Still, Maury was the third wealthiest county in Tennessee, after Shelby and Davidson.[7]

By the turn of the century, Maury County population had grown from 7,772 (whites) in 1810 to 42,703 (all races). Though there was some manufacturing prior to the emergence of the phosphate industry, the economy was still agriculturally based. Farmers used the excellent soil to grow cereals, grasses, fruits, and vegetables. Rich bluegrass pastures supported the horse-breeding business, as well as dairy and beef cattle. Before the turn of the century, a short-lived racing industry developed that featured a unique, kite-shaped track on which the world record was set for the paced mile. Phosphate mining was becoming increasingly important. In 1888, William Shirley discovered phosphate rock, a product of materials deposited in the water occupying the central basin in the Paleozoic era, while digging in an old Yankee breastwork. Initial mining of several quickly discovered sites mainly employed men with picks. As digging and refining technology evolved, chemical companies, most prominently Monsanto, flocked to the county to produce both phosphate fertilizers and elemental phosphorous. By 1946, approximately 1.5 million tons per year were mined in Tennessee. Eight phosphate companies in Maury County employed about twenty-four hundred people.[8]

Yet, Columbia was truly famous for its mules. This peculiar product of a mare and donkey was the preeminent source of tillage and hauling power in the poor South until after World War II. Columbia had become a center for mule trading well before the Civil War. Acknowledged as the "largest street mule market in the world,"[9] the town was widely known for the selection and quality of mules available on its trading days, the first Monday of each month. By the late 1930s, some sixteen thousand to twenty thousand mules were sold each year in Columbia for approximately two million dollars.[10]

Celebration of this unique segment of the county economy was formalized in 1934 with the designation of the first Monday in April as Mule Day. By the next year, the festival was noted enough to draw the attention of Will Rogers. He turned down an invitation to be marshall that year but likened "Mule Street in Columbia for Mules to Maiden Lane in New York for Diamonds."[11] Postmaster General Jim Farley, Governor Prentice Cooper, and sixty thousand others attended the magnificent 1940 celebration, which featured "1,000 girls on 1,000 mules." Farley's address dedicating the new post office during Mule Day was carried on national radio—high cotton for a town of approximately ten thousand folks.[12]

Since before the Civil War, Maury County citizens had been proud of its numerous, high-quality educational institutions, some of which were

Mule Day in Columbia. (Picture postcard courtesy—Ridley Wills II)

well known throughout the South. Among these were Woodward Academy, Jackson College, Columbia Female Institute, Columbia Athenaeum,[13] Branham and Hughes Military Academy, and Columbia Military Academy. By the end of World War II, only the latter of these private schools was active. The county public schools were deemed good, though no one published extravagant claims about them. There was no evidence that general educational achievement was in any way exceptional. In the most recent census, only 488 people were known to have completed four or more years of college. By 1946, six public high schools for whites existed and two for blacks, College Hill in Columbia and Clark Training in Mt. Pleasant.[14]

In 1946, Maury County seemed prosperous, having a versatile economy buoyed by inexpensive Tennessee Valley Authority (TVA) electricity. Taxable property exceeded twenty-one million dollars. Total crop and livestock values were more than ten million each. The previous year's manufactures had been worth twenty million dollars. This economy was the product of a static World War II county population of 40,357 (74.8 percent white and 25.1 percent black) and a Columbia population of 10,579.[15] With the burgeoning phosphate industry, no one anticipated trouble in absorbing returning veterans. No clouds were apparent on the local economic and social horizons.

THE OTHER SIDE

After World War II, politicians and businessmen could honestly and proudly trumpet Maury County's past and confidently predict an even better future. Only careful attention to what was *not* present in such praises would cause an observer to recognize that the Dimple of the Universe was a typical Upper South, segregated society that did not advocate or anticipate any immediate disruption of its two tiers.

Publications rarely mentioned blacks except to enumerate their schools and churches. The prevalent assumption that they were suited for and should be happy with lives of agricultural or industrial labor had not changed since the turn of the century. Just as the officially sanctioned *Century Review* referred to "a gang of negroes" working the phosphate mines, a pre-1946 Columbia Chamber of Commerce pamphlet on Mule Day showed an old Negro in overalls with his mule above the caption, "A Nigger and a Mule, Companions in the Good Earth."[16]

Blacks were employed traditionally as laborers and domestics. Of 4,107 employed non-whites counted in the 1940 census, 60 percent of men worked as operatives or laborers, farm or otherwise. Seventy-eight percent of females were domestic workers. Ninety blacks were listed as professionals; most were probably educators.

Because of the increased opportunities for industrial employment in phosphate and other industries, people were moving to town. Urban population had increased 73 percent since the 1930 census, while rural population had grown only 2 percent. However, Maury was still a rural county. In 1946, 66 percent of people lived in the county; 45 percent of the total lived on farms. Though blacks constituted 25 percent of the population, they owned only 13 percent of the farms. These 460 properties were not choice either, representing only 4 percent of county-farm valuation.[17] Such data were typical for Middle Tennessee.

The history of race relations in Maury County, which one could not discern between the lines of any local newspaper or civic publication, was perhaps not so characteristic. Prior to the Civil War, there had been a small and ineffective manumission movement in the area. Possibly because of its relatively large plantations and slave population, the county was particularly sensitive to anything that might lead to rebellion. It had one of the few Tennessee ordinances prohibiting the education of blacks and enforced the mandate by whipping violators. Columbia was a federal garrison town after the war, and occupiers noted an especially angry lack of reconciliation among returning Maury Confederate veterans, who openly talked about restoring slavery.[18]

The Ku Klux Klan originated in Giles County, Maury's southern neighbor, in the spring of 1866. A chapter was established in Columbia by 1867, and Maury County soon became the "banner Ku Klux county in Tennessee,"[19] with a membership of several hundred. Regardless of its oft asserted original goals of fraternity, harmless mischief, and protection of southern womanhood, the Klan soon became an unlawful instrument to intimidate, torture, and occasionally kill blacks and their alleged allies.

The Maury Klan seemed to be pacesetters in these felonious regards. The local Freedmen's Bureau agent in December 1867 reported the first use of night riding for the purpose of terror. Robed in mysterious garments, they frequently patrolled Columbia's streets with the tacit and often official acceptance, through deputization, of local lawmen. The Maury Klan performed whippings and occasionally murdered. They apprehended Seymour Barmore, a white detective hired by Governor

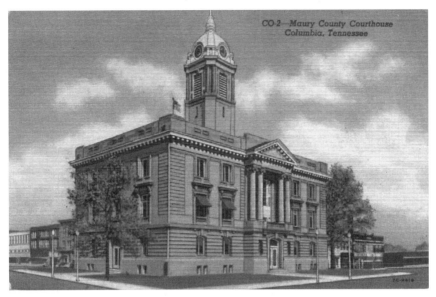

Maury County Courthouse. (Picture postcard courtesy—Ridley Wills II)

Brownlow to infiltrate the Klan. In January 1869 at midnight as Barmore's train passed through Columbia, they shot and hung him. Weeks later, his body was retrieved from the Duck River, a frequent terminus for Klan victims.[20]

Well into the twentieth century, the violent element of Maury County was still committing the ultimate act of racial terror, lynching, and getting away with it! On November 11, 1927, a young, black man allegedly attacked Sarah Harlan, a sixteen-year-old, white girl, as she waited for her school bus. A spontaneous posse apprehended eighteen-year-old Henry Choate. Though Harlan never directly implicated him, Choate had been in the vicinity and had scratch marks on his face. The angry mob reluctantly turned their captor over to Sheriff Luther Wiley, who promised a speedy trial in appreciation of their generosity. This was one day before the Democratic primary in which the sheriff sought reelection for, among other reasons, destroying lots of stills.[21]

That night, a mob of seventy-five to one hundred unmasked men broke into the county jail with sledge hammers. The sheriff's wife, the mother of the alleged victim, a Methodist minister, and an editor of

Nashville newspaper the *Tennessean* (who was in town for a speech) pleaded for calm and due process. A cowed deputy handed over Choate. The teenager supposedly confessed before being killed, either by blows to the head or from subsequent hanging from the west, second-story portico of the courthouse.

Various ministers and officials decried the act. While presiding over a grand jury, District Judge W. B. Turner spoke out against such violence yet exonerated the responsible officers. The *Daily Herald*, the principal county paper, shuddered at the breakdown of law enforcement by "solemnly sworn defenders of the state" who "stood supinely by." Sheriff Wiley lost the nomination by fifty-eight votes. The grand jury did not indict for murder because no one would positively identify any perpetrators.[22]

Six years later, an eerily similar lynching occurred in Maury County. A Negro woman, Tenny Cheek, had long worked for the Lauris Moore family of Glendale. Her son, seventeen-year-old Cordie, had been a childhood pal of nineteen-year-old Henry Carl Moore. By November 16, 1933, however, friction had developed between the two young men. Cordie cut some wood that day for the Moores and accidentally tore the dress of eleven-year-old Lady Ann Moore with a splintered log. Henry Carl persuaded his adopted sister to accuse Cordie of rape.

After Cordie Cheek was arrested, officials chose to sequester him in the Davidson County jail for his protection. The Maury County Grand Jury found no evidence to indict him, and the relieved youth left jail on December 15 to go to his aunt's home near Fisk University in Nashville. That afternoon, several armed, white men in two Ford cars "arrested" him and took him back to Maury County. Just after dark before a large crowd of people at the junction of the Lewisburg and Culleoka highways, the kidnappers dragged Cheek on the ground behind an automobile, castrated him, and lynched him. Several in the crowd shared a pistol, taking turns to shoot the lifeless body. After being summoned by an anonymous call, Sheriff Claude Godwin found him hanging from a cedar tree.[23]

Thomas Jones, president of Fisk, kept the story alive in Davidson County. He obtained the support of Nashville leaders, including prominent ministers, lawyers, educators, and the editors of both white city newspapers, the *Nashville Tennessean* and the *Nashville Banner*. He persuaded Governor Hill McAlister to offer a reward for the killers and Judge Chester Hart to concede that either Davidson or Maury County could claim jurisdiction in the case. Civic resolutions arose. The case seized the attention of the National Association for the Advancement of Colored People (NAACP) and the Inter-racial Commission. However, despite solid identifications of license plate numbers and several kidnappers, including Henry Moore, activity surrounding the case declined. Two successive Davidson County Grand Juries brought no true bills, and the governor lost his enthusiasm, expressing traditional southern resentment against outside interference.

The crime barely made a ripple in Maury County. Civic leaders concluded Cheek was guilty and deserved the mob's vengeance. Sheriff Godwin maintained that as long as Negroes raped little, white girls, nothing could be done about lynching! The *Daily Herald* editorialized that the lynching was cruel but that the authorities had not pressed hard enough to solve the original "crime against society."[24]

WHAT KIND OF PLACE?

In 1946, Maury County had obvious strengths—a strong agricultural economy producing diverse crops from good soil, emerging industries based on phosphate mining, and a historic interest in education. Author Erskine Caldwell could never have patterned *Tobacco Road* after this place, which was prosperous and apparently peaceful, without obvious class acrimony.[25] Maury County had a pleasant climate; the esthetic bonus of gorgeous, antebellum homes built by the county's second generation leaders; and Mule Day, a colorful, clever holiday.

Yet, this image must not have appeared so rosy from the economic and racial underside or for those with any future vision. Blacks remained notably poor and uneducated in Columbia. The first black admitted to a University of Kentucky graduate school, Lyman Johnson, grew up in Columbia and graduated from College Hill High School, where his father was principal. After obtaining fame and success in Kentucky, he swore never to return to Columbia, where "Negroes had no opportunity at all." Racial harmony was rooted firmly in caste, blacks and whites knowing their places and by all appearances living amicably within them.[26]

Behind the community closet door of peace, order, and prosperity, however, lurked some sociopathic skeletons. How civilized was it that the potential for lynching, whether as victim or executioner, apparently was still a part of the social equation to many Maury Countians? Whites had hung two young blacks within the generation, and in response, there had been protest from some pulpits and podiums but no general outcry. The justice system had failed to indict, much less convict, any killers. The county was, as most other communities, populated by people of diverse strengths, capabilities, honor, and courage. It was a place of contradictions from which had come both a president and lynch mobs—a place of amity and injustice.

Contrary to future accusations, no identifiable person or group could have imagined that this seemingly bucolic, relatively modern, and naturally blessed place would disrupt into riot. In the momentum of postwar adjustment, Maury Countians and their leaders had not remembered that the only predictable certainty is uncertainty.

CHAPTER TWO

More Than an Argument over a "Small Debt"

THE RADIO

February 25, 1946, was a mild, cloudy late-winter day in Columbia.[1] This was a "blue Monday" or "farmer's relaxin' day"[2] when farmers did much of their town business. Though perhaps not as busy as the first Monday of each month when mules were traded, the downtown streets were bustling. Columbia seemed to be emerging from the economic doldrums of the war. The *Herald* editor had noted just how crowded the streets had been with cars the previous "Saddy" and questioned how bad conditions would be when autos "really came on the market again."[3]

The courthouse square was typically busy for a blue Monday where folks gathered to shop the retail stores and socialize on the low concrete wall surrounding the lawn. Within the big stone building, legal business was also brisk. A new circuit court grand jury had just sat, and prosecutors representing citizens of the Eleventh Judicial Circuit, including Giles, Lawrence, Maury, and Wayne Counties, presented evidence before Judge Joe Ingram.

Gladys Stephenson was interested in none of this. The black, thirty-seven-year-old mother of four would never have been casually circulating among the white, mostly male crowd. A Columbia native, she was visiting from her home in Detroit, and with her son James, was trying to complete a prolonged and frustrating retail transaction. More than two months prior, she had taken her children's radio to the Castner-Knott appliance store on the square for repair and been given a cost estimate of eight to ten dollars.

11

However, she had not observed the sign stating that merchandise unclaimed after thirty days would be sold for charges. When her seventeen-year-old son, John, went to get the radio, it was gone.[4]

With neither family knowing it, the first interface between the Stephensons and the Flemings had occurred. Twenty-eight-year-old William "Billy" "Willie" Fleming was one of five brothers from the nearby village of Culleoka, and he had been in World War II. He had served in the Pacific and spent some time in a Veteran's Administration hospital in Memphis. After learning radio repair skills through the GI Bill, he had worked at Castner-Knott since December 1945.

Billy's brother, twenty-four-year-old Flo, had been a navy pharmacist's mate, second class, and had been discharged early because his twin was killed in the Pacific. He had run for the Democratic nomination for Maury County sheriff against the incumbent, J. J. Underwood, in October 1945 and won by 34 votes of 2,929 cast. In one-party Middle Tennessee such a

Gladys Stephenson and her
children, John and Lelia.
Photograph is blemished.
(Courtesy—James Stephenson)

victory usually guaranteed the same in the general election, and Flo would become the youngest sheriff in county history in August 1946. The primary election was marred by a recently passed state law allowing for somewhat imprecise registration of veterans and charges of fraud, particularly at the Culleoka box.[5]

The Stephenson family also had multiple members who had served in the military. Gladys's former husband, then living in Chicago, had marched across Europe in the Army Signal Corps. Her eldest son, James, also known as "Junior," "Jimmy," and "June Pie," had lied about his age, left College Hill High School, and enlisted in the navy at age sixteen. He was now nineteen years old, had been discharged in January after serving in the South Pacific aboard the USS *Prometheus*, and was visiting Columbia to see his mother. He had hated the lack of opportunity in the South and planned to live in a large northern city, perhaps pursuing a career in athletic instruction.[6] First though he was to make some history in his hometown.

When the Stephenson radio went unclaimed after thirty days, Billy had given it to his father, John, to sell to a worker on his farm for twenty dollars. Gladys still wanted the radio and achieved successful intercession with the store through a lady for whom she was currently doing domestic work. Although the merchant accommodated and retrieved the appliance, Gladys's ire was further piqued because repair cost was more than what it had been quoted. A new fee of a $13.75, $17.50 with batteries, was negotiated.[7] An imminent race-riot mountain was to proceed from a financial disagreement of truly mole-hill proportions.

James and John Stephenson picked up the radio for Gladys on Saturday, February 23, not heeding the clerk Lavala LaPointe's reminder that it would need batteries. The repairman had not fixed the wall electric cord as originally requested by their mother. Two days later, mid-morning on this blue Monday, James and Gladys entered the second-floor store to have their original request fulfilled. Though not belligerent, Gladys was clearly displeased. LaPointe, Canadian-born, had a French accent and was nervously having difficulty communicating with his frustrated customer.

It is unclear whether the AC cord was attached (LaPointe's assertion) or that it was bagged with the radio to be taken to another shop (Gladys Stephenson's version). Rising acrimony might have abated but for the intervention of another employee, Billy Fleming. As Gladys descended the stairway, she advised another customer disappointed in the quality of his repair service that he would do well to take his business elsewhere. James, waiting below in the stairwell, heard her tone as being "conversational." Billy Fleming said it was loud. As Fleming followed the

James Stephenson, top row, third from right and his U.S. Navy boxing team. (Courtesy—James Stephenson)

Stephensons out of the store "to get them started down the street," James recognized danger and had Gladys precede him out the door. The door closed between disgruntled customer and unsolicitous clerk. However, James looked back through the door pane in a "challenging" manner. Billy picked up the perceived gauntlet, opened the door, and pursued James onto the street.[8]

Fleming was unaware he was pushing not only another veteran but one of the better South Pacific navy welterweight boxers as well. The "slight, boyish"[9] Stephenson had confidence, courage, and experience. Billy asked, "What you stop back there for, boy, to get your teeth knocked out?" James responded, "Well, if that's what it takes." Fleming then punched James in the back of the head but had bitten off far more than he could chew. James quickly turned around and seized Billy behind the head, throwing three jabs into his face. For his last quick punch James released his clutch, causing Fleming to crash through Caster-Knott's front window.

A biracial scrum then developed on the sidewalk. As James pummeled Billy, a white man jumped onto his back. Gladys joined in to defend her son, and a heavy, white man hit her in the eye and tore her coat. James detached himself enough to protect her from this intercessor, and she ran away to Stephenson's Drug Store on the corner to ask the owner to call the police. The outmatched James, meanwhile, was told, "Boy, you better run!" Standing his ground, June Pie retorted, "Run where?" Returning from the drugstore, Gladys found officers had already arrived and without asking questions had attached their own interpretation to the fight. Police Chief Walter Griffin and Officer W. C. Frazier arrested the Stephensons for disturbing the peace. Bystanders had quietly removed a bleeding Billy back into the store, and from there he was taken to the hospital.[10]

ARREST, BAIL, AND RUMOR

The difficulty and manner in which the Stephensons were arrested varied with describers. The clerk LaPointe said that policemen gave James a "gentle slap" and hit Gladys "gently on the head with a club," depictions corroborated by Chief Griffin. James thought his mother to be excited but denied she resisted arrest. Both described the blows in harsher terms. Regardless the technique, villainy had been assigned. No officer asked details of the fight, and Griffin somehow believed the two Stephensons were fighting between themselves.[11]

The police took the mother and son to the city jail to appear before Magistrate Hayes Denton, a Culleoka politician whose car had allegedly been used in the 1933 abduction of Cordie Cheek from Nashville to his Maury County lynching.[12] At the jail when a policeman asked who the "gal" was, James responded that she was his mother whom he was defending in the brawl. Yet, both seemed resigned to their fates and did not inquire about counsel. When asked if she were guilty of fighting in the streets, Gladys responded that, yes, she was guilty of fighting *back*. James answered similarly, and each was fined fifty dollars plus costs.[13]

As neither could pay, they were taken to the more secure county jail. Shortly after noon, the ante was raised considerably. In spite of Billy's disapproval of "revenge against the darkies" and recommendation that his father not press charges, John Fleming wanted the Stephensons held for attempted murder. Denton canceled the original warrant signed by Griffin and issued one signed by John Fleming. When Gladys asked how long they might be held at the jail, a policeman told her that for what they tried, she was lucky to be living and that she and James would likely be held a long time.[14]

The first rumblings of potential mob action were heard throughout the center of town. A black woman in the jail increased Gladys's alarm by saying that "white people is raising hell uptown." Though less frightened than his mother, James also got an inkling of potential trouble from a

Julius Blair. (Courtesy—Addie Lou Flippen Blair)

member of the ubiquitous Fleming family, brother Flo in his highway patrol uniform. He solicitously inquired if James were hurt, then changed tack and informed the prisoners that "a lot of talk" was going around town. When James inquired just what kind of talk he meant, Flo explained it was "lynching talk."[15]

He also wondered how, not whether, James had cut Billy. Quick rumor had established that Billy had been cut either by James with a knife or Gladys with a sliver of glass. Gladys had iterated at the fight scene that James never carried a knife. James had not known that Billy Fleming had sustained a leg laceration when falling through the store window and tried to explain to Flo the likely etiology of Billy's injury.[16]

Those most vulnerable to mob action were now hearing things that reinforced their fears. Gladys's mother, Hannah Peppers, arrived promptly at the jail where Sheriff Underwood told her the bond had inflated from fifty to thirty-five hundred dollars. She reassured her daughter that she would find help and headed toward East Eighth Street, Mink Slide.[17] When unobtrusively crossing the square, she heard some white men promising to "take them two Stephenson niggers out of the jail and hang them."[18]

She sought aid from the "money men" of the black community, Julius Blair and his son, Saul "Sol," and James Morton. In the absence of elected black officials, these businessmen were recognized as leaders and frequently stood bail for their poor, unofficial constituency. Julius Blair, the seventy-six-year-old, black-community patriarch, had lived in Maury County his entire life. He had barbered since the turn of the century, serving customers of both races. Though he had operated shops on the square, he had purchased property and developed businesses on East Eighth for several years. In later years, he had preferred running his "drugstore" that was actually a soda fountain and confectionary. Saul Blair, a veteran of World War I, had taken over management of the family barbershop from his father.[19]

Thirty-six-year-old James Morton Sr. owned one of the oldest black funeral homes in Tennessee. He was active in civic affairs, including fund-raising for the Red Cross and serving as Negro chairman for the sixth and seventh war loan drives. He and his family lived at the northwest corner of East Eighth and Woodland, the foot of Mink Slide, in a house separated from the funeral parlor by an adjacent church.[20]

Shortly after noon on Monday in the Morton Funeral Home, Hannah presented the case for bail for her daughter and grandson to these men. Though all were initially hesitant, her recitation about a potential lynching persuaded Julius Blair; the others concurred. Picking up John Dudley, an elderly, respected Spanish-American War veteran, they immediately headed out to make bail. Julius imagined potential danger for the Stephensons but never for his community or himself.[21]

The "money men" posted bail, thirty-five hundred dollars each, for James and Gladys before Squire Denton, who had been told by Deputy Sheriff J. C. Goad of a rising hum of public conversation about the fight and arrests. Denton called Julius Blair aside and advised he leave the Stephensons in the jail for their protection. Julius had already considered and rejected this choice. He had learned from a lifetime in Maury County that neither the decrepit jail nor any sheriff could protect prisoners from a determined mob. Blair assured the magistrate that the Stephensons would be safer in hands of their own kind and uttered the unofficial battle cry for the subsequent black-community response: *"We are not going to have any more social lynchings in Maury County."*[22]

Rumors of the fight and potential consequences were also spreading among whites. Town and county officials recognized early the possibility of turmoil but just as quickly dismissed their concerns. In addition to underestimating the potential for danger on the basis of reassuring historic hegemony, they totally failed to communicate or coordinate. The police department, sheriff's office, and mayor were all working within a three-block area, yet there is no evidence that anyone knew what the others were doing.

Eldridge Denham was in his second, four-year term as mayor and, like other members of the local power structure, thought race relations in Columbia were fine. All afternoon Monday, he was working in his restaurant on South Main Street, one-half block from both the courthouse and East Eighth, and first heard about the fight from a lunchtime customer. There is no evidence of any conversation between him and the constabulary about an emerging, unprecedented community crisis until after dark.[23]

Police Chief Griffin was not sure whether crowds were greater than usual for a Monday, but he did ask some small groups to disperse that afternoon. He also heard some folks say that the woman and boy should be punished for knocking the white boy through the plate glass, but this caused him no alarm. The seventy-year-old police chief went home at seven o'clock, the end of his shift, for his usual supper and early retirement.[24]

The fifty-nine-year-old, lame duck sheriff, J. J. Underwood, had good relations with the black community. Several of them had urged "Mr. Jim" to run as an independent, hoping to thwart Flo Fleming, who was known to be hard on blacks.[25] Underwood left the courthouse around four o'clock Monday evening after attending circuit court all day. The top county lawman then first heard about the fight between "the two darkies and the white boy" that resulted in supposed serious injury to Billy Fleming. He was relatively more concerned than others in leadership and set out to calm matters. Events were, however, to stay at least one step ahead of him.[26]

Typical for the time, there were no blacks in local government. The white community viewed blacks as a homogeneous underclass led by a few relatively affluent businessmen. Elected leaders of Maury County thought that the actions of the mass of blacks were easily controlled by the "leading darkies." Morton and the Blairs were said to "rule the Bottom," another term for East Eighth Street.[27] Belying a later assertion that he did not believe there would be any trouble, Underwood quickly responded to a late-afternoon telephone message of concern from James Morton, one of these unelected leaders, and drove his Ford car down South Main to the black business and society street.

While sitting in his parked car at the top of Mink Slide, Underwood talked with the Blairs. The conversation was calm, friendly, and responsible. Julius Blair had known Underwood all of his life and had cut the sheriff's hair when he was a boy. When Underwood had run a meat shop, Saul had done business with him. They briefly discussed the upcoming election and whether the incumbent should stay in as an independent candidate. The prime topic though was trouble—real or imagined. Underwood reinforced the elder Blair's fears, admitting there was a "feeling" around town. The sheriff reminded the father and son of his good record with blacks, sympathetically remembered the 1927 and 1933 Maury County lynchings, told the story of his own father stopping a lynching in Arkansas, and said, "We ain't going to have no trouble."[28]

The Stephensons signed their warrants and were taken from the jail shortly after five o'clock by the Blairs and John Dudley. As night approached, both black and white leaders conveyed uneasiness in their parting. Underwood, who knew and liked Gladys's parents, told the

Stephensons' new protectors to take care of Gladys and James. Julius advised the just released prisoners his now certain belief that "Uptown, they are getting together for something."[29]

In addition to a local precedent for racial violence, Blair's conclusion was reinforced by perhaps the most frightening and stimulating rumor circulating about downtown since the arrests, that of an alleged rope purchase. Whites were said to be buying that lynching equipment in Porter-Walker Hardware store immediately after the Stephensons had been arrested. Two especially vocal whites, Joe Williams and Roy Scribner, were arrested that afternoon for attempting a "two-man lynching" and creating disorder, though they had no rope on them. A woman telephoned Saul Blair and told of unnamed whites asserting that if they didn't succeed in hanging the two Negroes, they would offer themselves for lynching. Whatever the validity of the rumors, blacks took them very seriously.

The ability to hear the rumor of the rope purchase seemed racially selective. Mayor Denham finally heard it in his restaurant that evening. If other white leaders heard it at all, the story did not disturb them.[30]

ALIGNMENT

Perception about the crowds on the square that afternoon and just how dangerous they might be varied considerably, again usually along racial lines. The police department seemed to neither hear nor see any turbulence. Chief Griffin, who had dispersed the small crowds of "youngsters," heard some reports of "resentment" toward the Stephensons but went home that evening without making any special provisions for trouble. At dusk, Patrolman Bernard Stofel thought there might have been seventy-five to one hundred seemingly harmless "pool-hall-type boys" milling about the streets.[31]

Blacks saw the square assembly somewhat differently. From the jail, the black leaders took Gladys Stephenson out West End to Happy Hollow, a small, black enclave where she was currently lodging. Reasoning that a mob was less likely to attack a woman, and James was more at risk, they took him back to Mink Slide for close protection. Besides, the laconic youth had a date that evening and wanted to be wherever any action might be. Though he had not shared the thought with James, Julius Blair had decided that things might settle down if the young veteran were removed from Columbia.

After depositing James Stephenson in the midst of bustling Mink Slide, Julius Blair began a reconnaissance from his car of the square geographically one block from East Eighth but ethnically a nonbridged, infinite distance away. On his first trip around, he thought there might be twenty-five to fifty whites, some now obviously carrying long guns. He noted increasing numbers on a second tour just after dark and decided that tactically the time had come to get Stephenson, the obvious target of any nocturnal mob, out of town.

A cool June Pie had meanwhile purchased a haircut in Saul Blair's barbershop and discovered that many on the crowded street were concerned for his safety. Whether because of his military experience, intrinsic confidence, or youthful ignorance, he and a few pals drove his girlfriend home via South Main and the square, where he also noted a growing crowd of people and at least three men with guns.[32]

Throughout the county, people of both races quickly heard about the unrest. Some approached and retreated. Others, whether for adventure, curiosity, or concern, headed for the action like moths toward a flame. James T. "Popeye" Bellanfant, a Negro driver of a school bus for College Hill High School, advised the rural youngsters Monday afternoon to tell their parents and brothers the story of the Stephensons and to "come to town and bring what they have got" (supposedly weapons). Most paid no attention to the request, and there was no evidence any families responded.[33]

Irena Shyers exited the Princess Theater around five o'clock, having seen *The Bells of St. Mary's* from the balcony section for blacks, and was amazed at the restless crowd on the square. When she heard that her College Hill schoolmate, Jimmy Stephenson, had been arrested and that trouble was stirring, she sought her boyfriend, Herbert Johnson, who had served in Europe and North Africa in the war. He advised her to take her mother to their home in the country. Herbert went to his house in Macedonia, a black residential area in northeast Columbia where freedmen had settled after the Civil War, and started back downtown with a weapon. His mother urged him to stay home for protection in case "they come through the neighborhood." He wisely obeyed.[34]

Irena's brothers, Lee and Earlie, heard about the matter from their cousin at their farm on Bear Creek Pike. They came down to the Bottom after dark, allegedly for a regular meeting of the Royal Dukes Club. They also were concerned for the Stephensons' safety and carried a rifle with them.[35]

John Finney, who had just returned to his desk at the *Daily Herald* from stateside service in the Marine Corps, went to pick up his daughter at a later movie that was playing to a packed house. He suggested to some members of the "curious" crowd on the square that they go home. Several "irresponsible" types responded that he should tend to his own business; so *he* went home.[36]

James Beard, a white mechanic, heard about the trouble around half past eight at a service station ten miles away in Mt. Pleasant. The rumors stirred him and three pals to high-tail it to Columbia. Borgie Claude, from Riverside, did likewise, arming himself with some beer and a pistol.[37]

Brothers Calvin and Raymond Lockridge, both black carpenters and ministers, had been told by their "baby brother," Albert, about the mounting crisis late that afternoon as they worked on a house in Riverside, a nearby white neighborhood. Calvin's wife was the first cousin of Cordie Cheek, the man lynched in 1933; and Calvin had sworn there would never be another lynching in Maury County as long as he lived. After finishing work, the brothers drove around the square to East Eighth, slowly working their way through clusters of milling whites on North Main.[38]

Meade Johnson noted the proliferation of race talk and guns from late afternoon and was worried for the safety of himself and his Mink Slide store, a pool-room restaurant that had been raided several times as a bootleg operation. He decided to close early and had his son, James "Digger" Johnson, drive him and employee Rufus Kennedy home at half past seven.[39] His prudence may have protected him from harm, but it would not keep him or his family out of tragic trouble.

The sheriff and his small staff (seven deputies, two of whom were in Columbia) were definitely quicker and more concerned with developments than the police department. Underwood and Griffin had briefly chatted before Griffin went home. Both then felt nothing would come of all this. Underwood, however, now faced real danger.[40] Just after dark, a crew of twenty to thirty young whites "with beer on their bellies" came to the jail and demanded they have the Stephensons, ostensibly for lynching. Brandishing a sub-machine gun, Underwood ran them off. Chasing the group away, he arrested James Scribner and Earl Tomlin, who were drunk and had approached the jail because they had heard some excitement was expected there.[41]

Deputy J. C. Goad further amplified Underwood's apprehension with a report that blacks were congregating in the Bottom. The two lawmen drove there and were shocked to find a big, restless crowd. Though there might have been uncertainty about the reality of a white mob, there was an obvious large concentration of seventy-five to one hundred black men on East Eighth. Some were armed, and many were angry!

Underwood tried to use his lifelong friendship with many blacks to restore control. Standing beside his car, the sheriff talked with those he thought might help defuse the ticking social bomb. Calvin Lockridge had been born on Underwood's farm, had helped the sheriff in his elections, and had purchased a 1937 Buick from one of Underwood's sons. Lockridge did not want any problems to occur on his friend's watch and promised to keep the blacks down in the Bottom if Underwood fulfilled his guarantee against any white invasion. Several parties heatedly agreed they would go home if the crowd on the square first dispersed.

Underwood also urged the Blairs to ask the crowd to go home. Julius said they had a right to be there to protect the Stephensons and were not planning to come uptown anyway. For the first time, Underwood realized the coloreds thought whites really would invade Mink Slide. He promised to "arrest the Hell" out of any whites heading toward East Eighth. The sheriff did not recognize he was the arbitrator in negotiation of an armed standoff.[42]

His assurance seemed lame and had little effect on the crowd. Several, among them an especially angry William Gordon who would play a tragic role, shouted that the sheriff would say anything to disperse them and that Underwood could not be trusted. From the depth of the crowd came a threat to "kill the son of a bitch." As they began to press onto his car, Saul Blair and Lockridge told them to back off, that to threaten a law officer was a mistake. Recognizing the futility of further street negotiation, Lockridge politely but firmly shoved Underwood into the auto. In parting frustration, the sheriff told Lockridge that if the sides could not be kept apart, he might have to call in "the militia," the first admission of possible local loss of control. Calvin replied that might just be the best thing to do. The sheriff drove away, another moment of potential disengagement having passed.[43]

Only eight policemen constituted the Columbia force, three of whom were more than sixty years old. The five on duty as evening descended sensed danger, though they did not discuss their concerns with their chief. None knew of the white crowd who sought the Stephensons at the county jail but had heard "a little whispering" around town. They began extensive patrolling. After supper, three of them drove through Macedonia in response to a rumor of guns being collected there. They saw nothing unusual.

Around half past eight, four of them—George Reeves, Frank Collins, Sam Richardson, and Bernard Stofel—drove south down East Eighth. They stopped in mid-block and talked with the crowd without leaving the car. The policemen saw several weapons, and the throng was confidently aggressive, "talking very smart." A "yellowish nigger" said "he had fought for freedom overseas and he was going to fight for it here." James Morton said they had done nothing wrong, but they had

Stephenson with them and intended to protect him. Saul Blair said they were looking for protection from the police, and Richardson said they would get it. All the blacks said to tell the whites not to come down to the Bottom, for they were ready for them. Morton and Julius Blair said they intended to "fight to the end."[44]

The ten-minute conversation conveyed a clear message of resoluteness by the blacks and heightened fear among the policemen. Their small coterie did not dare attempt disarming the throng outside their squad car. The increasingly nervous officers drove back to City Hall to report their findings to City Manager Ulna Swann and Mayor Denham, now at last somewhat aware, apparently concerned, and participating in decisions.

Perhaps because of his good relations with blacks, Underwood allegedly told the black leaders they should get James Stephenson out of town for his safety, a story the sheriff denied. Deputy Goad also denied making a later, solo trip down East Eighth and telling Saul Blair to remove James from the scene. During one of their trips to East Eighth, the sheriff's department had at least implied their support of this earlier idea of Julius Blair.[45]

A now thoroughly worried Underwood did make at least one more call to the Bottom. After his previous trip to the Bottom, he walked around the square and detected a similar though less-organized air of white unrest. He returned to the jail and phoned James Morton, asking if there were still men down there with guns. He asked Morton to clear them out and promised to arrest blacks who did not disperse. (His potential use of the arrest threat seemed to have turned 180 degrees.) Morton's noncommittal response did not reassure him. Around 8:30 and without consulting any other local officials, he called Governor James McCord and asked for state law-enforcement help.[46] He sought maintenance of peace but unintentionally assured that the racial drama was to play out on a stage far bigger than Columbia, Tennessee.

ESCAPE AND ENTRENCHMENT

James Stephenson had been at the absolute eye of the storm. Though June Pie seemed oblivious of his situation, both Julius Blair and the sheriff's department thought him in immediate danger as the target of a mob. Blair believed that removing James from the scene would protect him and prevent trouble. The patriarch asked his son, Saul, to make arrangements.

First though, Saul had to find the carefree alleged felon. After taking his girlfriend home, James had arrived back at Mink Slide around 6:50.

There he circulated among the crowd, which was bigger, more restless, and perhaps drinking more than usual for this time of day. A stack of long guns had sprung up like mushrooms in various places, especially at Saul's shop. James took one and joined twenty-five to thirty others on rooftops of stores on the south side of the street in order to assess the mob of which they had heard so much. Following consultation with his father and Deputy Goad, Saul called out for James to come down.[47]

Stephenson's exit from Columbia and segue to a historic secondary role had elements of strategic correctness, tactical ingenuity, and Keystone Kops performance. In addition to himself, Saul rounded up an escort of James Bellanfant, Robert Frierson, and Tommy Neely, who had plans to go to Nashville anyway that night for fun. They were armed with a couple of shotguns and pistols, including an Italian machine pistol with a stock. In order to avoid recognition by crowds in the downtown area, they started north by back roads, Iron Bridge Road and Bear Creek Pike, shortly before eight o'clock in Neely's Ford coupe.

They progressed only a couple of miles before that car broke down. After nursing it back to Neely's house, they boarded his Dodge car. Transportation uncertainty continued when that car blew a tire in front of the Haynes Haven mansion on the Nashville Pike.[48] Someone used the phone there to call George Nicholson, who came with his car. *That* vehicle was plagued by a tire rubbing a front fender. In order to avoid letting James be seen, Neely and he walked from Haynes Haven through the village of Spring Hill and waited on its north side while Nicholson's car was repaired at a service station.

The weary and wary travelers got to Nashville sometime after ten o'clock, bought a ticket at Union Station, went to the Dallas Eat Shop in north Nashville, and put James on the 2:00 A.M. (February 26) train for Chicago. While there they saw something that suggested they had not avoided trouble for their people by spiriting away Stephenson. Several Nashville policemen, while arresting a black man, justified beating him because they had heard four policemen had been shot in Columbia.[49]

As soon as Saul had left, Julius had called the sheriff's office and spoken to one of Underwood's sons. With relief, he had said Stephenson was out of town and "it is not necessary to have any trouble." Believing this truly the case, Blair had then turned to other responsibilities on his crowded civic agenda.[50]

Several black-community leaders had been meeting to raise money to buy land for a new high school. They did not detect enough unrest or danger to cancel a meeting that evening at the house of Miss Johnnie Belle Fulton, a teacher and school supervisor. Attendees included Julius Blair,

County Agriculture Agent for Negroes George Newburn, Mrs. James (Mary) Morton, Reverend Joseph Blade, College Hill Principal Samuel E. Jones, and real estate agent Andrew J. Armstrong. They proceeded about their business, electing Blair treasurer of the ad hoc group.[51]

Matters were not so orderly or constructive on Mink Slide. No identifiable leaders screamed at troops to either man barricades or invade the town. (Except when they went to make bond for the Stephensons, Morton and the Blairs had been together only moments all day.) Instead, a ferment of excited, angry, mostly young, black men, who collectively felt threatened, anticipated white invasion and brandished a motley collection of arms. Some drank booze in the spirit of carnival, others to gain false courage.[52]

In addition to carrying the prevalent feeling that there must be no more lynching in Maury County, veterans were angry that such events might still occur back home. Their military experience had shown them a different life and instilled both confidence and sophistication. Milton Murray had been back in Columbia two days, having served in the Army Artillery Corps in North Africa. He and several other black former noncommissioned officers supposedly constituted a very unofficial command structure. One of their first measures was to place men with guns on roofs for reconnaissance and sniping duty. They used a light-skinned Negro to infiltrate the crowd gathered on the square and bring information about the white men's intent.

Plenty of guns were available. Some young men though were not skilled in using them. Ed Kimes recalled one fellow almost killing someone when he accidentally discharged a shotgun. Kimes counseled his fellow gatherers to not shoot except in true self-defense should the whites come. He also suggested not drinking alcohol.[53]

There was sporadic firing into East Eighth. Shots were said to have come from the roof of the Dixie Manufacturing Company on the corner of South Main and West Eighth. Firing also supposedly came from a couple of vehicles driven by whites that raced down Mink Slide from South Main. Blacks were similarly trigger happy. A wayward tourist from California mistakenly drove down the street and was fired upon. Even black undertaker V. K. Ryan took a few shots into his car door as he went down the street on business. An alley entering the middle of the north side of the street provided easy access for any invader, and jumpy defenders allegedly saw several such aggressors.[54]

After taking his wife to the meeting, James Morton did not provide the street leadership later reputed to him. Instead, he hid himself in his home. When he emerged to investigate some shots, he saw the third lawman (after Underwood and a policeman) to make a trip down the street that day. Tennessee Highway Patrolman E. B. Noles learned about events from Morton and advised him to get everyone to break up. Another man told Morton that people were gathering on the square. He went to Fulton's house to retrieve his wife, advising the committee that things were getting out of hand and that real danger seemed imminent. "I understand that they are fixing to come down on us, and I think it would be wise for everybody to be home with their families." The meeting promptly broke up before nine o'clock.[55]

Morton decided to get his children away from East Eighth Street. "Johnny" Hewe Lockridge, a cousin of Calvin and Raymond, assisted Morton at the funeral home as well as doing farm labor. Earlier that evening, Morton had called for him to retrieve a body that was expected to arrive at the train depot from Wyoming at midnight. Now the worried mortician cancelled that assignment and asked Johnny to take the Morton children to a friend's house.[56]

Outside, the former servicemen felt darkness would be an ally. Several proprietors were persuaded to douse their lights. When Alldie Sharpgon drove his city bus down East Eighth at 8:22, he saw people with guns on a dark street. No one got on the bus. Shortly afterward he heard shotgun fire from Mink Slide as shooters blasted out the street-light in mid-block.[57]

When Chief Griffin called in at nine o'clock to check on matters before retiring, Sam Richardson said Griffin had better come back to town for "it looked like the gossip was going to give us some trouble." Griffin met his officers on the southwest corner of the square, where they heard further shooting from East Eighth and felt pellets rain down onto the street. The elderly and respected police chief felt matters had gone far enough. Commensurate with other officials' actions that day, he did not hesitate or consult. Neither did he recognize that this situation might be more dangerous than others he had faced. As chief constable of the town, the lifelong Maury Countian felt responsible and fully confident he could end the foolishness. He had dealt with Negroes all his life and would personally take care of the problem.[58] How wrong he was!

CHAPTER THREE

A Walk into Darkness

THE WALK

All streets except West Seventh leading outward from the courthouse sloped severely downward. One block from the square, East Eighth descended eastward off South Main, ending downhill at Woodland Street. People looking up the street at night would see descending pedestrians silhouetted against the sky, especially if the street were dark and those walking east were back-lit, a circumstance of some importance in imminent events and resulting trials.

The shots that Chief Griffin and his men heard had been used to destroy the streetlight in the middle of Mink Slide. Long awnings, attached sheds, and extending signs from several establishments also obscured vision at street level. With all store lights doused either voluntarily or after coercion, East Eighth was now a dark place. Lights on the upper (west) junction crossing South Main were out of harm's way and remained lit.

Griffin and Officer Will Wilsford, both born early in the last quarter of the nineteenth century, now proposed without apparent trepidation to walk down to the Bottom and end the foolishness. They felt they could talk some sense into the miscreants. Officers Bernard Stofel and Sam Richardson, who had been frightened on their earlier ride down East Eighth, counseled against such action. Griffin strode confidently down South Main through crowds of acutely interested whites, mostly "youngsters." He made no effort to organize the seven following officers. As he and Wilsford stepped onto the sidewalk heading down the south side of

27

darkened, volatile Mink Slide, Stofel and Richardson knew the two old fellows were heading into danger and joined them. Officers Collins and Reeves stayed at the northeast corner of Main and Eighth to hold back the increasingly excited white crowd.[1]

The officers wore blue overcoats with badges and carried no lights. Their sidearms were holstered. They could barely discern the bubbling knot of blacks clustered in front of Blair's barbershop halfway down the block. As they slowly advanced, Griffin and Wilsford shouted that they were there to help. Their reassurance had no effect on the nervous, angry, and suspicious crowd, which to Griffin sounded like a bunch of drunks. As Wilsford was asking them not to "draw," a voice called out for them to halt. In rapid succession, other voices said "halt, Hell," and "fire!" From approximately one hundred feet away, a fusillade erupted into the approaching officers. Richardson and Stofel dove between parked cars, minimizing their injuries. The blasts injured the older men much worse, with Wilsford being hit a couple of times in the face. All four men scrambled back up toward Main, none drawing his weapon. Several cars were commandeered for taking them to the hospital.[2]

Concerned bystanders stopped Sheriff Underwood from going onto East Eighth after he raced to the scene. He and others now prevented armed whites from going into the Bottom. Shortly before the shootings, Mayor Denham had, without recorded consultation, contacted Wayne Carlton, a local officer in the Tennessee State Guard, to enlist the aid of that agency. County and city leaders were rapidly admitting their inadequacy to handle the situation, over which they were to have less and less influence.[3]

Chief Walter Griffin was kindly, careful, widely respected, and obviously brave. His opinion that he could talk the mob out of its meanness was not unique. Mayor Denham had earlier considered going to Mink Slide with the city manager to personally calm the crowd. Those judgments disregarded the scanty but adequate intelligence of their own police force, which had recognized dangerous mob instability. More cogent, their judgments were based on anachronistic perceptions of Maury County blacks. The walk down Mink Slide and shooting of the policemen showed that the Bottom had changed and blacks would not be so easily managed as before. A new, unsettled, and unpredictable era had begun.

THE TENNESSEE HIGHWAY PATROL

Tennesseans had rejected several attempts to impose state police authority. Radical Reconstruction era Tennessee Governor William "Parson" Brownlow was infamously unpopular to the majority of state citizens. One of his most hated measures was the creation of the Metropolitan Police District of Memphis. Also known as "Brownlow's Band," this force had omniscient legal status, was above the usual law, and enjoyed statewide powers under the governor. After Brownlow's defeat in 1869, his state police force was promptly disbanded. Separate legislative acts in 1919 and 1926 again attempted the creation of state police. Both foundered because of strong-arm tactics of the lawmen, reinforcing the unpopularity of the state-police concept among Tennesseans. Politically, county sheriffs approved this, believing a weaker state law agency was no threat to their jurisdictional and patronage powers.[4]

Recognizing the certain danger of increasing automobile traffic on proliferating Tennessee roads, Governor Henry Horton signed a law creating the Tennessee Highway Patrol (THP) in 1929. Both the state legislature and the executive sought to assure that there would be no repetition of Tennessee's unhappy experience with state police. Though giving the patrol enough flexibility to respond to unpredictable lawlessness, their prevailing charge was to *enforce traffic laws* in a courteous fashion. Horton said they were to go "not as lords, but as servants of the people." Finance Commissioner Charles McCabe, known as the "Father of the Patrol," affirmed they were "not to be men of force whom the people fear" and reminded they certainly were *not* state police.[5]

Due to manpower shortage during World War II, the patrol took on new and varied tasks, including controlling prostitution (mainly around military bases), escorting navy vessels through inland waterways, and commandeering vehicles for fighting forest fires. The patrol's most lucrative new assignment was confiscation of bootleg whiskey, a task it used for its men's financial and social gain for a couple of decades.

Digressing from its initial, altruistically defined mission, the patrol had become a very political organ by World War II. The initial patrolman's salary of $125 per month was generous by depression standards. If retaining that security required doing a few political tasks of questionable legality, then so be it. Patrolmen's political connections and their willingness to nurture those connections after hire were critical to job retention.

Edward "Boss" Crump of Memphis was effective political czar of Tennessee in 1946. He notoriously used highway patrolmen to watch and, if necessary, intimidate voters at key precincts during elections. They usually performed such services in plain clothes with the requisite enforcement tools, i.e., blackjacks and guns, highly visible. With the apparent sanction and support of its director, Lynn Bomar, the patrol was not only political but had an unprofessional *gestapo* reputation.[6]

If in 1946 patrolmen were still ostensibly servants whose primary goal was to guarantee highway safety, events in Columbia would sully

Tennessee Highway Patrol Commissioner Lynn Bomar. (Courtesy—"*Servants . . . Not Lords*")

that reputation. In carrying out the Columbia assignment, the patrol would redefine the outer limits of their purported historic mission. As Safety Commissioner Bomar said, "Sometimes we assume some powers we really don't have."[7]

The patrol had less than 150 men in 1946. It suffered funding and manpower inadequacies as residua of a tight World War II state budget. Bomar had been director of the THP since 1942. When that position was elevated to cabinet status in 1945, he became the first commissioner and was to be the only one to wear a uniform. An all-around athlete, Bomar was widely known as Vanderbilt University's first football All-American in the early 1920s. After a short professional football career, he held various law-enforcement positions throughout the state. His public persona was one of conviviality, gentleness, kindness, and jollity.[8] The Columbia race riot highlighted some of his other leadership and personal characteristics.

THE TENNESSEE STATE GUARD

The Tennessee State Guard had a life span of only five years. Created by the Tennessee State Guard Act of 1941, its function was to provide military protection, especially against riot and sabotage, to the state while the National Guard, the traditional state militia, was mobilized for the international emergency. Its troops were teenagers and men ineligible for the draft, and its commanding officers were generally political appointees, some with World War I experience.

Training of the youthful cadre was inconsistent, and potential missions were uncertain. Its operation was grossly underfunded. Outdated weapons such as single-shot Enfield rifles were scavenged from other sources, for instance, National Guard storage depots. Observers with any military sophistication recognized this was not an imposing force.

Brig. Gen. Jacob McGavock Dickinson was the Second Brigade (Middle Tennessee) commander. A descendant of two of Nashville's

General Jacob McGavock
Dickinson (on left) and his
Tennessee State Guard staff.
(Courtesy—Mrs. Peggy
Dickinson Fleming)

leading families, the McGavocks and Overtons, Dickinson was a graduate of Hotchkiss, Yale, and Harvard Law School. He was a captain in World War I and returned to Nashville from a Chicago law practice in the 1930s to be a gentleman farmer and serve in various state offices. Governor Prentice Cooper had commissioned Dickinson to organize the state guard.[9]

SECURING THE TOWN

Commissioner Bomar had gone to bed early the night of February 25 because of a bad cold. Governor McCord awakened him around half past eight and told him "to proceed as quickly as possible to Columbia for protection of lives and property." Bomar and Patrol Sgt. Fred Waltrip raced the forty-two miles and met Sgt. E. B. Noles and Flo Fleming (the man was everywhere) at the city limit. The three lawmen's quick survey of the area revealed many armed, angry, and aggressive whites who bragged of their military experience and begged to be let loose on Mink Slide, the invasion feared and now anticipated by blacks.[10]

As martial law had not been declared, neither the patrol nor guard could legally supercede the authority of local law-enforcement agencies. Theoretically, the sheriff would need to deputize them before they could perform search, seizure, or interdiction. No one paid any heed to such legalities, however, as the local authorities acquiesced from fear or uncertainty, and the commissioner confidently took control.

Bomar immediately concluded that the prevalent threat came from the entrenched blacks on East Eighth, among whom were likely those who had shot the policemen. He saw only allies in the chaotic group of armed whites buzzing around the square. Without apparent concern for legality or *increased* danger, he and his men quickly demonstrated a penchant for vigilantism.

In a bizarre opening act of the patrol's Columbia reign, they led a white mob in seeking weapons from the local state armory. Between ten and eleven o'clock, some angry boys commandeered a Monsanto bus on the square and went to the armory a few blocks away. Having been notified about the emergency, several local guardsmen in civilian clothes had arrived to protect the home facility of the Tenth Machine Gun & Chemical Company. Patrolmen Noles and Griffin told State Guard Maj. William Cotham and Lt. Myron Peck that Bomar had authorized the deputization of the mob stirring outside the armory and that they needed arms for them. Additional pressure came from several of the mob who got into the armory and threatened to take weapons.

The scared but sensible guardsmen refused, despite a threat to call the governor and the haranguing of an excited and profane Bomar. Though they hid behind the true technicality of inaccessible firing pins and ammunition, they recognized the illegality and danger of this request from another arm of state law.[11]

The governor contacted General Dickinson at 10:15 P.M. By half past ten, he had begun mobilization of the Second and Tenth Regiments. Guardsmen from all over Middle Tennessee began to converge in Columbia. Unlike the patrol, the state guard had a contingency plan that had been available since 1943. Code named "Lakeland Problem," the plan was developed to isolate troublemakers, separating them and cutting them off from other armed groups. Specifically, guardsmen were to suppress rebellion and violence, protect life and property, and restore law and order.[12]

Though most Columbians slept in ignorance of events, their downtown was buzzing with danger and uncertainty. Mink Slide was dark and quiet, nothing indicating any offensive action by those hunkered there. Except for the Negro residential area east of Mink Slide, whites swarmed through a one-block perimeter around East Eighth in all directions. They were mobile, restless, and full of competitive juices. Either being on furlough or having just been discharged, several wore military uniforms. Only the absence of a leader seemed to be preventing their invasion. Sniping from cars, street level, and rooftops sporadically sang into the darkened street. Blacks returned fire, especially against a couple of passing cars.

Rumors spread haphazardly, including tales of strangers, sometimes carrying suspiciously heavy suitcases, coming in on buses and trains. Gauges of the size of the opposing camps varied tremendously. Estimates of entrenched Negroes ranged from seventy-five to three hundred men, and General Dickinson thought there were just as many or more whites when he inspected the area after one o'clock in the morning.[13]

James Beard and Borgie Claude typified the young whites who roamed free and armed. When Beard, the son of a former fire-department

A carload of volunteers.
(Courtesy—GJ files)

chief, arrived on South Main shortly after the shooting of the policemen, he quickly returned home to get a weapon, something most in the crowd were already brandishing. Many of the boys were reinforcing their bravado by drinking spirits. Around eleven o'clock, his pal Claude persuaded him to venture down an alley south of East Eighth off Main Street to retrieve Claude's truck, which was in a shop there. Though subsequent testimony was contradictory, Claude was apparently also toting a can of gasoline that was not intended to fuel his vehicle.

Some Mink Slide defenders discovered these infiltrators and welcomed them with buckshot. The two men hustled out after Beard was hit in the leg. While at the fire hall having bullet fragments picked out of his leg, he did not pretend to support the alleged purpose of their venture and swore he would return to Mink Slide to close other unfinished business. He intended to "burn them out." Claude warned Beard that he had "better shut up." Caution overcame bravado, and Beard went home, having done his share of civil defense.[14]

Amazingly, several blacks underestimated the danger on East Eighth, either not recognizing the volatility of the mixture of crowds and guns or somehow being unaware of the shooting of the policemen. Calvin and Raymond Lockridge sneaked into the Bottom the back way around half past eleven to get their entrapped nephew. After learning about the shooting, Calvin threw the carbine he was carrying into his car, and the Lockridges drove down the block to Woodland. They were apprehended by uniformed men whom Calvin had thought were a group of taxi drivers. They were Tennessee Highway Patrolmen, including Bomar, who promptly arrested them. The arrest became rough when Patrol Lt. Clyde Castleman saw a back-seat passenger fumbling with the carbine.

Feeling entrapped by the white mob and the newly arrived patrol, several men decided to spend the night in Odd Fellow's Hall above

Keeping an eye on Mink
Slide. (Courtesy—GJ files)

Lucille's Restaurant. Horace Gordon had brought his child to a 4-H
meeting that day and was eating in Brown's Cafe when the shooting of
policemen occurred. Charlie Smith lived only a block away but also chose
to hide in the hall. Elmer Dooley, who was going to school on the GI Bill,
was to meet a girl and had been on Mink Slide only thirty minutes when
the policemen were shot. John Blackwell had gotten a haircut and
encountered armed men blocking the way when he headed home. Henry,
Luther, and Charlie Edwards also partook of the social action that
evening and took refuge in their aunt's house around the corner on
Woodland Street after the shootings. Others hiding in that generous rela-
tive's domicile included Clarence Brown, Julian Myers, and the Shyers
boys. Hollis Reynolds, an assistant to the local veterinarian, lived in a
room above Albert Wright's cafe, but was blissfully ignorant of
surrounding chaos and turned in at his usual hour.[15]

Others were scared, sensible, or resourceful enough to escape.
Recognizing that the situation had gone beyond peaceful settlement and
that they were outgunned by two state law agencies, these men counseled disengagement and retreat. Many escaped via Helm's Branch, a
shallow, winding stream behind East Eighth that led into east Columbia,
Negro territory. By early morning of Tuesday, February 26, the creek was
literally crawling with black men.[16]

When General Dickinson arrived in Columbia at 1:20 A.M., he made a
personal inspection of the area and met with Bomar, Underwood, and
other local leaders. By half past two, they had agreed not to make any
action other than a cordon before seven in the morning. Dickinson would
not have enough troops available until then to control crowds and secure
order. The plan was for the sheriff to negotiate withdrawal. Guardsmen
would replace patrolmen in the blockade, and force would be used only
if absolutely necessary.[17]

The fourth estate was now on the scene. In addition to reporting, newspapermen were to have some influence on events. The first of these was
the raid on James Morton's home. Most reporters arrived before midnight

and set up a command post at a substation used by both Nashville dailies. After being told by a local reporter that Morton was a "leader," reporters made several calls to his home to get the black perspective on matters. Morton did not feel it safe to come out for an interview but suggested he would meet one of them, preferably accompanied by Sheriff Underwood, in his home. J. A. Kingcaid, a United Press reporter known as "Punjab" by his colleagues, took Morton up on the offer. A highway patrolman let him into the residence around three o'clock in the morning.

Morton, his wife, his mother-in-law, and a friend, Marcia Mayes, had remained clothed and huddled quietly in their dark house. Around half past ten, the undertaker had briefly turned on a back light to let in several armed men off the street who requested shelter from the cold. He agreed to do so if they would lie low in a dark back room.

After conversing with Morton, Kingcaid placed a call from the private home's front parlor. Then came Bomar! He thought it suspicious that the house was so quiet. Beaming his flashlight and without warrant, he burst in and strode through. In the back room he found his biggest catch since arrival, the men Morton had sheltered, their weapons, and numerous "intoxicants." He arrested Morton, John Lockridge, and the boys in the back.

This raid early in the events at Columbia typified patrol performance. They paid little attention to due process, had unequivocally judged the local blacks to be the only villains, and were consistently abusive. Bomar's alleged first statement to Morton after entering uninvited was "Morton,

A youthful guardsman and local officials. (Courtesy—GJ files)

you are the bastard leading these bastards." He advised his men that if anyone moved to "blow them off the earth." A patrolmen told Morton, "If you bat your eye, you son-of-a-bitch, you will lose sight on the world." One of them was also reported to have stolen some of Mary Morton's jewelry.[18]

Bomar almost immediately enhanced the arrest total for this early morning foray to the lower end of Mink Slide. As the patrolmen were herding the occupants out of the Morton house, they stopped Saul Blair's car. After dropping off the rest of James Stephenson's escort, George Nicholson and Saul had returned to the Bottom, allegedly to report to Sheriff Underwood about Stephenson's escape. The patrolmen arrested the armed men as well.[19]

Both patrolmen and guardsmen continued to arrive in Columbia. By early morning hours, a leaky cordon surrounded East Eighth. Firing had almost stopped. Armed whites continued to roam the area, often serving as unofficial deputies. Bomar had arrested the Lockridge brothers; a drunk, out-of-town white who mistakenly drove his truck down Mink Slide; the men in James Morton's house; and two of the guys who had spirited James Stephenson out of Columbia. There had been no deaths.

Though there were still signs of legal vigilantism and presumption of black guilt in mob action, the patrol and guard were gaining solid control as reinforcements arrived. The state might have momentarily concluded that its forces had done a great job of protecting property and saving lives. With things so obviously going their way, officials would surely end the crisis by morning—assuming there were no rogue peace officers participating in the mission.

A state guardsman holds back armed whites at top of Mink Slide. (Courtesy—GJ files)

CHAPTER FOUR

The THP Bull in a Racial China Shop

THE RAID

In a conference at half past one on the morning of February 26, local and state lawmen made plans for entering Mink Slide, controlling the blacks ensconced there, and seeking those who had shot the Columbia policemen.[1] A consensus emerged that trust should be established in order to comply with the goals of preserving lives and property. A daylight raid was therefore essential. Dickinson suggested using a loudspeaker to broadcast their intentions and calm the besieged. If necessary, he also thought noxious gas would be better than gunfire. The majority rejected both ideas.

Dickinson felt he did not have enough guardsmen on hand to control potential mobs from either side of the racial set-to. Troops were rapidly arriving though, and he believed that by early morning he could safely separate the potentially warring factions. The officials chose seven o'clock as the earliest hour for action. The guard issued official orders at half past five to that effect.[2]

Commissioner Bomar had a less-compulsive interpretation of the plan and promptly forsook it for his own agenda. At precisely 6:07, he signaled with a flashlight for Sheriff Underwood, an unknown number of semi-official deputies, and forty to fifty highway patrolmen to walk onto a still dark East Eighth. Bomar led a contingent from the lower end of the street, and Middle Tennessee Division Chief J. J. Jackson led one from the upper end.

General Dickinson (facing camera) enters command head-quarters at City Hall. (Courtesy—GJ files)

Halfway down the block at Saul Blair's barbershop, a gunfight ensued. Observers could not tell whether shooting began from outside or inside the shop. All lawmen on the scene said a single shotgun blast from within the shop elicited their return fire. Their response was overwhelming and unremitting. Officers blasted the shop's windows and locks and rousted its two cowed occupants, William "Rooster Bill" Pillow and Loyd "Papa" "Poppa" Kennedy. Blood-lust and/or fear rose in patrolmen's craws. Rampage replaced minimizing property loss in the mission. They began shooting out store windows and locks up and down the street. Hiding Negroes were in more danger than they had imagined the night before. The barrage, to which there was no further opposition, lasted an hour.

For officers, the yield was especially good at the Odd Fellow's Hall. Patrolmen beat down its door to find the several men who had hidden there through the night. They variously gun-whipped, stomped, black-jacked, cursed, and dragged Charlie Smith, Elmer Dooley, and Leonard Evans down the steps into custody. The most brutal treatment, resulting in one of the few serious injuries of the riot, was rendered to John Blackwell. The imposing J. J. Jackson made this arrest, dragging the Negro headfirst down the stairway after slicing his scalp with a gun butt. Jackson's actions were allegedly in response to Blackwell poking a rifle out the door, an act later denied in court by all the arrestees.[3]

Hollis Reynolds had slept through the night in his room in Albert Wright's cafe. Patrolmen broke in while he was dressing and shot him through both forearms as he raised them to defend himself. As he was marched up to South Main and then to jail, the arresting officers and various members of the white crowd beat him about his head and upper body.

Patrolmen similarly rousted all of the young men who had slept in Daisy Lee's house. They even flushed a couple who had slept under the church at the foot of East Eighth. Other than the single shot from Saul's shop, no blacks had returned fire. The state's officers had swept the supposedly organized rebels aside without resistance.

General Dickinson was furious and worried. When he surprisingly heard gunfire from Mink Slide at 6:15, he had only 211 men present and armed, not a sufficient force to control crowds, much less aggressors. He ordered all available soldiers to the area double quick. When he heatedly confronted Bomar at 6:40 regarding why the commissioner had jumped the gun in contradiction to the established plan, Bomar brushed Dickinson off, saying he had agreed only to go in "along about seven."

Dickinson's fears about crowd control seemed terribly accurate as armed, white crowds, excited by the sound of gunfire and the one-sided carnage on East Eighth, sought to join in the fun and bag a Negro. Spirited Col. Victor Wilson commanded the Second Regiment of the guard. As destruction by the patrol continued on Mink Slide, he tried to establish an effective cordon on South Main. He attained control of the surging crowd when he faced down a recalcitrant gun-toter, taking away the man's weapon and bending it around a post. From that moment, he more easily persuaded armed men to go home, though he could not successfully arrest any of them.[4]

During the next few hours, lawmen inflicted huge damage to the businesses of East Eighth. Other than highway patrolmen, the guard allowed only a handful of deputies and journalists into the Bottom—limiting the number of suspects who could have inflicted the subsequently well-documented vandalism on the street. Bomar and Underwood only stayed about an hour, but patrolmen roamed for most of the rest of the morning.[5]

A prone, unconscious John Blackwell. (Courtesy—GJ files)

An injured Hollis Reynolds is taken to jail, Flo Fleming on right. (Courtesy—GJ files)

Damage to Saul Blair's barbershop went far beyond the gunfight. Cushions on the four chairs were slashed, mirrors broken, linens scattered, and clippers and razors stolen. Various proprietors, including Julius Blair, later reported theft from cashboxes and jukeboxes, smashed mirrors and windows, and eaten or ruined food. Searchers threw all the instruments out of Dr. Frank L. Hawthorne's cabinets and demolished his equipment.

Both Mary Morton and various reporters saw patrolmen break into the Morton mortuary, where they created the most infamous damage, cutting drapes and furniture, putting a dress into a casket and pouring embalming fluid onto its upholstery, and destroying a rostrum—all amounting to over two thousand dollars in losses. No one could ever identify who defaced a closed, blue coffin by writing KKK in powder across its lid, which thereby intensified emotions and led to one of the most famous images of the Mink Slide riot.[6]

MOPPING UP

As guardsmen took over cordon duty, patrolmen gathered their catch of motley, scared blacks to incarcerate them on uncertain charges. The officers had adequately cowed them by beating and cursing them. John Blackwell lay prone in an unconscious state, his eyes swollen shut and blood flowing onto the street from the gash on his scalp. Several of

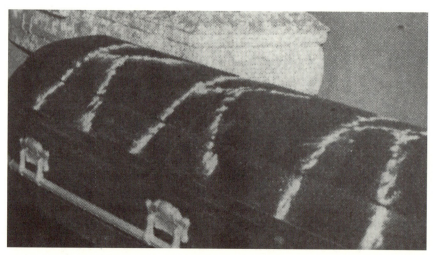

Defaced casket in Morton Funeral Home. (Courtesy—The *Crisis*)

Damage in Saul Blair's barbershop; note slashes in chair upholstery. (Courtesy— The *Crisis*)

A highway patrolman assesses the viability of John Blackwell, Police Officer Collins and Constable Copeland in background. (Courtesy—GJ files)

Blackwell's buddies heard a stream of profanity come from the guardsman standing over him and thought the officer kicked their friend. However, he was just turning Blackwell over with his foot to see if the black man were dead. A photograph of this scene created national stir, mainly through its publication in *Time* and *Ebony*.[7]

Though Bomar and his men might have bagged the policemen's assailant(s), the arrest total was disappointing. By half past nine on Tuesday morning, the patrol had arrested 31 people, far less than the predicted 150 to 300 supposedly holed up in Mink Slide. They retrieved thirty to forty guns (totals were rarely precise) and commensurate ammunition.

Bomar now belatedly used the loud speaker recommended by Dickinson. Wearing a yellow scarf, he rode through the embattled block in a jeep with the general, promising to provide "the same protection as the people on the other side of town" and asking the few nonarrested blacks to let him "see you smile." Everyone appreciated the apparent end of hostilities, no matter the uncertainty of final resolution. One grateful black bystander said, "Okay, boss, that is right, thank God."[8]

As the Negroes were marched up Woodland to the county jail, they could not seem to get their arms high enough to suit their guards. Any hint of arm dropping was met with curses, kicks, and whacks with gun butts and blackjacks. Patrolmen continued abusing their captives within the jail.[9]

Meanwhile on East Eighth, Chief Jackson heard the phone ring in Morton's establishment. After receiving permission from Bomar, he

began gathering intelligence from various callers. Using his best collo-
quial dialect and end-man voice, he chatted with several callers, much to
the amusement of his troops. He said callers from Chicago, Nashville,
and Columbus, Georgia, expressed concern and offered help, including
men and weapons. He attempted entrapment of a local woman by asking
her to bring guns to a nearby church crawl space.[10]

Around mid-morning, Bomar sought something he had not heretofore
been particularly concerned about, legitimization of action. He called
Nashville to get permission to search homes and businesses in the "riot
area" for weapons. Attorney General Roy Beeler said this was permissible
only if the sheriff deputized the searchers, a point of law that had not yet
deterred any of the state forces. Beeler felt society must be protected from
such riotous behavior by "niggers." Although Dickinson had initially
resisted the idea because of its questionable legality, he now acquiesced.[11]

Approximately seventy-five deputized patrolmen and seventy-five
guardsmen fanned out into all black residential areas of the town—east
Columbia, Macedonia, Happy Hollow—confiscating ammunition and
three hundred to four hundred weapons. Despite later claims of their
high-powered capability, most of these were old squirrel and rabbit guns,
.22-caliber pistols, and a few old shotguns. The blacks had well hidden
their more dangerous weapons. Authorities made no searches of any
white neighborhoods.[12]

Criteria for arrest of blacks during the next two to three days occasionally included suspicion of felony, but some were arrested for simply
being melanotic and ambulatory. The gendarmerie were rounding up the
usual Negro suspects, many of whom had a past history of liquor
running.

A policeman rescued the janitor at City Hall who had been
surrounded and threatened with lynching. Joe Calloway was arrested
early Tuesday morning as he walked to work. Walking along Woodland
that morning, Hiawatha Leftrick was arrested and knocked unconscious
with a blackjack. Deputies arrested Alexander Bullock and tattooed him
across the face with a blackjack when he came to City Hall. He was only
trying to claim his stalled car he had fled on Mt. Pleasant Pike when some
black fellows shot at him the night before. The grocer, James Martin, was
arrested on Thursday because the police had heard he expressed the
sentiment that all the "laws" in town should be shot.

John Dudley had "raised" and worked for numerous prominent
Columbians. A policeman and Billy Griffin saw the seventy-four year old
coming out of the courthouse after picking up his pension check. They

Onlookers look over a pacified Mink Slide. (Courtesy—GJ files)

After the round-up, William Gordon in light coat, Leonard Evans to his right, Chief Griffin's son, Billy, second patrolman from left. (Courtesy—GJ files)

Keep your arms up! (Courtesy—GJ files)

Mink Slide roust. (Courtesy—GJ files)

Confiscated weapons; Sheriff Underwood on left, THP Sgt. E. B. Noles to his left, Constable Copeland on right. (Courtesy—GJ files)

Sgt. Dave White guards prisoners at foot of Mink Slide; Clarence Brown in combat boots. (Courtesy—GJ files)

Joe Calloway getting arrested. (Courtesy—GJ files)

Heading up Woodland Street to jail. (Courtesy—GJ files)

shoved him into their car, told him they were tired of his showing his "importancy" to white folks, and arrested him.[13]

Julius Blair, who had slept through the night but unfortunately had been designated as a ringleader, was finally incarcerated after several *faux* arrests. He had tried to make bond for Saul on Tuesday morning but was told by Underwood that the highway patrol was not allowing any bond. Patrol Sgt. Noles apprehended him as he was going home. Underwood freed him, but later several other patrolmen braced Blair against his car and demanded to know where his gun was. When he replied he did not have one, Flo Fleming retorted, "You ain't too good to have one, you old, gray-headed son-of-a-bitch," and arrested him.[14]

By Wednesday, the final contingents of more than eight hundred Tennessee State Guardsmen and approximately seventy-five Tennessee Highway Patrolmen were well in place and in total control. Governor McCord had toured the town Tuesday afternoon and expressed his satisfaction with how state forces had responded. Local papers praised the restoration of order. There were no white mobs, and most of the blacks were incarcerated. Though Negro property had been damaged, state lawmen had apparently stopped the civil disturbance without fatalities.[15]

DEATH IN THE JAIL

By Thursday, over one hundred prisoners were stuffed into a couple of cells in the county jail, an old, two-story house that had been converted into a lockup as well as a home for the sheriff and his family.[16] Underwood and his staff were overwhelmed and seemed to make little use of the swarms of visiting state lawmen. Technicalities and details slowed procedures; just processing the prisoners took two days. District Attorney General Paul Bumpus and the sheriff were also inundated with requests for interviews by out-of-town newspapermen, some black, from all over the country. This was bigger than Mule Day but much less fun.

Authorities had never anticipated and were not remotely capable of caring for this many prisoners. They kept the Blairs and Morton in a separate room, apparently because of their perceived rank. There were only four other beds. Most prisoners squatted or stood, whether asleep or awake. Their menu included two daily meals of old bacon, syrup, partially cooked beans, and corn bread. Leaky buckets served as common toilet facilities. Prisoners spat tobacco juice onto the cold, wet concrete floor to kill maggots.[17]

Patrolman Don Kelly
questions James Morton.
(Courtesy—*NB*)

Patrolman frisks James "Popeye" Bellanfant.
(Courtesy—GJ files)

Searching for weapons, William Gordon
fourth from right. (Courtesy—GJ files)

Patrolmen view a cleared Mink Slide; note Castner-Knott sign in background. (Courtesy—GJ files)

Many of the prisoners were scared; some were passive. Others seethed because of the terrible conditions, the dubious grounds upon which most of them had been arrested, and raw racial anger. Authorities felt strangely secure and apparently did not recognize any persistent danger.

Those prisoners who were sophisticated enough to want representation were not allowed to seek it.[18] Neither were their families allowed to see them. No prisoner could make bail, as authorities had refused to post any. Beginning on Thursday morning, two days after the majority of arrests, a "commission" consisting of District Attorney Bumpus, Sheriff Underwood, Commissioner Bomar, and Assistant State Attorney General Ernest Smith (representing Governor McCord) began interrogating prisoners. Those arrested could not be freed until they had appeared before their captors and potential prosecutor, Bumpus. The panel questioned prisoners in the jail dining room. They either freed, re-incarcerated, or assigned bail to the prisoners.[19] Again, all were without counsel!

One of the first prisoners called was James "Digger" Johnson, son of Meade. Johnson had an arrest record for bootlegging and gambling. As a known acquaintance of Underwood, he was afraid his early summons would look to his friends as if the sheriff were doing him a favor. Underwood thought Johnson would cooperate and that the state would get some information from him.

Willie Gordon and Johnson were acquaintances but not close friends. Gordon also had a record, but most of his arrests were for violent acts. Unlike his six younger siblings, he was an angry, volatile individual. He had once been arrested for fighting a man, paid both his and his victim's fines, and then shot the man. Gordon and Johnson had apparently bragged that they were among the police shooters. Believing the law was after him, Gordon was fidgety and morose and would not eat during his incarceration. He gave his wallet to his brother, Horace, who was also imprisoned. He also allegedly sought a razor and said that if the law took him out, some of them would go with him.[20]

Digger Johnson's testimony was circuitous and self-serving and would later play an important role in legal proceedings. Gordon had reason for concern. Sadie Flippin had implicated him before the interrogators as one who shot the policemen. However, his testimony was terse and unrevealing. The board felt sure he was withholding information and set his bail at five hundred dollars, a figure they thought might encourage cooperation but which he might also meet because he worked for wealthy white people.

The fatal fiasco that followed was at least in part due to crowded facilities and carelessness by lawmen. Johnson, Gordon, and Napolean Stewart were taken to the sheriff's office to await bail. Also in the room, which was between the lockup and the family's living quarters, were

Deputy Tom R. Darnell, the sheriff's just deputized son-in-law Ed Pennington, and *Nashville Banner* photographer John Morgan. They were distracted from the prisoners as they casually pursued various activities: Pennington lounging on a cot and the deputy talking on the telephone. More ominous (and hard to believe), guns were stacked everywhere—in corners, behind chairs, and under beds.

Somehow Gordon and Johnson quickly loaded a couple of guns; Gordon's was a bolt-action .22 rifle. Sheriff Underwood thought the shells might have been in a hanging mackinaw. His son Jimmy believed Gordon had them in his shirt pocket. John Morgan believed they were brought in with some cigars by Pennington. Others said that initial frisking of the prisoners was just inefficient. Each probably got off one shot, grazing the deputy on the arm.

Several patrolmen were walking in the corridor outside the parlor when the shooting began. They had come to identify the prisoners who had purportedly wounded their men from Blair's barbershop the morning of their Mink Slide raid. They had removed their side arms as they approached the cell block. J. J. Jackson grabbed Underwood's pistol as the sheriff ran toward the shooting. Other arms were quickly passed to patrolmen. Jackson, Dave White, Billy Griffin (the police chief's son), and others filled the doorway and blasted away at Gordon and Johnson.

Napoleon Stewart sought safety by running to a corner and raising his hands. The ever-present Flo Fleming shouted that Stewart was going for his gun and knocked the prisoner down with a blow to the face. The hapless Stewart then felt the toes of numerous THP boot tips kicking him and felt the weight of Bomar's foot on his neck. He had no problem concurring with the burly commissioner's suggestion that he "lay still."[21]

Though barely alive, the two perforated prisoners were taken to Meharry Hospital, an all-black institution in Nashville, for care. Later critics said the two men were allowed to die because of a whites-only policy at the Columbia hospital. Local authorities said the transfer was necessary because the victims were too seriously injured to benefit from local care. The "bad" and "dangerous" Negroes, Johnson and Gordon, died in transit to Nashville.[22]

ENDING THE CRISIS

Before the killings, Attorney General Bumpus had recognized potential problems caused by the jail being overcrowded. Afterward, all authorities

Patrolman frisks William Gordon. (Courtesy—GJ files)

Deputy Tom Darnell shows the gunshot wound to his forearm. (Courtesy—*NB*)

Calvin Lockridge (with cap) and group of prisoners in Nashville jail. (Courtesy—*NB*)

Patrolman Billy Griffin inspects confiscated weapons. (Courtesy—*NB*)

agreed the boiling pressure in the jail needed to be relieved. The prisoners were scared and restive, and their response was hard to predict. Their keepers were also somewhat unpredictable. Just after the shooting, a highway patrolman had opened the main cell, waved an automatic weapon, and suggested they should all be similarly mowed down.

Late that afternoon, a cattle truck, with manure still carpeting its bed, was backed up to the jail. Forty-two prisoners were packed in to be taken to a jail in Nashville for twenty-four hours. The trip was terrible. Prisoners took turns breathing through a slit to the outside. Once in Nashville though, things looked up for them. They could bathe, had individual beds, and were served warm food. Raymond Lockridge thought he had gone from hell to heaven.[23]

From a maximum Maury County jail population of more than one hundred prisoners, all were released by March 7. They had either made bail or been released due to lack of cause for incarceration. Bonds varied from $250 to $5000, the latter applying to "big shot" leaders such as James Morton and the Blairs. The state guard left town on March 3; and authorities lifted curfew the following day, one week after William Fleming and James Stephenson had their disagreement. Mayor Denham spoke over Nashville radio station WLAC, extolling his town and the good conditions there. The *Daily Herald* editorialized that the city had returned to normal and asked all good citizens to "pitch in."[24]

Despite the brief coverage of the riot's legal ramifications, a couple of such features that were uncharacteristic of trouble in these parts were noteworthy to locals. One was that Horace Frierson, a Columbia native and current U.S. attorney in Nashville, had felt compelled to make an early statement that no civil rights had been violated by authorities. A week later, he reported that he had requested Federal Bureau of Investigation (FBI) agents to investigate the riot, unusual activity from the federal government's prosecutor in Middle Tennessee.[25] A second peculiarity was that among the many strange faces in town just after the riot were lawyers, some black and one conspicuous white, who were clamoring to defend those arrested. Who were these people, and just what business did they have in Maury County? The battle was over, but the legal war was just beginning.

CHAPTER FIVE

Big (and Strange) Fish in a Little Pond

LEGAL REPRESENTATION

Maurice Maxwell Weaver arrived in Columbia the evening of February 26. The NAACP had retained the thirty-three-year-old, white lawyer from Chattanooga. Weaver was a graduate of the University of Tennessee Law School, where his liberal political inclinations and concern for the downtrodden had been reinforced by a sympathetic faculty. The navy veteran had worked for numerous left-wing causes and organizations, including the Congress of Industrial Organizations (CIO).

A field representative of the NAACP in Chattanooga had recommended Weaver to its executive director, Walter White, who had phoned him before flying to Tennessee from New York City. The NAACP also sent Z. (Zebulon) Alexander Looby to the scene. The native of Antigua, British West Indies, practiced in Nashville and was a member of the NAACP National Legal Committee.

Walter White reasoned that a white lawyer would be less controversial than a black one in Columbia. That was a misjudgment. The soft-spoken and gentlemanly Looby was to be far less disputatious than his white colleague. Weaver's friends and opponents recognized not only his brilliance but also his questionable ethics and morals. With his disruptive methods and as a perceived traitor to his race, he was to quickly become an effective nuisance to prosecutors and a legal lightning rod in the Columbia matter.[1]

Weaver was at Sheriff Underwood's office at seven o'clock on the morning of February 27 and had no initial trouble attaining access to Saul Blair and James Morton. Sheriff Underwood told him later that day that he could not see any more prisoners until an "investigation" was completed. Underwood also assured Weaver that they would soon release the prisoners. With that promise, Weaver went home to Chattanooga.[2]

When he returned on Thursday, however, no prisoners had been released, and Julius Blair had been arrested. The elder Blair had taken Weaver to interview Mary Morton during the lawyer's initial visit. This fraternization had raised local authorities' hackles, who asked Blair when they arrested him why he was "running around town with these white lawyers from Chattanooga."[3]

Weaver encountered official obstruction wherever he turned. Squire Denton refused to let him see any arrest warrants, saying there had already been too much interference. The first fractious interface between the interferer and Commissioner Bomar occurred that Thursday afternoon after the jailhouse shootings. Bomar was clearly in charge at the jail. He told Weaver that the sheriff was elsewhere though Underwood was obviously there. When Bomar said Weaver might be in some danger of being shot on the street, Weaver responded he had no apprehension for his safety with Bomar's ample protection. In questioning why Weaver should be so interested in these matters, Bomar told him "you will find out the Negroes were trying to set up a dictatorship." As suggested by Bomar, Weaver returned later that day to see his potential clients only to find they had been shipped to Nashville.[4] Feelings between the commissioner and the aggressive attorney were to bloom from antipathy to hatred.

Forty-five-year-old State District Attorney Paul Bumpus had an excellent reputation. He was honest, conscientious, and persistent. He grew up in Mt. Pleasant, "read" the law with local lawyer Mr. Joe Garner, and was admitted to the bar in 1921. He overcame a stuttering impediment and was considered an effective courtroom presenter. The district attorney truly believed the county and nation were facing a civil war and was, therefore, all the more diligent on this case.

The board of investigation that questioned prisoners in order to establish bail and investigate the riot was proceeding slowly before the killings of Gordon and Johnson. When the situation was further compounded by that crisis, big-city reporters, and the obnoxious Weaver, the interviews and continued imprisonments were only prolonged. Bumpus was orderly and thorough as he built his investigative case. Keeping out defense lawyers surely aided the prosecutor's discovery. He apparently did not

imagine that forbidding representation during these proceedings
might be a key element in later
plaintiffs' defenses.

Looby and Weaver threatened to
file *habeas corpus* writs while the prisoners were in Nashville and did file
several in Columbia early the next
week. Whether this pressure had
any effect on state officials is unclear.
As prisoners were systematically
examined, they gradually dribbled
out of jail throughout the next week.
Authorities released some prisoners
because they obviously were not
involved in the shootings. Both the
Mink Slide "money men" and some
sympathetic whites provided bail;
defendants allegedly refused proffered NAACP money.

Two late arrests took place on
March 8, those of Robert Gentry and
John McKissack. Looby and Weaver

Attorney General Paul F. Bumpus. (Courtesy—
MD)

immediately filed *habeas corpus* briefs on their accounts. Since they were
considered prime suspects by prosecutors, Ingram set their bail bonds at
the highest level, five thousand dollars. Defense attorneys in this early
skirmish showed different personalities and professional styles that
would carry through two trials over several months. In conciliation and
compromise, Looby argued that bail be lowered to a more affordable five
hundred dollars for the poor men. In contrast, Weaver swung for the
fences and asked the charges be dismissed because the state could not
place the defendants at the crime scene. Ingram retained the high bond,
and the incarcerated men were promptly bailed out by Julius Blair, James
Morton, and Jim Martin. Authorities had not yet arrested any whites,
despite continued public reassurances by Bumpus that they would do so.

As defendants watched the frenetic Weaver and persistent Looby,
they forsook any previous lawyers they may have had and turned their
defense over to their new barrister friends from the NAACP. Looby excit-
edly proclaimed, "These are the new Negroes of the South." No more
Booker T. Washingtons would patiently work and wait.[5]

OUTSIDE AGITATORS

The Mink Slide riot and its controversial end were tailor made for the NAACP, and the leading national advocacy organization for blacks committed itself to the duration of legal resolution. The organization's board set up national steering and advisory committees, hoping to defend those indicted, identify and punish those they felt were the real villains, obtain compensation for physical damages, and alert the nation to avoid such conflicts in similar settings. The call went out to chapters to help finance the effort, and the chapters responded. The association assigned audacious, brave, and increasingly successful Special Counsel Thurgood Marshall to the case and continued to use the services of Looby and Weaver. In addition to pamphlets, they planned a movie about the matter.[6]

The riot attracted quick attention from various other regional and national organizations. Some of their opinions were studied and balanced; others were regionally patronizing, sanctimonious, disruptive, and/or dishonest. Among the established civil rights organizations looking into the riot and occasionally influencing its outcome were the Southern Conference for Human Welfare (SCHW), the Southern Regional Council (SRC), the American Missionary Association, and the Chicago Civil Liberties Committee. Perhaps the most interested of the overtly rabble-rousing groups was the American Communist Party.

Though some of these groups could influence matters by fund-raising, others' greatest effects were through their publications. Among the screeds that began popping up within days of the riot was an especially locally unpopular one, written by Clark Foreman, president of the SCHW. "The Truth about Columbia Tennessee Cases" pointed blame at state and local officialdom and became, itself, an issue to be considered. The SCHW was immediately active on the national front as well. Foreman wired his organization's irateness to Attorney General Tom C. Clark, and its New York Committee endorsed an angry wire from the NAACP's Walter White to President Truman.

The SRC was more moderate and less interventionist or controversial than the SCHW, which had some tenuous ties to the Communist party through its frequently changing leadership and served as a continual target for white, southern editorialists. Guy Johnson in *New South*, the journal of the SRC, later examined the Columbia event more thoroughly and dispassionately but still blamed Tennessee's politicians and lawmen.[7]

Black newspapers such as the *Chicago Defender* and *Pittsburgh Courier* reacted along racial lines in a predictable fashion. The *Louisville Leader* right away sent reporters, who were among the first journalists to draw

Thurgood Marshall, c. 1945.
(Courtesy—The *Crisis*)

Bumpus's time and ire. The national Negro magazine *Ebony* published big, gory pictures but was very temperate in its reporting. It noted the unfortunate parallel with racial outbreaks in 1919 and assigned biracial responsibility for the riot.[8]

Northern liberal publications also responded predictably, occasionally accurately, but usually without the benefit of investigation. For example, The *New Republic* pessimistically predicted the law-enforcement reaction was symptomatic of the militant spirit sweeping the country.[9]

Some of the most interesting and voluminous early coverage, particularly by Harry Raymond,[10] was in the *Daily Worker of New York*, a Communist publication. The *Worker* had a stringer in Middle Tennessee for many months and published much more than did the local papers on the riot. Some of its coverage was inaccurate. All of it was inflammatory. The newspaper's journalistic persistence led to some scoops, including interviews of both Gladys and James Stephenson, obvious and attainable stories that no regional paper seemed interested in pursuing. In addition to Bomar, the *Worker* consistently singled out Flo Fleming as one of the villains of the piece. It called him a "leader of the lynchers," described him strutting down

Mink Slide, and printed the recurring story of his needing a bandage on his hand because of an injury sustained from beating Negroes in the jail.

The Communist party recognized the propaganda value of the Mink Slide riot. Community schism reinforced the party's message of class struggle and seemed to bode well for its recruitment of blacks. Communists generously conceded Columbia was not a totally bad town because of a union presence in many of its industrial plants. To them, though, there were good and bad unions. The Mine, Mill, and Smelter CIO workers, mainly at the Armour plant, were pitted in their scenario against the "Jim Crowed" workers of the Victor and National Carbon plants.

The party also sponsored a shrill pamphlet by Robert Minor. *Lynching and Frame-up in Tennessee* hyperbolically recounted Maury County and Tennessee's twentieth-century repression of Negroes, describing in detail the lynchings of Henry Choate and Cordie Cheek. Though slanted heavily in favor of Negroes' perspectives, its account of the Mink Slide riot was as accurate as any other by "outsiders." In seeking a cause for the catastrophe, Minor blamed Monsanto (part of a "vast, worldwide monopoly"); the "great trusts" of the north, who needed unorganized, low-wage southern workers; and all sitting politicians, from southern racists to northern Republicans. His solution to race and labor problems in the South and elsewhere was membership in the Communist Party.[11]

Within a month of the riot, the NAACP sent several of the Negro principals on speaking tours around the country to tell their version of events at Columbia and raise money for their defense. They addressed church congregations, civil rights organizations, and political rallies. Calvin Lockridge spoke in Chattanooga to ministers and representatives of the Highlander Folk School, then headed up the East Coast. After attending meetings in Norfolk and Baltimore, he and Saul Blair addressed a conference of 150 delegates in Washington, D.C. Calvin returned to Washington in April to speak to the National Negro Conference.

Called by the SCHW, the National Federation for Constitutional Liberties, and various CIO unions, this polyglot conference in Washington on March 13 demonstrated the rapid, passionate, and general reaction of leftist organizations to the riot. Among those sending representatives were the NAACP and the Chicago Civil Liberties Committee. A thirty-three-member entourage from Chicago rode a B & O Railroad "Civil Liberties Car" to Washington.

Both Stephensons spoke in Chicago and Detroit. Gladys, along with Marshall, Weaver, Looby, and Leon A. Ransom, also addressed the Thirty-seventh Conference of the NAACP in June.

Raymond Lockridge fondly recalled his magical train tour. Starting in Rochester, New York, the laborer/minister took the message across the

Editorial view of the *Nashville Banner* on "outside agitators" of the Columbia race riot. (Courtesy—*NB*)

upper Midwest through Youngstown, Akron, Cleveland, Toledo, Detroit, Chicago, Milwaukee, and Minneapolis-St. Paul.[12]

Of national groups dabbling in the Columbia affair, the most interesting and potentially influential was one whose executive committee was co-chaired by Eleanor Roosevelt and Channing Tobias. The National Committee for Justice in Columbia, Tennessee, formed to act in conjunction with the NAACP. Whether for efficiency or maintenance of organizational turf, Executive Director Walter White felt that all funds should be raised by the NAACP or the National Committee for Justice and managed by the former. The 110-member committee contained many of the prominent liberals and Negro rights advocates of the era, e.g., Eleanor Roosevelt, Mary Bethune, Bette Davis, Albert Einstein, Clark Foreman, Oscar Hammerstein II, Fiorello LaGuardia, Sinclair Lewis, Adam C. Powell Jr., and A. Philip Randolph. In addition to raising money through the committee, Negro leaders used its propaganda and Mrs. Roosevelt's access to important national leaders, particularly Attorney General Clark. Though not as controversial as Robert Minor's pamphlet, this organization also put out an inflammatory, inaccurate tract called "Terror in Tennessee."[13]

The committee's obvious regional constituency and anti-segregation philosophy made it instantly and continually unpopular among most southerners. Roosevelt was an especially red cape to segregationist bulls. Despite her husband's continual electoral capture of the South, her efforts for integration had not gone down well in Dixie. Though they were apparently mythical, her detractors continually referred to the notorious "Eleanor Clubs," alleged groups of Negro women who were inspired by Eleanor Roosevelt to end their traditional domestic employment to white women.[14]

Governor McCord was an immediate recipient of northern and Negro pressure. He received Walter White, Looby, and Reverend William Faulkner the afternoon of the February 26. His secretary, Bayard Tapley, treated the notoriously pale-skinned White brusquely but was absolutely rude to his darker companions. White denied the accuracy of subsequent Nashville newspaper versions of this meeting, which described NAACP acceptance of state actions in the riot as necessary and appropriate.[15]

Later in the week, leftist strangers Samuel Neuberger and Reverend Joseph Moore of the National Federation for Constitutional Liberty and Ira H. Latimer, executive director of the Chicago Civil Liberties Union, visited McCord. In spite of the state's critical involvement, the governor was now taking a hands-off attitude, asserting that the Columbia affair should be handled locally. Black editorialists immediately expressed disapproval, a policy that was to continue into the imminent gubernatorial election.[16]

This unusual interest by outside agencies was, however, no more surprising and unsettling to locals than actions of the federal government. The U.S. Department of Justice had not, to any significant extent, intervened in local disputes since the Reconstruction. That executive arm of federal law was to forsake such policy in the Mink Slide matter, portending an active role in civil rights struggles in the last half of the century.

FEDERAL INVOLVEMENT

U.S. Attorney Horace Frierson's motives in making an early statement about the non-abridgement of civil rights in the Columbia race riot are unknown. Critics said he was trying to protect his hometown's reputation with a hasty and erroneous application of legal whitewash. On the other hand, his quick reaction to the situation served to officially bring it to the attention of his superiors in Washington and guaranteed a federal role of some sort.

After the two jail slayings, Frierson requested regional FBI agents investigate the riot. They were interviewing participants in Columbia within a week of its outbreak. Local papers did not respond to the FBI appearance, but the *Nashville Globe*, a weekly Nashville black newspaper, was exultant. *Globe* journalists believed this meant the federals were taking over the situation, and therefore blacks would more likely receive justice. Of more significance was an apparently changed attitude on the part of the big, daily *Nashville Tennessean*. *Tennessean* editorialists felt that Attorney General Clark should assign a U.S. attorney other than Frierson, i.e., one without any potential conflict of interest, to investigate the Columbia riot. This suggestion was a largely unnoticed but significant break in the traditional attitude of major southern newspapers toward the correct use of federal authority in racial matters.[17]

In early March, Attorney General Clark began releasing strong statements about the violation of civil rights during the riot. He ordered that a special grand jury look into such alleged violations. Federal Judge Elmer Davies instead turned the issue over the federal grand jury then sitting in Nashville. The FBI findings in Columbia were to provide appropriate material for their deliberations. Again, the Nashville black paper saw nothing but good for Columbia blacks coming from this source of justice, calling the pending proceedings "one of the most historic legal battles ever fought."[18]

Negro editorialists were writing from their hearts and not their heads. As already seen in the Columbia incident, this was an era in which law officials with different jurisdictions had similar attitudes and cooperated without rivalry or burdensome organizational barriers to seek public safety and justice as they perceived them. Just as he certainly did over the highway patrol, Boss Crump supposedly had considerable influence over the Memphis-based FBI agents who investigated the riot. Perhaps the journalists should have wondered if hazy jurisdictional lines and the exigencies of regional politics would have any effects on things so supposedly sacrosanct as the FBI and a federal grand jury proceeding.

LEGAL MANEUVERING

On March 22, Bumpus presented several indictments to the Eleventh Circuit Court Grand Jury. Case 4718, *State of Tennessee* v. *Saul Blair, et al.*, charged Saul Blair, Julius Blair, James Morton, Meade Johnson, and James Bellanfant with inciting Robert Gentry, Luther Edwards, Paul Miles, Raymond Lockridge and certain other persons to commit murder in the first degree. Other defendants were William "Moot" Bills, William Dawson, Horace Gordon, Milton "Toady" Johnson, John Lockridge, Willie Pigg, Early Scott, Napolean Stewart, and Gene Williams. They allegedly attempted to kill Will Wilsford with malice and forethought with shotguns, rifles, pistols, and machine guns.

Case 4719 indicted whites, Carl Kelly, Roy Scribner, Earl Tomlin, and Joe Williams, for the assault on the jail to snatch the Stephensons. Case 4720, *State of Tennessee* v. *William Pillow and Loyd Kennedy*, charged the alleged shooters from Saul Blair's barbershop with injuring Patrolman Ray Austin. With Case 3721, the state accused John Blackwell of attempting to murder Patrolman C. A. Cartwright. Case 4722 included those luckless hiders in Morton's funeral home. Finally, Case 4731 indicted Gladys and James Stephenson. Bonds ranged from $250 to $5000 for several of the alleged "inciters."[19]

The NAACP had expanded the defense legal team. It now included Leon A. Ransom. The forty-seven-year-old Negro graduate of Ohio State Law School was a law professor at Howard University and a member of the NAACP legal staff. Walter White felt the case was ideal for defense because of the absence of sex charges and the high character of the defendants.[20]

This respected team set to work establishing the principles of their defense and, much to the displeasure of Judge Joe Ingram and the prosecution, stringing out the proceedings. Though anticipating the worst outcome of the trials, the defendants were absolutely delighted with the persistence and pugnaciousness of their lawyers. The local white press called their tactics "filibustering." Jubilant black editorialists questioned in headlines whether prosecutors could "Take It as Well as You Can Dish It?" In spite of their tenacity, all these crack barristers seemed to be accomplishing was trial delay. In May, Ingram denied pleas for continuance and separate trials.

Typical for the region, Negroes had not served on many Maury County juries. A week after the indictments, Weaver and the other defense lawyers signed pleas of abatement on the grounds that their clients could not get a fair trial because blacks had allegedly been systematically excluded from the indicting grand jury. The prosecution countered with testimony from three blacks on the tax files who had been summoned by postcard when the last jury pool had been created in 1944. Though he really did not know what was going on, one of these fellows had found his way to the courthouse but was told there that his name was nowhere on the list. The other two did not understand their responsibility, seemed ill-at-ease with legal proceedings, and had their employers get them excused from the summons. This hardly seemed a representative call of informed Maury County Negroes to jury duty.

Thurgood Marshall inveigled the jury commissioner, Joe Taylor, to admit they always "tried to pick large taxpayers" for juries. Looby immediately sought case dismissal on this ground. Judge Ingram denied the abatement plea, a frequently used defense measure calling to quash a trial. The judge averred that jury commissioners had acted in accordance with state laws when they replaced the jury box in 1944 and pointed out that the resultant 1946 list contained ten Negroes. The defense had, nevertheless, begun establishing substantive grounds for the appeals they thought would inevitably be necessary.[21]

The defenders attacked every possible weak detail of the legal actions against their clients. They filed a misnomer plea on behalf of William Pillow, who had been called "Willie Pigg" in the original indictment. Ingram quickly dismissed these pleas as trivial.

In late June, defense attorneys argued for a change in venue, hoping for Williamson or Davidson County.[22] They felt that both these counties north of Maury were less hostile to blacks and that they might be able to

Attorneys before the bench of Judge Joe Ingram: Left to right—Maurice Weaver, Howard Ransom, Z. Alexander Looby, Paul Bumpus. (Courtesy—*NB*)

place some blacks on a jury in either place. This was especially true of Davidson, home of State Capital Nashville.

Ingram granted the change of venue motion on July 2. To defense lawyers' utter horror though, he moved the trial to Lawrence County. That county, just south of Maury, had very few blacks and had an even more racist reputation. The 1940 census showed a county population of 28,025 people, 2.4 percent of which were Negro. In 1946, a sign was allegedly posted on the outskirts of Lawrenceburg, the county seat, which read, "Nigger, read and run."[23] Ingram denied a hasty withdrawal of the venue-change motion, asserting that Lawrence County's contiguity to Maury made it perfect for a trial site.

On July 23, Ingram gave defense attorneys sixty days to prepare and file their wayside bill of exceptions. This was a defense summation of evidence presented in the absence of a court reporter the substance of which must be accepted by the presiding judge and which can be used to justify retrial in another court. Despite Looby and Weaver's continued pleading against moving proceedings to Lawrenceburg, Ingram set a firm trial date there of August 8.[24] The time for maneuvering was over. Prosecution and defense now had to toe the legal line.

CHAPTER SIX

Federal Grand Jury

THE CHARGE

A judicial hearing had already occurred in late spring 1946, which perhaps predicted for both prosecution and defense their possible hopes in the pending criminal trial. This was the federal grand jury hearing in Nashville that investigated the Columbia riot. A barrage of political pressure had descended on President Truman and U.S. Attorney General Tom Clark in the weeks following the riot. Letters, petitions, and telegrams came from academics, businessmen, congressmen, ministers, municipalities, private citizens, and labor unions—the sleeping car porters auxiliary, transportation workers, steelworkers, and autoworkers. The attorney general felt the pressure and issued a press release on March 7 announcing that the Justice Department intended to investigate whether federal laws had been violated during the riot.

In the manner of such prosecutorial proceedings, testimony was secret and publicity scant. Still, Bumpus and Weaver and the other attorneys probably honed their cases from the direction and outcome of the federal grand jury deliberation. Regardless the judgment reached by the jury, a federal hearing of a case on civil rights violations in the South was most unusual. It is uncertain whether any of the participants recognized that the hearing was a harbinger of similar events that would transpire in coming decades, after several critical U.S. Supreme Court decisions and legislative actions.

TESTIMONY

On April 8, 1946, only six weeks after the Mink Slide riot, testimony began in Nashville before the Grand Jury for the Middle District of Tennessee "In the Matter of Columbia, Tennessee, Investigation." Federal Judge Elmer D. Davies charged them to make a "full, complete, fair, and impartial investigation," especially into potential violations of civil rights alleged to have occurred in the Columbia riot. He counseled that the supposedly violated rights were defined in the Fourteenth Amendment to the Constitution and clarified in Section 41, Title 8 USCA, Section 52 Title 18 USCA, and case law. These statutes addressed due process and equal protection in general and the legally defined rights of non-white Americans in particular. He stressed that a public official must *willfully* violate civil rights while performing his duties to be in violation of the law.

This grand jury had apparently finished its work several weeks prior, and Davies apologized for calling them back. He also addressed an emerging bone of contention: why he had not called a *special* grand jury as requested by Clark. Applying some tortuous reasoning, Davies said he did not do so in order to avoid the appearance of rigging the proceedings after the considerable publicity that had followed the riot. The judge went beyond Clark's wishes and introduced an additional issue, the inflammatory pamphlets that had flooded Columbia.

J. F. Richardson of Hohenwald was chairman of the twenty-three white men on the panel. In addition to District U.S. Attorney Horace Frierson and his assistants A. O. Denning and Z. Thomas "Tommy" Osborn Jr.,[1] three representatives from the Department of Justice in Washington, John M. Kelley Jr., A. B. Caldwell, and Eleanor Bontecou, were to participate in the proceedings.[2] Several distinct groups testified before the jury for the next two months.

Investigators

W. E. Hopton represented the FBI agents who had interviewed about 390 people in their investigation. On the first day of testimony, he said the Department of Justice's mission consisted of two parts: They intended first to determine whether any civil rights had been violated and second to determine, if possible, what was the cause of the disturbance. He synopsized the event as he had come to understand it, including several themes that would recur throughout later versions and various trials. These included the February 26 indiscriminate search for guns in only Negro homes, the official version of the jailhouse slayings, the presumptive guilt of black "leaders," highway patrol denial of vandalism, and the early prevention of NAACP attorneys communicating with prisoners.

Hopton confirmed that the white men milling around the square in the early evening of the twenty-fifth were armed and many were drunk. He felt that the damage in Saul Blair's barbershop could not have all been done by gunfire from the street. The vandalism in James Morton's funeral parlor was also mischievous and extensive.

After comprehensive investigation, he definitely felt no organized conspiracy existed among blacks for either offensive or defensive purposes. The FBI looked into various rumors surrounding the riot and could find no substantiation for prevalent stories about the alleged rope purchase and multiple killings of blacks by authorities.[3]

Fight Participants

The jury heard a reconstruction of the riot-precipitating fight from the combatants and one onlooker. This testimony varied according to race. The nervous clerk, Lavala LaPointe, and a polite Billy Fleming said James Stephenson struck the first blow. A contrite Fleming said the disagreement would have ended had he not hastily opened the outer store door and pursued the Stephensons.

Gladys Stephenson denied hitting or cutting Fleming, denied cursing or resisting arrest, and said she fought to protect her son from the police. Her son James said Fleming struck the first blow and that he fought to protect himself and his mother. He cooly described his escape to Chicago, about which Gladys learned three days after he left. When asked about his contacts since the event, James said he had talked in Chicago to a NAACP lawyer, a "Mr. Thoroughgood" Marshall.[4]

The Law

Police Chief Griffin conveyed an air of calm detachment. He admitted he had experienced some unease in February; this sort of activity was unusual in Columbia. Still, in spite of rumors about racial revenge against the Stephensons and growing white crowds around the square, enough to create a traffic jam from illegally parked cars, he saw no need to modify the town's security that evening. He also did not recall an impromptu speech allegedly given by City Judge Will Fleming (no relation to Billy or Flo Fleming) urging calmness and lawfulness. He could not explain why only the Stephensons were charged after the sidewalk fight, reassuring the jury that some whites would yet be arrested.

After giving his account of events, Sheriff Underwood elaborated on several points. The many arrests were overwhelming to the facilities and peacekeepers of Maury County. Despite the relatively massive presence of law officers, Underwood did almost all of the prisoner processing until Bumpus began to help on Wednesday. Underwood strongly adhered to

Patrolman inspects Blair's barbershop as guardsman looks on. (Courtesy—GJ files)

Some of the damage in Morton Funeral Home. (Courtesy—GJ files)

Some armed volunteers with highway patrolmen at top of Mink Slide. Officer with stripes on sleeve is J. J. Johnson. (Courtesy—GJ files)

the formulated "leader" thesis as a cause of the alleged insurrection, believing the crowds on Mink Slide had been mobilized by these alleged commanders, Morton and the Blairs. He was generally proud of law enforcement during the crisis, pointing out the low mortality rate. He agreed with Department of Justice official John Kelley Jr., who questioned, in a leading fashion, if blacks did not get more leniency than whites in crimes of violence.[5]

The investigation headed in a different direction with Commissioner Lynn Bomar's appearance. In several hours of effective testimony over two days, Bomar began a diversion away from possible errors of law-enforcement officials to alleged ones of numerous other agencies. He curbed his well-known temper (which would diminish his effectiveness in subsequent proceedings) and was courteous to all, apologizing to a woman transcriptionist for salting his testimony with the word hell. He said all actions by him and his agency were done to save lives as they faced unknown numbers of rioters in a racially volatile situation. He felt his intentions justified various acts, such as searching James Morton's house without warrant and invading Mink Slide before the appointed hour in violation of the plan made with the state guard. He *knew* Morton was a leader in the riot and expressed incredulity that folks in the under-taker's house would not want to immediately come out and offer themselves into the protective custody of the highway patrol. He admitted to only two personal physical contacts with prisoners, saying he "nudged" Calvin Lockridge with his knee and stepped on Napoleon Stewart's neck in the jailhouse after the shootings there.

He instructed his men to always be polite and would never have toler-ated racial discrimination. His only regret was not having enough men on guard duty at the jail in order to avoid the fatal shootings. It was beyond his comprehension that his men could have done any of the extensive destruc-tion to Mink Slide businesses. As for the despoliation in Morton's funeral parlor, both he and his men were too superstitious to mess with caskets.

In addition to establishing his virtuous professional motives by having his oath of office put in the report, Bomar read a long list of accusations against those outside elements whom he felt were responsible for the civil disorder in Columbia. These included Communist publications and a recurrently implicated demon, James Dombrowski, executive secretary of the SCHW. Bomar was especially incensed at and introduced into the record a copy of a political cartoon in the *Washington Afro-American* that depicted the THP rampaging through the funeral parlor.

A questioner queried the absence of an official written report by Bomar to Assistant Attorney General Ernest F. Smith, Governor McCord's

Political cartoon in *Washington Afro-American*, unfriendly to THP. (Courtesy—*WAA*)

representative in Columbia. Bomar dismissed this implied aspersion on his professional performance by saying that, although he had not interviewed all his men, he had talked with Smith for hours about the patrol's role in the matter. By introducing new and unfamiliar villains during the first week of testimony, Bomar had deflected the jury from its primary missions of investigating civil rights and what happened before and during the riot toward discovering just what happened *after* it.[6]

This shift in emphasis was reinforced by Ernest Smith's testimony. He bemoaned the introduction of communistic influences from other parts of the country, to which the "better class of Negro" did not subscribe. Among the outsiders he implicated were the Highlander Folk School and Dombrowski, who had allegedly called Morton in Mink Slide the night of the twenty-fifth. He introduced the statement of Digger Johnson, made shortly before he was killed. In a self-serving response to the interrogation of Bumpus's investigative panel, Johnson had told of planned black mobilization that was to be implemented in the event of racial conflict. This statement was to be repeatedly invoked as a substantiation of the recurring thesis that black leaders were prepared for rebellion and that the response to the Stephenson arrest and alleged lynch threat was orchestrated.[7]

State Attorney General Roy H. Beeler was prolix, imprecise, and contradictory. He cited some cases to justify emergency actions without warrant by the THP in order to protect citizens. He was unsure whether the raid on Morton's house represented unlawful search and seizure but believed the sheriff was the ultimate local authority and had been issuing warrants throughout the crisis. He thought blacks were treated fairly in Tennessee courts but that they would have even less trouble if they left white women alone. He ended his confusing diatribe by saying that wartime had given outsiders too much encouragement to know others' business.[8]

District Attorney General Paul Bumpus's testimony reflected the man's personality—careful, polite, compulsive, suspicious, and confident in his cause. Three interrogators spent little time on the specifics of the case and allowed Bumpus a pulpit to expound his relevant social views. He excused the slowness with which prisoners were processed by referring to the need to satisfy outside journalists and lawyers with uncertain jurisdictions. He agreed that conditions in the Maury County jail were horrible and that new facilities would be needed for the supposed coming crime wave. Bumpus joined the now rising crescendo against outsiders, particularly "foreign elements and agitators." He felt the riot was representative of a national problem and that it would not end until the federal government stopped it. Because of their political homogeneity, blacks, he believed, received special treatment, such as lower fines and bail bonds, from politicians. Both he and an interrogator, Assistant U.S. Attorney General Thomas Osborn Jr., agreed that the "white man's problems" included the prevention of undue influence on blacks by outsiders. Osborn closed by congratulating Bumpus on his "fairness."[9]

General Dickinson was precise and dignified, befitting his social and military status. He told of Bomar's premature invasion and their disagreement over the commissioner's forsaking of the joint plan. He had sought to avoid the use of firearms and reported his belief that a show of force and perhaps noxious chemicals would have prevented destruction and danger. He further distanced himself from the highway patrol with the first official testimony about the attempted confiscation of weapons from the armory by patrolmen who had lied saying he had given them permission to obtain them. He strongly defended his troops, whom he called "little kids," against the accusations in such documents as Clark Foreman's "Truth about Columbia." During six days of occupation with 802 troopers, his men fired only seven shots, five accidentally while cleaning guns. He did not believe any guardsmen vandalized Mink Slide.[10]

Several other guard officers testified in circumspect fashion, not giving much information and implicating no one. They were not sure the damage on Mink Slide was any worse later in the week than it was just after the THP raid. They entered only a couple of white homes during the search for weapons and stated that occupants of the searched homes were generally polite. These military types neither saw, heard, nor spoke any evil. Their testimony likely had little effect on the jury.[11]

Newsmen

The grand jury interviewed several photographers and reporters who had observed the riot and its aftermath. Their observations varied

Youthful Tennessee State
Guardsmen. (Courtesy—GJ files)

somewhat but generally were critical of the THP. John A. Kingcaid, the free-lance writer representing the United Press, was one of the earliest on the scene and most involved in the action. He had been in James Morton's house in the early hours of February 26 when Bomar walked in *sans* warrant. He then trailed Bomar until the Mink Slide roust was finished after daylight.

Kingcaid had a unique and relevant relationship with Maurice Weaver. He had met and partied with the Chattanoogan at a state legislature session in 1939. When Weaver saw Kingcaid at Columbia, he began calling him in Nashville. After several overtures, they had some drinks, and Weaver proposed the writer make a "statement" about what he had seen in Columbia, particularly the abuse of Negroes and property destruction. Weaver would of course meet Kingcaid's "expenses" for any information that might be helpful for the defense. Kingcaid shook him off by saying he had seen no abuse and only gunfire damage to store windows.

John Morgan, a *Nashville Banner* photographer, had also been close to a critical event. He was in the jail parlor when the gunfight resulted in the death of the two black prisoners. He recounted confusion, noise, and uncertain perpetration. He could not tell who fired the first shot, though he thought it was one of the prisoners. He said the two lawmen in the room had been distracted and were attending to matters other than guarding prisoners amidst stacks of confiscated weapons.

Most of the print journalists were appalled at the violence and destruction that characterized the THP Mink Slide raid. Both Ed Clark, photographer for *Life Magazine*, and Henry Schofield, photographer for the *Tennessean*, thought patrolmen fired first into Blair's barbershop. Certainly there was no return fire to the patrol's hour-long bombardment. They also supported testimony concerning gleeful beatings of arrested blacks with blackjacks, gun butts, flashlights, and feet. When asked why he did not capture any of this on film, Clark replied the actions were quick and surreptitious. This pair identified the highway patrol as those who wrought destruction in Morton's funeral parlor. Neither photographed any damaged coffins because the caskets were covered with paper when the newsmen entered.

John Thompson, reporter for the Associated Press, entered the Morton house while Bomar was making his multiple arrests there. He tarried to interview the weeping, hysterical women left behind. They told him of black fears arising from racial events during the last twenty years. He, too, could not understand the necessity for the patrol's ballistic rampage down Mink Slide. Reporter Beasley Thompson and photographer John Malone, both of the *Tennessean*, seconded these impressions of wanton destruction and bullying long after the situation was under control. Officials' fears of armed resistance seemed to have been proved invalid.

These *Tennessean* employees had briefly pursued a story implicating Sheriff Underwood as a contributing cause to the civil disruption. In the early morning hours of the twenty-sixth, Malone had heard a deputy tell someone at the jail that the sheriff was too easy on blacks and "would buddy with them." Thompson claimed tenuous corroboration of this belief and planned an article criticizing the sheriff for making political hay out of chaos. The newspaper allegedly did not run the story because of fears of libel. One observer felt this peculiar slant came from the rivalry between the Nashville newspapers. The *Banner* supported the sheriff, and the *Tennessean* was out to get him.[12]

White Boys

It is hard to understand why several white men who hustled into the action on February 25 were called to testify. Their stories were those of young men seeking excitement or mischief. In no way did the men represent the number of whites participating in the nocturnal events. The actions in the riot of those who testified were insignificant. Perhaps prosecutors saw them as typical of the people law officers were dealing with that night or were seeking some balance to subsequent testimony of multiple blacks.

Thirty-year-old Roy Scribner told of his early evening arrest by Underwood when Scribner drunkenly approached the jail to look into the "row" he had heard about. James Beard and Borgie Claude told their story of meeting up on South Main, loaded with beer and bullets. From their disjointed testimony, their sole aim did not appear to be to retrieve Claude's truck. The gasoline they carried was not for the vehicle, it seemed, but to help them burn Mink Slide. Yet to Columbia officials, whites gathered in town were only curious youngsters.[13]

Negroes

Several of the leading blacks began testifying during the second week of proceedings. The Blairs gave their versions of events. Saul was polite but evasive. After he said authorities would not allow him to contact a lawyer, the questioner asked if it might not have been for his own good to stay safely in jail. He described the damage in his shop and admitted blacks had stored some guns there the afternoon of the twenty-fifth. Saul's only contact with the alleged ultimate outside meddler, James Dombrowski, was at a March meeting at the Nashville Young Men's Hebrew Association.

Julius was dignified and occasionally hazy about details. He told of his efforts to protect the Stephensons and the final decision to get James out of town. He told of his arrest, his meeting Weaver, and the highway patrol being in charge. Reflecting his distrust of Magistrate Hayes Denton and Denton's supposedly racist district, Julius implied that Denton might have been responsible for the rumors of white mob violence. According to the elder Blair, the sheriff and police could and should have stopped the trouble before it got out of hand.

Calvin Lockridge recounted his complicated travels during the fateful day and night. He genuinely did not want any harm to come to Sheriff Underwood. He had not stayed on East Eighth that evening because he feared his new home would be burned by white mobs. His timing had been bad when he returned to Mink Slide to retrieve his nephew and there encountered Bomar. He described Bomar as kicking, not "nudging," his brother, Raymond.[14]

Late in the proceedings, the jury took testimony from a score of other Negroes. Some of this concerned clarification of Popeye Bellanfant's alleged call to arms given the young people on his school bus. The rest dealt with details of various men being flushed out of hiding places and arrested. All blacks denied shooting at patrolmen and gave recurring versions of beatings from them. John Blackwell denied having a gun, had no idea how cartridges came to be found on his person, and had little memory of events after he was hit in the head with a gun and bounced down the Odd Fellow's Hall stairway.[15]

The Defender

Apparently much to his pleasure, the grand jury called Maurice Weaver to the stand. He lengthily described his difficulty in getting through the legal maze to his new clients, elaborating on the machinations he and Looby used to try and free them. In order to prove that a dangerous white mob had been at the jail, he tried to have a transcription of his interview with Underwood on the afternoon of February 26 admitted into evidence. The jury refused to accept it.

Weaver's loquaciousness and aggressiveness got under the skin of Thomas Osborn. Osborn asked whether Weaver was actually denied access to any potential clients. In court, Weaver did not question the size of prisoners' bonds; he questioned the reason the prisoners were held. According to Weaver, retention of the prisoners was strictly for officials, through coercion, to create evidence for a criminal conspiracy invoked by the Blairs and James Morton. Weaver offered for investigation the names of several men who were not only coerced but beaten in jail. The jury dismissed him and his suggestions.[16]

The Outsiders

Less than a week after Lynn Bomar's testimony, the grand jury had diverted from its initial charge toward the allegedly disturbing outsiders and their inflammatory literature. James Dombrowski initially declined an invitation to appear. Instead he sent a letter saying he would be glad to assist the jury in any way he could. He admitted he had never visited Columbia and that his material for Foreman's most disturbing pamphlet, "Truth about Columbia," derived from culling various news organization and statements by Weaver, Underwood, and several Negroes. When interviewed by Thomas Osborn late in May, Dombrowski admitted he had made some errors in the pamphlet and planned to publish another article after the grand jury completed its work.

The jury also courteously examined black reporter Oliver C. "Ollie" Harrington, who had a public-relations job with the NAACP and had written several articles on the riot. His work was not so controversial, and no one suggested he need retract any of it.[17]

Ira Latimer, executive director of the Chicago Civil Liberties Committee, politely testified in a balanced manner. He described an interview with Underwood on March 3 in which the sheriff unburdened some of his thoughts about race relations and politics in Maury County. Underwood had said he had been too easy on veterans of both races and that this laxity had led to some lawlessness. He also confided his suspicion that fraud had been a big part of Flo Fleming's Democratic primary victory over him.

Latimer felt that the crisis could have been prevented by someone bridging the communication gap between blacks and whites. Underwood had at least tried but failed. No other leader had attempted to come between the two hostile, armed, and rumor-fed camps. That gap had allegedly continued after the riot as an approach to white clergymen by their black peers in Columbia had been rebuffed. When pushed by a questioner concerning someone who had contributed to the chaos and remained unindicted, Latimer nominated Flo Fleming, who he believed had battered Napoleon Stewart and others.

Latimer's investigation of the riot was careful. He felt the account reported in his organization's newspaper, the *Civil Liberty News*, was complete and fair, unlike those by the SCHW and Committee of 100, for which he had no journalistic respect. Though the jury's curiosity about outsiders may not have been satiated, Latimer's appearance helped convince them that all intruders were not necessarily ogres or unbalanced by prejudgment.[18]

THE U.S. DEPARTMENT OF JUSTICE

Whether in response to political pressure or because it was right to do so, General Clark, presumably with President Truman's blessing, immersed the U.S. Department of Justice into this regional conflict with cautious but unprecedented interest. The department seemed leery of crossing jurisdictional barriers or too quickly finding fault with Tennessee officials who had supposedly prevented greater chaos. Department lawyers aided Judge Davies in preparing instructions to the jury on the civil rights issues. Horace Frierson sought to minimize his role because of perceived conflict of interest, delegating the majority of investigation and interrogation to his assistants.

Soon after arrival, the visiting attorneys noted what they considered an unbalanced legal approach to the case. Local officials apparently intended for Bomar to receive no criticism. Davies was responsible for laudatory remarks about the commissioner being placed into the hearing transcript. Bomar had convinced everyone that his men did not destroy Mink Slide property. Rather, he asserted, the immature soldiers of the state guard were probably responsible.

The Washington lawyers, Kelley, Caldwell, and Bontecou, saw other biases in attitude and procedure. Davies and the U.S. attorneys seemed obsessed with the propaganda tracts that surfaced in Columbia. Witnesses were, in apparent collusion, telling different stories than those they had given the FBI just after the riot. Frierson's staff seemed intent on depicting black leaders as guilty revolutionaries. After extensive interviews and a trip to Columbia, the Department of Justice attorneys found no bases for any of these attitudes.

Clark's emissaries could not establish a harmonious working relationship with the Nashville-based U.S. attorneys. Both groups had agreed upon a sequence for questioning witnesses. Interrogation by the department attorneys was so different from that of Denning and Osborn, however, that it sounded like cross-examination. Clearly the staffs were working against each other. Department attorneys wanted to squelch the local agenda that was unsubstantiated by proof, and the Nashville-based U.S. attorneys sought justification for all actions by state officials during the riot. In an attempt to record what they perceived as objective testimony, the Department of Justice interlopers were responsible for calling several newspaper men and photographers before the grand jury. Unlike Bomar, these witnesses thought the highway patrol was responsible for the destruction on Mink Slide.[19]

Early on, the department staff did not believe the grand jury would bring any indictments. The D.C. lawyers then became concerned about whether it was desirable for the jury to file a report, and if so, what its content should be. Though initially uncertain of the propriety of intercession, the lawyers in the civil rights section of the department finally decided to influence any such document produced.[20]

During a jury recess in late April and early May, Assistant Attorney General Theron Caudle traveled to Middle Tennessee to negotiate with Davies and Frierson and his staff. He remonstrated with Frierson, who was embarrassed about the antipathy between the two groups of attorneys. Caudle and Frierson visited Davies in his remote cabin in the Cumberland Mountains and asked him to delay in order to modify an imminent report by the jury. Both the Department of Justice and the FBI had received considerable pressure from civil rights advocates about the direction the probe was going. Judge Davies felt no such pressure and resented Washington influence on his grand jury turf. He resisted Caudle's suggestion that the judge delay the jury report, which the Department of Justice official felt was slanted and a whitewash.

On return to Nashville, Caudle's pressure resulted in the jury delaying a final report and urging the FBI to more thoroughly investigate state officers before the panel reconvened in late May. In the meantime and without any apparent qualms about interfering with Judge Davies' Nashville operation, department lawyers in Washington wrote a final report for the grand jury's consideration.[21]

The FBI subsequently reported no evidence to implicate Tennessee officials. The Department of Justice wanted the jury to make a final report rather than reporting a no bill and continued to participate in composing that document. Though ameliorated by the department influence, the jury report showed that Judge Davies and the U.S. attorney's office staff got much of what they apparently wanted from the proceedings. As initially anticipated by Caudle and Turner Smith, chief of the department's civil rights section, the jury called no indictments.[22]

THE JURY REPORT

The initial enthusiasm for Tom Clark and the federal grand jury recorded in the spring by the Negro *Nashville Globe* editorialists had with passing weeks given way to skepticism about the frequently delayed final report. That concern proved well placed when on June 14 the jury reported to Judge Davies that they had heard no evidence that would warrant indictments for "violation of any federal statute."[23]

The major portion of the report was a recording of their understanding of events. They reasonably concluded that, in light of conflicting testimony, they really could not assign blame in the initial fight between the Stephensons and Billy Fleming. They also found no evidence for the malicious rope purchase or an organized lynch mob action. In disagreement with some black witnesses and Agent Hopton, they noted no proliferation of arms among whites until after the shooting of the policemen. They disregarded General Dickinson's story of Bomar forsaking the plan of joint daylight entry into Mink Slide and consequences of the highway patrol raid. They reported a unique story of continued firing from within the Odd Fellow's Hall, something not previously recorded elsewhere.

As had been the case with most of the testimony, the jury did not pay much attention to possible rights violations in the final report. The record did not mention the controversy about whether the highway patrol had a right to enter and seize without warrant, as they had done in James Morton's house. The panel similarly disregarded testimony dealing with the inability of the arrested Negroes to attain legal representation in the early days of the crisis. Alleged mistreatment of arrestees was justified by supposed failure to comply by the prisoners. The jury concluded the shootings of William Gordon and James Johnson were justifiable homicides.

Near the end of the report, the recorder applauded local and state authorities for minimizing mortality and morbidity and preventing "a bloody race war." In closing, they criticized the misrepresentation of the riot by various pamphlets and distant journalists, especially the Communist press. Jurors were certain such works were disseminated for purposes of increasing racial disharmony and fueling further class strife.[24]

The closure warned both blacks and whites against propaganda. "In the opinion of this grand jury nothing is so likely to erode and ultimately destroy peaceful and friendly relations between the races as the dissemination of half-truths and falsehoods such as have been so freely circulated in relation to the events occurring at Columbia." Judge Davies gave his grateful benediction to their conclusions, "Your official action should put an end to the irresponsible and scurrilous rumors that have been so freely circulated over the entire country and should be a reassurance to those of both the white and Negro races who sincerely desire to live in peace and harmony."[25]

Be that as it may, Tom Clark had not initially asked the grand jury to investigate the insidious influence of propaganda on Maury County race relations. The panel had quickly taken the bait proffered by Davies and Bomar to pursue and indict mysterious (yea, Communist) outsiders, targets less challenging than the technicalities of civil rights abridgement and incontrovertibly evil of their white constituents. Their conclusion that quick state response to the crisis had perhaps prevented worse chaos was theoretically correct. In apparent gratitude for that success, they disregarded the messy side issues of due process, vandalism, denial of counsel, lack of coordination between the THP and the Tennessee State Guard, and brutality.

Regional newspaper response was ecstatically provincial. The Columbia daily applauded the jury's conclusions and said that those spreading falsehoods about the county would be unsatisfied by the report. In high dudgeon, the *Nashville Banner* noted that the South had its own customs and no intention of letting what he believed to be ignorant outsiders and the "slime" they perpetuated interfere with its affairs. Besides, Attorney General Clark had ordered the investigation only because of the continual bombardment of his office with stories from Communists and fellow travelers.[26]

Blacks were sorely disappointed. They wondered again why the jury had not addressed the needless destruction, mistreatment of Negroes, Weaver's inability to reach his clients, unwarranted arrests and indictments, and unlawful search and seizure. Why had Davies instructed the jury to pursue the issue of inflammatory literature? Finally, why had he not impaneled a special jury, as ordered by Clark, instead of one that had no blacks on it? All these acts by the judge, his known close political alliance with Boss Crump, and his admission during his confirmation hearings in 1939 that he had briefly been a member of the Ku Klux Klan during his young manhood had made the him a suspect jurist in the Negro community.[27]

These latter points were reiterated later in the year by Thurgood Marshall in furious correspondence with Attorney General Clark, sometimes through Eleanor Roosevelt as a conduit. From a federal viewpoint, Clark felt the grand jury had rendered justice, and to answer critics he repeatedly referred to its conclusions. On the matter of indicting those who wrecked havoc on Mink Slide property for instance, he asserted that since no one had identified any such vandal to the jury, the government had no apparent jurisdiction. Marshall cynically questioned why the FBI, with its tremendous reputation for tracking down spies, saboteurs, and other violators of federal law, could never seem to perform so well in Negroes' rights issues. He also questioned the proceedings of the grand jury. Alleged errors

Nashville Banner interpretation
of grand jury results.
(Courtesy—*NB*)

he complained about to Clark included black witnesses' lack of consultation
with Department of Justice lawyers, the hearing of state officials before
complaining witnesses, the absence of blacks on the jury, and the suitability
of Horace Frierson's calling a grand jury after he had already issued a statement that no civil rights had been abridged in Columbia.[28]

These were the same misgivings Marshall had discussed with
Department of Justice officials in the spring.[29] After involving the department in the Nashville Grand Jury proceedings and partially influencing
its work, Clark now stood firmly behind the final report. In response to
all entreaties, he emphasized that a properly constituted jury had found
no breaches of federal law. In particular, he reiterated that no one had
identified those responsible for acts of vandalism.[30] The U.S. Department
of Justice was finished with the affair in Columbia.

As the racially charged summer of 1946 progressed and after this
failure, from the Negro perspective, of federal intervention to produce
justice or redress, Middle Tennessee blacks looked with dread toward the
pending criminal trial in Lawrenceburg. They anticipated no help from
Harry Truman and his U.S. Department of Justice. The alleged murder
attempters of Mink Slide were to face trial in a reputedly redneck town
before a likely all-white jury.[31]

CHAPTER SEVEN

The Trial in Tennessee

UNHAPPY TRIAL TOWN

Apposition of the Trial in Tennessee[1] of the alleged attempted murderers of Mink Slide and events associated with World War II was continuous and, according to some, meaningful. V-J Day, August 14, was being celebrated in Columbia as the trial of *State of Tennessee* v. *Sol* [sic] *Blair, et al.* began in the Circuit Court of Lawrence County, Tennessee. Litigants repeatedly sought to parallel the case with international events to emphasize their views. Though occasionally melodramatic and overwrought, the metaphors were sometimes accurate.

Most people of the town of Lawrenceburg were not happy to host the notorious trial. Petitions circulated throughout the county asking Judge Ingram to rescind the venue change. Mayor R. O. Downey lashed out at the court and Bumpus. He bemoaned the perceived snobbishness of the richer, more populous Maury County, whose people supposedly called Lawrence a "Blackberry County." Yes, he thought the defendants could get a fair trial in his town, but they could just as well do so in Columbia. In expressing distaste for all aspects of the situation, he said, "We are not for the Negroes, but we don't want to wash the dirty clothes of Maury County." As for Bumpus, Downey promised that voters in Lawrence County would assure the district attorney's reelection defeat.[2]

Bumpus did not select Lawrenceburg as the new venue, and he did his best to smooth ruffled feathers. Noting that he was just doing his duty to punish the felons and prevent further such insurrections, he doubted

79

Lawrence County Courthouse.
(Picture postcard courtesy—
Ridley Wills II)

he would stand again for public office. In a long letter to a supporter in Lawrenceburg published in the local paper, he praised Lawrence County, noted the difficulty of success in such a trial without a united citizenry behind the prosecutor, and described an imminent national danger that events such as the Mink Slide riot portended.

After a confidential meeting in Columbia between Bumpus and Lawrence County leaders, the outcry subsided. Lawrence Countians were asked to be hospitable and polite and make the best of the situation. Though bemoaning the probably pending journalistic colorization of events and their county, they would do their civic duty since Columbia was neither capable nor courageous enough.[3]

In addition to the late-summer discomfort of working in the small courtroom, the defense panel faced significant logistical difficulties. They had no place to stay or eat in Lawrenceburg. None of the defendants or their Negro lawyers could use the segregated Lawrenceburg facilities. The food problem was solved by members of Columbia black churches, who brought picnic fare. Neither Looby nor Ransom could comfortably or safely stay in Lawrenceburg. Weaver, an alleged traitor to his race, was also unwelcome anywhere south of Nashville. Therefore, he and his nineteen-year-old, pregnant wife, Virginia, stayed at the Andrew Jackson Hotel in Nashville and commuted the seventy-four miles to Lawrenceburg on a daily basis.

An innocent controversy arose from one of these trips. Virginia Weaver rode to the trial in a car with one of Looby's young associates and Oliver Harrington, a colored correspondent for the *Pittsburgh Courier*. Locals looked askance at this scandalous, casual racial mixing. Thurgood Marshall, who could be as polite and deferential as necessary while in the

South, strongly advised Virginia Weaver not to do that again. It would, he said, be better to ride the Greyhound bus.[4]

In addition to this inconvenience and discomfort, the defense team seemed at a critical disadvantage in several other regards. The trial was, after all, being held in *Lawrenceburg*, a supposedly archetypal racist town in the racist South. The federal grand jury result had gone badly for blacks. The panel had barely looked at the question of civil rights violations, choosing instead to wax hot about seditious interlopers who poisoned local minds after the riot. Though the defendants did not know their defense team, they had come to appreciate their new, hot lawyers. Unfortunately they would be testifying to white prosecutors, long known to them and with whom they would subsequently have to live as traditional underlings on the social ladder. Not surprisingly, the defense decided that a reasonable long-range goal would be to win an appeal trial after anticipated defeat in Lawrence County.

Bumpus and assisting private attorney Hugh T. Shelton lived in Columbia and traveled thirty-three miles to Lawrenceburg each day. Assistant Attorney General W. A. "Bud" Harwell lived in Lawrenceburg. Buoyed by the grand jury results, confident in their case, and promising some surprises,[5] the prosecution team had no reason to anticipate anything other than success as they prepared to present the case for the State of Tennessee.

JURY SELECTION

A central element of the defense's case was to challenge the traditional, inequitable, and seemingly inevitable absence of Negro representation on southern juries. Should this happen in Lawrenceburg, the lawyers intended to challenge what they deemed a fundamental legal flaw, thereby assuring that jury selection would be one of the most critical and certainly one of the most quarrelsome features of the proceedings. It would also be a keystone in any subsequent appeal.

Defense attorneys were immediately surprised to see 10 Negroes in the 312-man jury pool. The defense asserted that these men had only been added after it became clear the trial would be in Lawrenceburg and questioned whether blacks had ever been used before on local juries. A member of the jury commission said they had been added earlier in the year to give them a proportional representation in the pool. Bumpus testified as a witness that he had seen one black on a Lawrence County jury.

As the prosecutor, he said that whatever was practiced in the past, the current panel obviously adhered to the law since it contained Negroes. Ingram quickly denied a motion to quash the trail based on past jury-selection practices.

Perhaps due to the absence of appropriate jury racial representation, the defense conjecture that a fair trial for their clients was impossible was possibly incorrect with blacks in the jury pool. That hopeful assumption was only a pipe dream. The state immediately used one of its allotted one hundred preemptory challenges to eliminate the first Negro examined. Considering the small black population in Lawrence County, prosecutors would have no trouble attaining an all-white jury.

The defense questioned veniremen in detail, especially about their racial views, and began depleting their two hundred preemptory challenges. After a couple of weeks, lawyers were deep into the initial *venire facias* before the first juror, W. E. Staggs, was accepted. Staggs admitted he believed in separate justice for Negroes and whites. The defense approved his acceptance only because it seemed an obvious trial error, yet another to justify an appeal.[6]

As the slow selection process *voir dire* dragged on, tempers frayed, none more so than Judge Ingram's. The thirty-four-year-old jurist had never presided over a trial with so much national importance or with such an obstreperous defense team. His anger descended most often on them. In frustration over their prolonged interrogations, he took the unusual step of not letting them ask veniremen about their social views. Lawyers could submit such written questions to the judge, who *might* ask them in an expeditious fashion. Though he was somewhat flexible about this, the

Defense lawyers question a venireman: Left to right— Z. Alexander Looby, Maurice Weaver, Howard Ransom. (Courtesy—The *Crisis*)

ruling was still a setback for the defense. The judge exposed himself to considerable journalistic ridicule when he questioned a potential juror who sought dismissal on the basis of a psychoneurosis. Ingram asked him, "Where does it hurt?"[7]

As his frustration with the slow pace increased, Ingram began liberally levying fines in all directions. Much to defense lawyers' chagrin, he raised the bail on defendant Clarence Brown when Brown stayed in Columbia because of illness. Irritated at Weaver and Looby's recurrent tardiness, he fined them twenty-five dollars after their sixth such transgression. Their excuse of a flat tire did not placate the angry jurist. Perhaps the defense attorneys' antipathy toward Ingram was transparent. Looby thought him "a

Judge Joe M. Ingram. (Courtesy—*MD*)

cracker who didn't know anything about the law." After the incessant disallowance of defense objections, Weaver said that Ingram, not the NAACP, was the "outside agitator."[8]

In addition to the defense's repeated challenges, selection was also impaired by Lawrence Countians' unwillingness to serve because of an anticipated long trial or their anger at having it foisted on them. The boys in the overalls, sweat-stained fedoras, and brogans may have seemed unsophisticated to outsiders, but they were not stupid. Their passive-aggressive responses were frustratingly effective. Some called for examination simply did not show up, and the court replaced those panelists by dragging people in off the street. Those who appeared greatly resented the wait at the courthouse. Many found unique reasons why they should be rejected for "cause."

The gambit that most irritated Ingram, however, was their feigning racism in order to inspire defense rejection. His anger created a comic moment when he forcefully called some veniremen to "this bar"; several promptly attempted to balance on the rail. Still trying to reign in a trial that continuously threatened to get out of hand, he fined and sentenced to jail more than one hundred recalcitrant locals for obfuscation, disrespect, and failure to appear after summons. All of these penalties were delayed or later suspended.[9]

Selection crawled at a glacial pace and in a hostile manner. Ingram's patience with defense delay came to an end by the first week in September. He threatened to jail the irritating Weaver for contempt and would not allow any more questions about race from the defense panel. Ransom harangued about Ingram's inflection and his commandeering of questioning about racial matters. One Lawrenceburg wag suggested the solution was to seat an all-black jury. He thought that would be fair, and then the defense would have no reason to further extend the process.

By mid-September, the defense had only thirty-three of its preemptory challenges left. It had used them to reject a variety of veniremen considered unsympathetic to the defendants, including illiterates, Klan sympathizers, obvious racists, one man whose father had been killed by a Negro, those who always referred to blacks as niggers, and a kinsman of Will Wilsford's. They had been forced to use up preemptory instead of cause rejections for such cases as those who felt the colored should stay in their place and for a man who handled Negroes on a chain gang and would always accept the word of a white man over a black. The state had rejected nine of the final fifteen blacks on the restocked panel, one for cause and eight by preemptory challenge. They had ample challenges left to frustrate any futile defense ambition to seat a Negro juryman.[10]

After refilling the jury box and six weeks of questioning more than five hundred persons, a panel of twelve white men was selected. Ingram, himself, had chosen the last two, saying all defense challenges had been exhausted. Though the people of Lawrence County were now bored with the process and more interested in the pending county fair, many outside the South wondered if the trial could be as interesting as jury selection and were excited at such a prospect. Reporters from, among others, the *New York Herald Tribune, Chicago Tribune, Daily Worker, Pittsburgh Courier*, Associated Press, United Press, and International News Service often outnumbered local onlookers in the courtroom. They were about to get their money's worth of newsprint and legal surprises from the Trial in Tennessee.[11]

THE PROSECUTION CASE

Public opinion before the trial agreed with that of the defense attorneys, i.e., there seemed no way the state could lose in Lawrenceburg. However, dispassionate examination of the spring federal grand jury report, with which both prosecuting and defense attorneys were thoroughly familiar, might have raised some skepticism about that anticipated result. True to its traditional function, the grand jury had been a prosecutorial discovery proceeding. In this case, the focus was to have been on alleged civil rights violations against Maury County blacks. Bomar, Davies, and others had redirected the Lawrenceburg jury toward outside meddlers. There had been plenty of testimony though about activities of the pending criminal trial defendants the night of the policemen shootings; and nothing had been presented that physically placed them there at the critical hour. Aside from the obvious facts that some colored people had shot at some policemen in the dark and then been arrested and indicted en masse, what facts did the state have to prove fact, motive, or methods of attempted murder?

On September 19, 1946, Harwell read indictments on two counts against twenty-five men. They first accused Sol Blair, Julius Blair, James Morton, Meade Johnson, and James Bellanfant of inciting Robert Gentry, Luther Edwards, Lewis Miles, Paul Miles, Raymond Lockridge, and "certain other persons" to commit first degree murder against Will Wilsford. The second count accused all these and Tommy Baxter, William Bills, Clarence Brown, William Dawson, Clifford Edwards, Horace Gordon, Milton Johnson, Calvin Lockridge, John Lockridge, Webster Matthews, John McGivens, Willie Pigg [*sic*], Early Scott, Charley Smith [*sic*], Napoleon Stewart, and Gene Williams of carrying out the attempted murder.[12]

Bumpus began by showing that East Eighth Street was 417-feet long, 75-feet wide, and sloped severely, west to east and north to south. Most establishments were on the south side of the street and included restaurants, pool rooms, barbershops, a couple of offices, a church, a shoe store, and a pressing shop. The defense submitted there were sloping awnings or sheds over many more storefronts than had been originally shown by the prosecution, a topographic feature bearing on visibility from and into the street.[13]

The prosecution called several policemen to relate the events of the night of February 25. Will Wilsford described the four officers clad in uniforms with topcoats descending into a darkened street, telling the indistinct cluster of blacks more than one hundred feet away in front of Saul's shop that they were there to keep them out of trouble. After his injury from a hail of gunfire, they retreated back to South Main. Bernard Stofel recounted the earlier events of the evening, including his impression that the Blairs and Morton used a "loud" tone in speaking for those around them and warned him that they were prepared if whites came down there. Sam Richardson identified several defendants he saw on the street during the inspection from a police automobile well before the shootings. Chief Griffin said that as he went home that evening, he doubted anything would come of the unrest following the Stephenson arrest. After being recalled downtown, he led the impromptu visit to Mink Slide and was shot in the leg. Bumpus and his men had thus established the sequence of events, that the corner of East Eighth and South Main was well lit, that there had been an angry crowd of blacks on the street, and that four policemen had been shot as they descended the sloping street toward a group of black people half a block away from them.

During this event reconstruction period, the defense was alternately pesky and constructive. Weaver failed to get introduced the now famous photo published in *Ebony* of a bleeding John Blackwell lying on the street under the gaze and feet of law officers. He and Looby taunted the officers for testifying in uniform, saying they otherwise never wore them except when on duty. Defense attorneys stalled, challenged details about East Eighth topography, and objected to seemingly trivial matters.

They also impelled the officers to admit to several things for the defense. Except for several arrests of Saul Blair for gaming, the Blairs and Morton had excellent reputations in the community. Because of the doused store lights, destroyed streetlight in mid-block, and overhanging awnings, Mink Slide was dark. The crowd of blacks, therefore, just might not have been able to identify those approaching from above as policemen. Columbia policemen had sought to reassure Negroes that they were there to protect them from whites, whether they could be characterized as a mob or not.

In the first of many attempts to introduce the issue of Maury County lynchings recent enough to be well remembered by Negroes, Weaver asked Wilsford on the first day of testimony if he remembered the killing of Cordie Cheek. After the judge sustained Shelton's objection, the jury was dismissed. In their absence, Looby cited considerable case law to argue that the defense should be allowed to introduce the plea of group self-defense based on these lynchings in which law officers had allegedly participated. Ingram sustained the objection to the introduction of such material.[14]

In his initial testimony, Sheriff Underwood told of his futile late-day efforts to defuse hostilities, including his trip to East Eighth with Deputy Goad and his phone call to James Morton to determine if blacks had disbanded. He could identify six of twenty-five defendants who had been on the street when he had faced the angry black crowd. After his frustrating call to Morton, he had independently called Governor McCord for help.

In the absence of the again-excused jury, Looby discussed the story of the group of whites who had come to the jail that evening, seeking the

Stephensons but being run off by Underwood. This was an attempt to establish that, on the basis of this and other rumors, Columbia blacks really thought a white mob had been formed. Once more, Judge Ingram disallowed the introduction of any material that might establish a basis for communal response to perceived danger.

Underwood told the defense that he had excellent relations with the black leaders, but he also felt they could have stopped the trouble had they so desired. In contradictory statements, he insisted that guns began appearing in white hands only later in the night but that shots had been exchanged between South Main and East Eighth immediately after the assault on the policemen. The sheriff admitted he did not arrest any whites carrying guns illegally because he was concerned the blacks were about to take offensive action out of Mink Slide.

For the prosecution, Underwood had verified the hostility of the black crowd on the Bottom, identified a few defendants who had been there before the shootings, described his efforts to stem the tide, and endorsed a hallmark of the prosecution case, the Negro-leader thesis. Despite the defense's inability to introduce evidence substantiating that there might have been a white mob on the night of the twenty-fifth, they had gotten the sheriff to testify that those identified as leaders among the defendants were good men.

Surely to the prosecution's disappointment, city bus driver Alldie Sharpgon could not certainly place any defendants other than the Blairs on East Eighth that night. During his tedious examination, the almost palpable acrimony between opposing attorneys surfaced. Ransom took umbrage at an alleged aspersion by Bumpus. The ever rancorous Weaver rose to his defense, objecting to white lawyers intimidating black ones. Opposing lawyers believed in the causes they advocated and truly disliked each other.[15]

Two days into the trial, the prosecution introduced a string of colored witnesses who proved mixed blessings to their case. Bumpus even asked the court to consider them hostile because they were colored. Doubtless ecstatic at his ambivalence, the defense argued that race alone should not automatically qualify a witness as hostile. The witnesses were poorly educated, having at best completed eight grades. Most were uneasy and confused on the stand. They mumbled, having to be repeatedly reminded by attorneys or the judge to speak up. Their testimonies were often inconsistent, usually allowing the defense to turn them to their advantage. Not one was a strong witness.

First came the Shyers brothers, Lee Andrew and Earlie. As with many other witnesses, Bumpus clarified that no one had either mistreated these witnesses *in his presence* or offered leniency for sympathetic testimony. He elicited specific identification of several defendants whom these young men had seen in the Bottom before the shootings. They had seen guns in Saul Blair's barbershop.

Weaver and Looby easily compromised the Shyers' testimony and its motivation. They used the brothers' experience to introduce a major fly into the ointment of several prosecution witnesses. Bumpus and his interrogation board had obtained statements from such witnesses after they had been arrested and variously beaten by the highway patrolmen, after days of incarceration in the filthy Maury County jail during which time they could not see family or counsel, and after the jailhouse slayings of Digger Johnson and William Gordon. Lee Shyers had enjoyed all these experiences and was so scared when he was called for questioning almost a week after his arrest that he cried. The court overruled Bumpus's objection to the irrelevance of Shyers's state of mind. Weaver had thus successfully shown how fear motivated these (and later) witnesses.

Looby further undermined their value by introducing the story of an alleged bribe of fifty dollars by the FBI for testimony by one of the Shyers boys before the federal grand jury. Paul Bumpus must have wondered why he had called these brothers.

Leonard Evans, William Pillow, and James Alderson likewise yielded bitter fruit for the prosecution. Although Evans said he was not coerced to testify, he also reported being "stompted" by the highway patrol. He saw guns in the hands of some defendants that night but also saw whites with them as he went to East Eighth from his work at Columbia Military Academy. "Rooster Bill" Pillow was an extremely compromised witness. Weaver was to represent him in a later trial stemming from the riot and counseled him against answering certain questions. Though Pillow was a prosecution witness, Bumpus and Shelton openly disagreed about his certitude. Finally the court ruled him a hostile witness.[16] Again, these were prosecution witnesses!

Alexander Bullock and Mamie Lee Fisher had implicated defendants Robert "Bob" Gentry and John McGivens with statements they had signed prior to release from jail. These defendants had allegedly told Bullock at the Ritz Cafe that they had been on the street when the policemen were shot. Mamie Fisher had left the Ritz with Bob Gentry and McGivens in a car driven by Bullock. After a week in jail, she also had signed, allegedly without pressure, a statement implying that McGivens had shot at the policemen.

The defense once more played the fear and coercion cards, and both witnesses reneged. Bumpus had not related that Bullock had given his statement in front of T. I. Shaw. Shaw and a ubiquitous TVA guard called "Mr. Smitty" had beaten Bullock with blackjacks the morning after the riot when he went to claim his commandeered car. Fisher blithely admitted there were contradictions between her signed statement and her Lawrenceburg testimony. She was less scared than when she signed her statement and reported that the lawmen had threatened her with three more months of jail if she did not sign the statement.[17]

Two more prosecution witnesses of dubious veracity had blown up in Bumpus's face, and he was beginning to show frustration. During Weaver's dismantling of Bullock's statement, he used colorful language that had to be stricken from the record and obliquely accused Bumpus of unfairly eliciting witness statements. The district attorney claimed to have no previous knowledge of Bullock's beating, resented the "gratuitous insult," and asked Weaver to make the same aspersion outside the courtroom. Such behavior was uncharacteristic of the usually polite state prosecutor.[18]

In an attempt to substantiate a conspiracy-to-revolt theory, the prosecution took three students from College Hill High School to testify about Popeye Bellanfant's recruitment of "your people" as they rode his school bus the afternoon of February 25. Horace Snipes, George Watkins, and Audrey Claiborn gave similar accounts of Bellanfant's story and their reactions. They had understood there was a danger of lynching, but none of their family members took up arms that evening. The defense evoked all to say they were scared at being brought to the trial by highway patrolmen and that their parents did not know they were in Lawrenceburg.

James Beasley, a man currently in jail for robbery, was the last of the string of colored prosecution witnesses. He said he had seen guns in the hands of Bellanfant and Calvin Lockridge and thought that perhaps Morton had told everyone to stay in the Bottom after Sheriff Underwood asked the crowd to disband. For the defense, Ransom confused the witness about chronology and identification of defendants. Beasley also said a Columbia policeman had told him that his testimony might make things go better for him. September 24 was not a productive day for the prosecution.[19]

The next day, Looby once more pleaded for the opportunity to introduce the history of Maury County lynching, feeling that the defense had laid adequate groundwork for this with the preceding testimonies based on fear. Bumpus objected that black-on-white historical killings could just as well be used. Looby clarified that they wanted to present a picture of group fear, to which there was nothing analogous for the whites. The court again refused the request. The defense again excepted.

The redirect examination of Sheriff Underwood yielded little new information but clarified just who was in charge in Maury County after

the riot. He reiterated that Bumpus had scrupulously informed all prisoners appearing before the investigation board of all their rights, except
that of counsel. Looby tried to show a connection between a prisoner's
making of a statement and his subsequent opportunity to make bond.
Bumpus noted that the Blairs and Morton had been freed without the
requirement of making a statement. Despite *habeas corpus* applications by
the defense team and local lawyers, William Fleming and C. D. Hopkins,
both Bomar and Bumpus had instructed the sheriff not to allow prisoners
access to the lawyers.

The defense won a rare victory away from the jury when Ingram
refused to allow the deceased Digger Johnson's statement to be introduced
by the prosecution. This statement was intended to support the prosecution's "leader" thesis, i.e., all the ruckus could have been prevented had the
leaders exerted their responsible authority. Again Bumpus and his
colleague Shelton disagreed in court, the latter admitting that Johnson's
statement was hearsay, *ex parte*, and inadmissible. The disagreement and
judgment clearly tickled Weaver and embarrassed Bumpus.[20]

Hayes Denton remained a controversial character throughout proceedings. Bumpus brought him forth to testify that he had witnessed Alexander
Bullock's statement, now the best indication the prosecution had to an
admission of any involvement in the shooting. After Denton's testimony, the
jury was dismissed, and Looby again vainly tried to get the court to introduce information about this witness's alleged involvement in the Cordie
Cheek lynching. On the jury's return, Weaver tried to obliquely sneak this
information into the trial. Ingram sustained several Bumpus objections to the
repetitiveness, obtuseness, and length of Weaver's questioning.

The prosecution used Police Officers G. I. Reeves and T. F. Collins to
reconstruct the department's activities the afternoon and night of the
twenty-fifth. Their consistent stories included the observed determination
of blacks to protect the Stephensons, the lack of any hint of offensive activity
on their own behalf, the observation that James Morton had a shotgun, and
the absence of arms among the whites on the square before the shooting.
The officers recognized that blacks on Mink Slide had heard and believed
the rope story. Once more Ingram would not allow any testimony regarding
the whites who came to the county jail to get the Stephensons.[21]

The state called several witnesses on its last day of direct presentation.
None was more interesting or potentially important to lawyers, journalists, and railbirds though than the first, Commissioner Lynn Bomar.
Unlike the grand jury experience, where he was treated as a virtual friend
of the court, Bomar was opposed in Lawrenceburg by Maurice Weaver,
who despised Lynn Bomar's integument and all that was in it.

Bumpus did not get beyond Bomar's credentials and his call from Governor McCord to go to Columbia before the jury once more was excused. (They never lacked exercise as they paraded in and out of the courtroom.) Looby had quickly established one of the more controversial aspects of Bomar's Columbia performance, the raid on James Morton's house without warrant. Looby felt testimony on this matter would compromise later trials on other indictments now held by Morton. The West Indian and Bumpus exchanged a flurry of precedents of the situation before Ingram made a strange decision. Since Bomar had no warrant and Morton had not invited the commissioner in, no questions about Morton could be asked, but others arrested in his house were not immune. Back came the jury.

The production became entertaining with Weaver's cross examination. First he provoked the commissioner to admit the THP sometimes engaged in activities they were not authorized to do—all in the spirit of saving lives. Eschewing remorse, he assured, "I won't get a search warrant the next time, either." After Weaver chided him for wandering about in his testimony, Bomar admitted the story about a white man needing help to get his stranded truck off South Main was bogus. He did not disarm whites because he did not know "what was coming out of Mink Slide." Besides, he had heard nothing about any whites shooting policemen. Bomar circumvented the issue of disregarding the plan carefully made with Underwood and Dickinson. He was certain the THP did no damage except with gunfire. Pictures suggesting the contrary apparently reflected damage by others. In discussing the jailhouse slayings, he said he should have killed Napoleon Stewart instead of just putting his foot on his neck. In redirect, Bumpus got him to revise that statement to, "If you don't lay there I am going to kill you."[22]

By mid-testimony, all parties were fuming, and decorum was nil. Bomar rose from his chair in a threatening manner toward Weaver and shouted his answers. Bumpus suggested the barbershop damage may have been done by some foreign or local subversive organization, which Looby took as an insult to the NAACP. When Weaver asked Bomar in closing if he had anything against the defendants, the flushed lawman retorted, "I don't care for you a darn bit." Those who had anticipated with interest the commissioner's testimony had not been disappointed. For the prosecution though, his appearance had been an ignominious failure.[23]

Freelance reporter J. A. Kingcaid told several cogent tales. To Hugh Shelton he described his 3:00 A.M. visit to James Morton's house, which was interrupted by Bomar's entrance and subsequent arresting of Morton and eleven others. The prosecutor sought to impugn Weaver by having

Armed white crowd with highway patrolmen looking into darkened Mink Slide night of 25 February 1946. Lawman in center staring at camera is Flo Fleming; man at left with gun is Orville Wagner. (Courtesy—GJ files)

the reporter relate the defense attorney's request that he would "make it right with you" if Kingcaid signed a statement regarding various depredations done to defendants. Looby sought to soften this damage by implying that Weaver was referring only to any expenses Kingcaid might have incurred. Also, Kingcaid had allegedly been told he could cross out any material in the statement with which he disagreed. Maurice Weaver was not on trial; but, in the absence of other provable allegations, his professional behavior offered a continually tempting target.[24]

Lynn Bomar was not the only professional athlete who found employment in the THP. Bumpus called Lt. Clydell "Clyde" Castleman, a former pitcher for the New York Giants, to testify about the visibility of the upper part of East Eighth from its lower juncture with Woodland, where he had been the night of the riot. Castleman insisted that light was sufficient to allow discernment of uniforms, a contention supported by testimony of another patrolman, Sgt. Greg O'Rear.

Patrolman Theo G. Fite, a former Columbian and acquaintance of Popeye Bellanfant's, reported finding a loaded "machine gun" in the house of Bellanfant's mother during the search for arms on February 26. Weaver got Fite to clarify that the complete search had consisted of several black neighborhoods around town, including Macedonia and Happy Hollow in west Columbia, not just those contiguous to Mink Slide. They only searched the rare white homes that happened to be in those black neighborhoods.[25]

After Bumpus presented some confusing and questionably relevant information about the Blairs and Morton having signed various defendants' bonds, he focused again on the nocturnal visibility on East Eighth. During an evening session, Will Wilsford testified about a recently staged duplication of his walk down Mink Slide. At three o'clock on a cloudy September morning and with the lights as they were the night of February 25, a photographer stationed in front of Blair's barbershop had taken a picture of him as he strode onto the street from South Main. Although he and other walkers were supposedly identifiable in submitted photographs, photographer Roy Staggs said the men were even more visible with the naked eye that night.

Weaver and Looby swarmed this expert and the staging. In addition to obtaining an admission that Wilsford had not been wearing an overcoat as he had in February, they scattered lots of distracting detritus about film speeds, flash bulbs, and the source of the witness's income. Only the jury could decide whether the reenactment was relevant.[26]

With this testimony about light and visibility, Bumpus thus ended the prosecution presentation. He had tried to show that the hostile Mink Slide crowd should have been able to recognize those approaching them as responsible lawmen and not a white mob. He had shown that several defendants had been on Mink Slide the night of the shootings. However, he had not placed guns in their hands at the time of the alleged crime. He had outlined a scenario of preplanned Negro response to be instituted by recognized community leaders. He had no confessions other than the vague, late-night braggadocio of Robert Gentry and John McGivens. Conviction of the purported black rioters did not now seem so inevitable.

THE DEFENSE CASE

The morning of September 27 was taken up with procedural matters. Yet again in the jury's absence, Looby argued the case should be dismissed on several grounds. First, Bumpus had failed to present evidence that placed any defendants on Mink Slide when the alleged crimes were committed. Second, Bumpus had given no proof that certain principal defendants had coerced others to commit a crime. Third, the district attorney had failed to mention several defendants in his presentation. Judge Ingram, whom the *Daily Worker* now characterized as "bigoted and blind," predictably denied the motion.[27]

That afternoon, the defense called the Blairs. Father Julius effectively presented himself as a respected community patriarch who had no interest other than maintaining peace so he could continue to make a

Scene in Lawrence County Circuit Court during Mink Slide trial. (Courtesy—The *Crisis*)

good, honorable living. He patiently told his version of Hannah Peppers's plea, the decision to bail and protect the Stephensons, and his activities the night of the riot. He stressed his good reputation among whites, his good opinion of Sheriff Underwood, and his history of making bond for deserving colored folks. Bumpus could not rattle him with questions about alleged conspiracy or about an old indictment against him for bonding without a license.

Son Saul recounted the tale of sneaking James Stephenson out of town and returning to report to "Mr. Jim" (Underwood) that the sailor was bound for Chicago. He continually dissimulated as Hugh Shelton tried to pin him down about times, weather conditions, and weapons. The court actually sustained a defense objection about self-incrimination when the prosecutor asked what kind of gun he had when he was arrested. Court adjourned a tad early that day so the jury could be shaved by a local barber.[28]

Numerous witnesses testified that various defendants had no motive to shoot the policemen and were elsewhere when the shooting occurred. Meade Johnson denied that he carried a shotgun that night as Officer Collins had testified. Johnson said he had gone home just after dark, an assertion substantiated by his employee Rufus Kennedy and his wife.

Billy Griffin and others arrested Johnson for having a derringer and some shotgun shells in his house on Thursday, the same day his son was killed in the jail. Shelton sought to impugn him by bringing up his record of serving six months in 1934 for selling whiskey.

Principal of College Hill High School Samuel Jones, Johnnie Belle Fulton, Negro Assistant County Agent George Newburn, Andrew Armstrong, and Reverend Joseph Blade all told consistent versions of the meeting at Fulton's house the night of the twenty-fifth concerning land purchase for a new colored high school and Julius Blair's attendance at the meeting. They also testified to his good reputation for "peace and quietude."[29]

Jennie Arnell, a College Hill senior, said defendant Webster Matthews was at her house for a study-date at the time of the shootings. Mary Morton, Marcia Mayes, and Mattie Smith, James Morton's mother-in-law, reiterated the now-familiar story of events in the Morton house that evening—Kingcaid's attempted interview, Bomar's intrusion, their rough treatment by highway patrolmen, and the fact that neither Morton nor they had left the house after he took his wife from the school building committee meeting at Fulton's house. Rosa Lee Calloway, defendant Eugene Williams's mother, said her son was home by half past eight that evening. Prosecutor Shelton marvelled at the precision with which she and Meade Johnson could time the homecomings of their family members.[30]

Saul Blair's version of the dicey flight of James Stephenson to Nashville was affirmed by co-travelers and observers in Nashville and Spring Hill. They admitted having some firearms but denied knowing the contents of a mysterious, long wood box that was transferred between the several cars they used. Despite some inconsistencies brought out by the prosecution, a neighboring white farmer and the family of "Moot" Bills, one of the fellows found by Bomar in James Morton's house, placed Bills at his rural home until ten o'clock the night of the twenty-fifth.[31]

As the trial wound down, the prosecution called a few more witnesses. Deputy J. C. Goad retold about Underwood's efforts to get the Mink Slide crowd to disperse and disarm, but he denied telling Saul to get Stephenson out of town. In cross-examination, Ransom affirmed Julius's reputation for "truth and veracity." Underwood had promised those with whom he conversed on Mink Slide he would "handle" the angry white folks. Lewis Hargrove, a Spring Hill policeman, cast doubt on the precise hour Saul and his merry band passed through the village on their way to Nashville.

Underwood's son S. W. had gone home to Culleoka around five in the evening and had not received a call at the jail from Julius Blair.

J. J. "Jimmy" Underwood Jr., however, did receive a call from a man identifying himself as Julius who told of getting James Stephenson out of harm's way. Jimmy was not certain this was Julius because he was distracted, being the only man at the jail with his mother, sister, and wife.[32]

IT'S CLOSIN' TIME

A flurry of last-minute legal housekeeping set the stage for closing arguments. The court overruled a defense request for a directed verdict on the basis that the prosecution had proved nothing. In response to a query by Weaver, the prosecution had to clarify that they were proceeding against Julius Blair and James Morton as principals and the rest of the defendants as accessories to attempted murder. Ransom argued that one had to have a principal, a shooter in this case, before one could have an accessory. Bumpus said an accessory could be tried even before a principal had been identified, a point Ransom did not concede.[33]

Journalists flavored their articles with cynical, almost raucous anticipation. Regional papers were respectful, but publications north of the Mason-Dixon line denigrated the court and state prosecutors, often in physical terms. In addition to sneering at Ingram for his ignorance about psychoneurosis, *Time* described him as pink and plump. Because of his personality and role in the riot, Bomar was a prime target of outsiders. The *Daily Worker* described him as big, bald, and pink faced.[34]

The commissioner's main national antagonist was Vincent Sheean of the *New York Herald Tribune*. These two were social polar opposites. Bomar was an autocratic, provincial segregationist with violent tendencies, which were doubtless helpful in his football-playing days. The forty-six-year-old, distinguished-looking Sheean was cosmopolitan, literate, humorous, socialist, and pacifist. He had been a foreign correspondent and was to write thirty books before his death (in Italy).

As did most northern writers, he had prejudged the South and the Lawrenceburg verdict. In one of his more mournful articles during the trial, he had described Bomar as "a stout, ruddy man with a bald head and an irascible temper." He had also contrasted him with the "venerable" Julius Blair and opined there was no doubt which of the two was the happier man. For this reason, Bomar called Sheean a "lying, Communistic son-of-a-bitch" during a recess. Sheean blithely replied, "Thank you very much, Mr. Bomar. I would not want you to say anything else. Any good word from you would be the worst possible condemna-tion." When Weaver objected about Bomar's behavior to the nearby Ingram, the judge said this was an affair between Bomar and Sheean.[35]

As summation loomed, Sheean noted that attorneys seemed to be conducting themselves with more decorum than they had throughout the trial.[36] Perhaps they were ashamed of their previous unprofessional conduct. More likely they were completely focused on the closing argu-ments of the biggest trial of their lives. These pleas communicated their personalities and prejudices more than any legal points they wished to convey to the twelve rural, white males before them.

THE FINAL ARGUMENTS

Harwell

W. A. Harwell reminded the jury that the state sought conviction of only Julius Blair and James Morton on the first count of inciting to murder. The policemen's testimonies had placed these leaders in the Bottom that evening. James Morton's family had said he remained in his house all night, but no one could explain why the armed men were found there. Testimony had placed Saul Blair on the street around 8:45 P.M., and Harwell noted inconsistent testimony about times during the trip to Nashville with James Stephenson. Policemen also saw Meade Johnson on the street late that night. The Negro crowd could obviously have seen to the top of Mink Slide and knew Columbia policemen, with weapons holstered, were descending onto the street. He said no one had the right to "mow down upon the streets of Columbia." He urged moderation, asking the jury to "try it like twenty-five Lawrence County people were being tried."[37]

Ransom

Leon A. Ransom argued that the black community response to a possible lynching was reasonable, understandable, and correct. The defendants had the same rights as all Americans. They congregated on the only black business street to protect the Stephensons. They had heard talk of lynching, rope purchasing, and a white mob accosting the sheriff at the jail. There was gunfire into Mink Slide. Itchy-fingered, nervous shooters certainly had injured officers as they advanced en masse. Ransom apologized for that.

The records and character of Morton and Blair were exemplary. It was unimaginable they would incite a riot, Ransom argued. The state had not placed them at the scene of the crime and had brought no weapon or other tangible evidence. Popeye Bellanfant committed no crime in talking to the children on the school bus about the situation.

The search for weapons and mass arrests on February 26 were done to intimidate and instill fear and helplessness into the Negro community. The true mob, as recognized by Underwood, was on the square, not in the Bottom. The jury should convict only it they thought lynching was not a crime.[38]

Shelton

Hugh T. Shelton contended that the trial was not about racism but the taking over of a city street and firing at policemen. Lynching had nothing to do with it. The state did not have to prove who fired the shots. Conviction was correct if a defendant was concealing himself for the intended killing of another. One did not need to be on the scene to aid and abet a crime. Various opinions supported that "commission of an offense by any one of the party in pursuance of that purpose is the act of the whole."[39]

Blair and Morton had been seen on East Eighth around 8:45. The Shyers saw Saul there. He questioned that if Meade Johnson's wife went to sleep, how did she know where Meade was the balance of the night? If Calvin Lockridge had a gun, he was guilty whether or not Wilsford was shot with it! The officers not only could be seen but were fired upon even as they retreated.

Weaver

Interestingly, the defense did not choose to end their presentation with the hot-headed, controversial, white lawyer, Maurice Maxwell Weaver. They knew his argument would be memorable, but it would also surely be antagonistic. True to his reputation, he hit the jury right between the eyes with satire and invective during his two-and-a-half-hour summation.

He began by applying a little soft soap, recalling his own rural, East Tennessee heritage and begrudging that he had to visit the lovely town of Lawrenceburg on such a mission as the case. Aggressive, angry advocacy quickly followed this uncharacteristic attempt at diplomacy.

The state, he said, had not shown that any of the defendants were in the Bottom at the time of the shooting and had not placed guns in any of their hands. There was a white mob—Hannah Peppers, Julius Blair, and Sheriff Underwood had seen it. Though the sheriff had described no guns "showing" in their hands, he had also said, "The white mob up there hasn't sense enough or guts enough to cause any trouble." Hayes Denton admitted warning Julius about a mob when Denton testified "with his long fingernails scratching his twitching face." The state's own witnesses Lee Shyers and Leonard Evans had seen the white crowd and were scared of them.[40]

Why did not the state indict Evans, Mamie Fisher, and the Shyers boys? Weaver asked. The state had softened up such witnesses by prolonged incarceration and beatings. "The finger of the state was on [them] until [they] testified" under fear. The state was persecuting the defendants by asking the jury to finish what the mob could not do in February and make this a legal lynching.[41]

The depiction of a convenient character contrast was easy, he said. One of the state witness softeners was Bomar, the "burly football player" who could not stay calm in the witness chair, instead showing his hate. Julius Blair *was* a leader—for principles, democratic rights, and right-eousness. There was no proof that in his declining years he "suddenly turned into a vicious mad dog."[42]

Finally, Weaver invoked World War II with a palate of metaphors. Whites and blacks had just fought side by side to preserve democracy. He, himself, had served on a minesweeper. Now the State of Tennessee was behaving in a fascist fashion to subvert the Negro by making examples of the defendants. Columbia must not assume the status of Lidice, the Czech village destroyed by Germans in 1942. The Nuremburg Trials had ended forty-eight hours prior, and this jury had the opportunity to make commensurate history by defending Tennessee democracy. They would *not* send this old man or this young boy (the oldest defendant, Julius, was seventy-six years old; the youngest was seventeen) to "a cold, barren cell in order to justify a lynching that failed up to now."[43]

Looby

Z. Alexander Looby, the black barrister with the distinctly non-southern accent, was as calm as Weaver was passionate. Pleading softly from a chair because a leg was in a cast, he expressed appreciation for the courtesy given defendants and their Negro lawyers in Lawrenceburg.

The crux of his rambling argument was that ignorance and inefficiency of public officials were the root causes of the whole affair. He said that there would have been no problem if the fight on the square had been between people of the same race. If Squire Denton knew trouble was brewing what did he do to stop it? What did the sheriff or police department do? The early morning arrests and incarceration in the Maury County jail were analogous to British imperial actions at the black hole of Calcutta.

Looby was not sure what Shelton meant when he talked about taking over a street. The defendants were being tried for shooting Will Wilsford. If Morton and Julius Blair were talking to policemen on Mink Slide at 8:45, what was illegal about that? The shooting took place at 9:37, and the state had not proved who the shooters were. Instead, they had tried all these people as goats.

There was no conspiracy. Indictments were against individuals committing crimes, which the state had not proved. Carrying arms for self-defense was legal. Looby believed the state's reenactment of the shooting to be bogus. In the "cave-like darkness" of the twenty-fifth of February, could not those on Mink Slide think the people coming down there were the mob?[44]

In closing, the lawyer became theological. Differences between races were God's business, which Looby did not understand. We could not afford another world war, and we had to learn to live together. No place was better to begin than in the South. The whole episode was the symptom of a disease. When that flared up, scapegoats were inevitably sought. That, of course, was what the unlucky defendants were.

Bumpus

After thanking Looby for his sermon, District Attorney General Paul Bumpus opened with a brief expression of courteous flattery of Lawrence Countians. He then launched into the longest, most passionate closure of all. The speech communicated his anger, earnestness, suspiciousness, sectionalism, xenophobia, demagogism, and ethnocentrism.

Bumpus covered a few technical points before dissolving into diatribe. He did not think James Stephenson had left Columbia until after the shootings, as testified to by the Spring Hill policeman who saw Saul in his town later than others reported. Several witnesses had said there was not a white mob.

A real fear the blacks would come shooting out of Mink Slide existed, he said. They were actually *luring* whites to the Bottom by saying they had the Stephensons and then firing shots. Only the brave and good work of Bomar and his fellow officers had prevented this. Morton and Julius Blair were obvious leaders. The former refused to order blacks to go home at Underwood's request, and both signed many of the defendants' bonds. They were taking charge when they spirited the Stephensons away. Just like Goering, these leaders must be punished.

Negroes were intimidated by their own, not the law. Just look at Mamie Fisher's fluctuating testimony, he said. Surely the jury would believe her and Alexander Bullock about the role of Gentry and McGivens, both of whom were armed.

He described the horror of police officers being shot and why the court must prevent any recurrence of this. Until this crime was avenged, Tennesseans could not hold their heads as high as accustomed.

Then he turned against the outside press, a group bound to inflame locals but of little relevance to the trial. Those people cast slanders and bred racial hatred, all for their own purposes, he said. They were nothing but dirty rats. Saying the South could solve its own problems, he impugned those journalists who "poured out upon the American public a flood of sewage that would nauseate even a skunk." They were "pinks and pimps and punks." Looby objected to this and was overruled. Bumpus regathered steam.[45]

In a flagrant call for the jury's revenge on outsiders, Bumpus described such bogey men as dogs, sticking their noses into everybody else's business. These "long-nosed men and short-chinned women" were depraved, but the South would deny their wishes. He described these "Browskis," "Grontskis," "Eleanorskis," and "Stinkskis" as anarchists, traitors, and subversive vermin. In a rare moment of humor, he said the South could handle a "Bold Weaver" as well as the "boll weevil."[46]

In an overtly electoral passage, he said it was fortunate there were public servants who were willing to stand up for what was right rather than worry about losing votes. We must place such people in positions of trust. With the aid of local patriotism, not prejudice, we would then have nothing to fear.

Pulling out all the traditional stops, Bumpus recalled his humble beginnings, the recent valorous service of Volunteer State soldiers, and the love of home. In the names of the traditions of our people, common decency, chivalrous manhood, and precious womanhood the jury should bring justice for Tennessee by convicting the defendants.[47]

THE VERDICT

Looby was more confident of acquittal than his colleagues. After recovering from depression following the federal grand jury result and observing the Lawrenceburg trial, the *Nashville Globe* writers were optimistic, stating that Bumpus's case had wilted. Sheean also compared Lawrenceburg to Nuremburg, saying there was a regional, naive negation of common law in the U.S. trial. With his prevailing angst and citing

Ingram's disallowance of any testimony about lynchings, he predicted loss for the defense.[48] The issue though was clearly more doubtful than before the trial when the short odds were on conviction.

After a two-week trial, the jury took less than two hours to return a verdict of not guilty for all but two defendants. They found Gentry and McGivens guilty of attempted murder and recommended the men serve no more than twenty-one years. The majority of spectators were Negro, and they were jubilant. The few whites were quiet. The attorney general and his assistants appeared stunned. Ingram set October 18 to hear a motion for a retrial for the two men.[49]

Local response to the surprising verdict was muted incredulity. Citizens of Lawrenceburg were pleased no violence had erupted. Those excited by the outcome agreed that Bomar and Bumpus had been "thrown for a loss." Bumpus received some local applause for his closing statement. Others called it bigoted and hateful.[50]

The NAACP was surprised and grateful, especially to defense attorneys, but restrained in its celebration. After all, Negroes still could not publicly eat or live comfortably in Lawrenceburg. Others still faced trial in the matter of the Columbia race riot. Drawing from their experienced perspective, the association felt the trial was more ludicrous and racist than any other, including the Scottsboro trials,[51] and believed that the way the trial was conducted, rather than the verdict, represented the norm for southern race relations in 1946.[52]

The Lawrenceburg jury. (Courtesy—The *Crisis*)

Reporters were as floored by the verdict as the prosecution. They were certain of conviction. When the daily sojourn back to Nashville had ended, Vincent Sheean broke out a fifth of Napoleon brandy. He had been saving it for years for a "really special" occasion. He had gotten emotionally involved in the trial and at no time in his interesting, nomadic life had he seen or felt anything more special than this mass acquittal.[53]

With surprise and joy, Sheean provided a thoughtful conclusion. He thought the "bizarre" trial was the sort of experience that caused Americans to "realize the full splendor of our destiny as a nation." He exulted over the successful defense, noting the effective closing chronology of Ransom's reasonableness, Weaver's passion, and Looby's simple religiosity. Though the proof against Gentry and McGivens had been tenuous at best, Sheean did not think it possible for all defendants to be freed. After describing Bumpus's amazing summary, Sheean noted that an unexpected band of outsiders, not the carpetbagger journalists against whom the district attorney had railed but the twelve good, true men of Lawrenceburg, had foiled the prosecution. The jury judgment had disappointed some but had reinforced Vincent Sheean's faith in the participation of good citizens in a democracy.[54]

Monday morning quarterbacks suggested various reasons for the acquittals. The Nashville Negro newspaper thought the pamphleteers and some courageous journalists such as Sheean, Harold Ickes, and Martin Agronsky managed to broadcast the truth. The jury though had no access to articles in northern papers and would have scoffed at the inflated versions in most of the pamphlets. Even Looby and Weaver thought the unpopularity of the change of venue and the district attorney associated with it may have influenced the jury. This should not have persuaded the jury though if they were as racist as advertised.[55]

No single, superficial reason could explain this verdict. Rather, the jury had just fairly assessed the information given them and the manner in which it was presented. The man or men who shot Will Wilsford may have been among the defendants. Several were proved to be elsewhere at the time though, and the prosecution never identified a gunman. Because they had no specific evidence to bring, prosecutors relied on the conspiracy theory and the umbrage good whites were bound to feel about a gang of Negroes shooting policemen. That argument was imprecise and demagogic. Bumpus's rambling, illogical closing was directed more against people about whom the jury knew nothing (e.g., syndicated journalists) than against the defendants.

The defense had been just as emotional but had easily shown the fallacies in the opposition's case. Reporter Sheean estimated the prosecution

Acquitted defendants pose in front of statue honoring Davy Crockett in Lawrenceburg. (Courtesy—The *Crisis*)

had totally failed to mention five defendants and had addressed fourteen others only in passing. The lack of evidence substantiated the defense assertion that these defendants were selected as scapegoats. Why, for instance, were only two of the four men who took Stephenson to Nashville tried? Similarly, some of the fellows found in James Morton's house were tried while others were not. The failure to indict those who testified for the prosecution was transparent, and the defense's success in showing the uncommitted nature of their testimony was ruinous. The only weapons introduced by the prosecution were a carbine and a "machine gun," yet Will Wilsford was injured with bird shot.[56]

Late in October, Judge Ingram awarded a new trial to Robert Gentry and John McGivens. Neither they nor the Stephensons ever came to trial though, as charges were quietly dropped for lack of evidence.[57] The Trial in Tennessee was over.

CHAPTER EIGHT

One More Time

ANTICLIMAX

O ne more trial would stem from the Mink Slide riot. On March 22, the state had, in Case 4720, indicted Loyd "Papa" Kennedy, a twenty-one-year-old bootblack, and William "Rooster Bill" Pillow, a thirty-eight-year-old stonemason, for shooting Highway Patrolman Ray Austin. The state said Kennedy and Pillow allegedly fired on the officer from the dark interior of Saul Blair's barbershop in the dawn of February 26. After that alleged opening shot, the patrol did, depending on one's perspective, either its systematic search or rampaging depredation.

After initially scheduling the trial for late July, the court had delayed it, first because of Thurgood Marshall's illness and then because of the Lawrenceburg proceedings. Much less public or legal enthusiasm surrounded this hearing, which many thought would never take place. Some local lawyers opined any new trials would be settled by a motion of *nolle prosequi*, for the state did not have any new evidence.[1]

The trial did proceed though and was a microcosm of that earlier one in terms of number of defendants, duration, interest, fireworks, and publicity.[2] The *Nashville Tennessean* barely covered the trial. The *Nashville Banner* covered it closely but, unlike before, took no editorial stand. Only the persistent Harry Raymond of the *Daily Worker* returned to represent the distant journalistic corps that had crowded the Lawrenceburg courtroom.

105

William Pillow and Loyd Kennedy. (Courtesy—*NB*)

His paper apparently still saw propaganda grist to be ground in a southern judiciary mill.

This trial was nevertheless an important event with an unexpected, contradictory, and almost decrescendo outcome. Its interesting coda provided a real threat to one of the defense attorneys, Thurgood Marshall. Had this event turned out differently, it might have considerably modified the history of adjudication on race and other issues in the United States.

JURY SELECTION (AGAIN)

Defense strategy was no different than that of the just finished conspiracy and murder trial. As before, Weaver had submitted in July a plea of abatement based on the absence of Negroes on the grand jury indicting Kennedy and Pillow. Looby had offered a motion of severance based on statements the two defendants had made implicating each other. Ingram had denied both motions.[3]

Four months later, the conspicuous Marshall replaced Ransom in the defense triumvirate. He arrived late Friday evening, November 15, after the jury had been selected and prosecution testimony had begun. Though his presence was well recognized, Marshall was to serve mainly an advisory role, with Looby leading the questioning and Weaver once more being the professional irritant. Whether for symbolism or substance, the defense frequently consulted the venerable and just acquitted Julius Blair. Once during jury selection when Looby had to leave, Weaver had the old fellow sit beside him at the defense table.[4] W. A. Harwell again assisted Paul Bumpus with the prosecution.

If the defense motion to quash because of the absence of Negro veniremen failed, the defense intended to seek a change of venue from Columbia to Nashville, saying that local conditions precluded a fair trial. They specifically cited a *Daily Herald* editorial stating that "people of Maury County were combatting the Communistic spirit that had been injected into the earlier trial of Negroes from outside."

Ingram refused the admission of a *Time* article, saying the magazine had "falsified" about the previous trial. The judge agreed to testify from the bench concerning the absence from the *venire facias* of anyone who had served on the grand jury for this court term; he would accept no questions concerning previous sessions. The defense futilely quizzed Circuit Court Clerk Dabney Anderson concerning the historic absence of Negroes on Maury County juries. Various county officials and leading citizens testified for the prosecution that certainly a fair trial could be held in Maury County. Newt Howell revealed the prevalent local opinion about Weaver when Howell admitted he would not be able to address the attorney as "mister." Ingram denied all defense objections to a local trial, and it was time to select a Maury County jury.[5]

Jury selection was not to be as prolonged as it had been in Lawrenceburg, perhaps because of defense exhaustion, but more likely judicial impatience. Beginning on November 12, defense attorneys adhered to their practice of lengthily questioning panelists about their racial views. As at Lawrenceburg, Ingram said to move along or he would in quick fashion ask defense questions submitted to him in writing. Prosecutors again rejected all blacks drawn from the pool. The judge used the interesting expedient of having a ten-year-old boy draw names from the jury box in open court. After the third panel had been exhausted, only six jurors had been chosen. They were Ronald Jackson, Mark Bryant, Henry Gilmer, J. F. Dowell, Eulus Fox, and W. B. King.

Ingram then took the matter completely out of the lawyers' hands. Supposedly with the aid of *Daily Herald* editor John Finney, he made a list of "outstanding and leading citizens" from which he completed the selection. As president of the Lion's Club, Ed Coker was conducting a luncheon meeting when a deputy entered, handed him a subpoena, and told him to be at the courthouse that evening. Throughout the day, Coker rehearsed a litany to the effect that the Monsanto plant simply could not run without him, and therefore he should be excused for cause. On arrival though, he found that the chafing Ingram had already sat his boss, the plant manager John Christian. Coker was cooked! The other four leading citizen selectees were Richard Haynes, J. W. Russell (elected foreman), Frank Murphy, and Randolph Loftin. Ingram picked J. Mike Blair as an alternate. Jury selection had taken less than seventy-two hours.[6]

THE TRIAL

Ingram moved the trial just as briskly. On the morning of November 15, Bumpus called the first of only five prosecution witnesses. Patrolman Ray Austin said that a shotgun blast, which slightly wounded his leg, first came from within the barbershop. Then those officers at the site fired away through the storefront. Patrolmen Dave White and Fred Waltrip faithfully reiterated that sequence of events.

The next day, Sheriff Underwood told a similar story, saying he gave a warning knock on the store window and then a shot came from within. Underwood jumped out of the way, and the patrol took over. After they rushed in, they found Pillow under a cloth at the front of the store and Kennedy huddling in the back. As the only non-lawman patroller that morning, John Kingcaid testified to the accuracy of that account. He also recounted Weaver asking him to sign a statement verifying THP brutality during their time in Columbia.

On cross testimony, Underwood confessed that even more physical evidence, the shotguns supposedly used by the defendants, had not been tagged and were lost. Looby got him to admit that there had probably been excessive mayhem during the Mink Slide search. Marshall revealed that Kingcaid had known Weaver since 1939 and had talked to Bumpus, Bomar, and Underwood before his testimony.

The defense only used Saturday afternoon for its presentation. Each defendant denied the prosecution version of the shoot-out, insisting the patrolmen fired first. The only other defense witnesses presented were three character witnesses. Julius Blair stood up for both defendants. Prominent white citizens, automobile dealer Jack Carlton and clothier Clifford Parsons, testified to Pillow's good character.

Loyd Kennedy's recalcitrant courtroom behavior, especially when contrasted with that of Pillow's, presented a real problem for his attorneys. The bootblack had only three years of schooling and sometimes seemed confused. His answers were evasive; Pillow's were direct. The "impudent" and argumentative Kennedy once told Bumpus to shut up, much to the discomfort of Looby and Julius Blair. Judge Ingram told the jury to disregard his demeanor and attitude when considering the evidence.[7]

CLOSURE AND JUDGMENT

Continuing his efficient trial management, Ingram gave defense and prosecution only one and a half hours each for summation; he had allowed six hours per side in Lawrenceburg.[8] Except for Bumpus's, none of the closing arguments were nearly so tense or interesting as the soliloquies delivered in the big trial.

They began Monday morning, November 18. Marshall said the trial served two functions for the state: to "give out" yet unremitted justice for the riot and to justify the destruction of black homes and businesses on East Eighth. He never took a case unless he believed his client innocent (a rather unrealistic professional assertion) and was "shocked" that Bumpus would dare bring trial on such flimsy evidence.[9]

Weaver applauded the attentive jury. He again painted a patriotic picture of World War II, noting that no questions had been asked about race when all were fighting for democracy. He could not understand why Bomar or J. J. Jackson had not been called as witnesses.

Looby honed in on Bumpus's alleged political aspirations, saying there would have been no trial except for "ambitious politicians." He urged the jury not give the attorney general a political victory. Concerning just who shot Austin, the state had asked the jury to play "eeny, meeny, miny, moe."[10]

Bumpus was typically prolix but much less scattershot in his argument than he had been in Lawrenceburg. He said this was no minor affair and any thoughtful district attorney must complete the proceedings, regardless the threat to his health. The peace of the community depended on the protection of its law-enforcement officers. He baited Marshall, who had emphasized he was not from New York, by calling him the "Southerner" from Baltimore. He did not care who was "shocked," saying cases of this

In The Circuit Court
Of
Maury County
IN THE MATTER OF:
STATE OF TENNESSEE
vs.
William A. Pillow, Alias "Rooster
Bill" and Lloyd Kennedy, Alias
"Papa Lloyd"

PAUL F. BUMPUS

Closing argument of District Attorney-
General Paul F. Bumpus, of Columbia,
Tenn., delivered on November 18, 1946,
at Columbia, before the Court and Jury
on the trial of the above styled case.

Reported stenographically and transcribed by
Kelley R. Hix, Stenotype Court Reporter, 202 Y. M .C. A.
Building, Nashville, Tennessee.

Published closing argument of Attorney General Bumpus in Pillow/Kennedy trial. (Courtesy—Paul Bumpus)

ilk would always be prosecuted in Tennessee. Officers gave adequate warning and responded with gunfire only in self-defense. He contended he had never seen any witness display so much malicious hatred as Loyd Kennedy and related that Pillow knew what he was doing when he fired on the patrolmen. He said that presentation of the weapons with which they shot Austin was unnecessary. Officers had observed them at their sides with empty shells nearby.

The attorney general said he sought no glory from conviction. He had done his duty by investigating and legally presenting the case. No jury could ever know the future effect of its decision, which is why they must weigh this one deliberately. A foreign war could be ended with victory, but the emerging struggle against crime would be ongoing. He asked for a decision for law and order, for which future Tennesseans would express appreciative love.[11]

After instruction, the jury departed for deliberation around suppertime on Monday evening. They took one hour and twenty minutes to return verdicts. Pillow was acquitted; Kennedy was convicted of attempted murder in the second degree. Ingram sentenced Kennedy to not more than five years imprisonment.

Defense attorneys declared their intention to appeal the conviction. As a footnote to the proceedings, Ingram ordered the cases against John Blackwell and the Stephensons extended to the next term of the circuit court.

The jury had not disregarded Loyd Kennedy's deportment as a witness. He had paid the price for being uppity.[12] How else could the jury have convicted him and acquitted his emergency nocturnal roommate of February 25 after hearing this proof? Looby drew a parallel with the Lawrenceburg convictions, in which the jury convicted the defendants against whom there was the least evidence, making in his opinion reversal in higher court more likely.[13]

GET THE "YALLER NIGGER"

Sulking in defeat, the Maury County law-enforcement establishment decided, while there was still opportunity, to strike back against those obnoxious outsiders. Just who authorized the action, whether it was impetuous or organized, or its planned extent, remained debatable. This petty grasp at retaliation did, without question, make a lasting impression on Thurgood Marshall.

Looby had noticed a "police car" staying close to him as the lawyers and Harry Raymond prepared to leave from the Bottom for Nashville soon after the trial ended on Monday night. Marshall was driving Looby's automobile as they crossed Duck River into suburban Riverside when three cars, sirens wailing, pulled them over. Eight officers, supposedly including policemen, patrolmen, and sheriff's deputies, presented a warrant to search the car for liquor. The occupants carefully watched the search in order to prevent planting of "evidence" in the auto. Marshall was light skinned, and officers repeatedly referred to him as the "tall, yellow boy."[14] Since the warrant covered only search of the vehicle, the lawyers would not allow search of their persons. Finding nothing, the officers allowed the car to leave, with Looby now at the wheel.[15]

Again they stopped the car, this time asking for Marshall's driver's license. Finding no violation, the frustrated peace officers let them go. Yet again, they pulled the car over, arresting Marshall for drunk driving (though he was now a passenger in the back seat) and taking him away in a squad car.

Looby and others followed the car through dark back streets to town. The gendarmes presented their prisoner to a doubtless puzzled Magistrate Jim Buck Pogue. This practical official asked to smell Marshall's breath. Though his full opinion of the examination is unavailable, the olfactory impression was instructive enough to convince him the counselor probably had not even had a drink and was certainly not drunk. He shook Marshall's hand and ordered his immediate release.

The defense retired again to the Bottom. They still believed officers were acting suspiciously, so they had someone else drive them to

Nashville. Popeye Bellanfant returned Looby's car the next day.

When asked about this episode, Sheriff Flo Fleming said the warrant had been issued by constable A. M. Butts on the basis of information received from "some colored person" that the Marshall party was transporting liquor to Nashville from Maury County. The arresting party included Deputies Curtis Lentz and Malcom Gray and Constable T. I. Shaw. Though Weaver said highway patrolmen were among the first to surround the car, Officers W. E. Smith and McGlothlin assured Bomar that they had just stopped to see what was happening.

The patrol and Columbia police had apparently been maintaining their distance from the defense team since the trial in Lawrenceburg. Patrolmen had several times observed the team's car speeding between Nashville and Columbia but had not apprehended the drivers. Chief Griffin had also cautioned his officers not to interfere with these visitors. He quickly distanced his department from the Marshall affair, reminding the public that a city constable was an elected official and not under his command.

With the support of the NAACP, Marshall immediately wired Attorney General Clark to ask for an investigation. Weaver also sought redress for alleged intimidation of Harry Raymond. Some observers thought their appeal was more likely to be heard because the Republican Party had just gained control of Congress. President Truman and General Clark received some pressure to indict the Tennessee lawmen, and the Department of Justice looked into the matter for some months. There was a suspicion in the department that various complainants, especially Maurice Weaver and Harry Raymond, were more interested in publicity than justice. No further investigation was ever made after mid-1947.[16]

The episode faded except for a continued debate among stalwarts regarding just "who saved Thurgood Marshall." Virginia Weaver felt that all remotely associated with the episode sought credit for saving the future justice. She believed that a vehicle loaded with journalists, which stayed with the action, prevented anything serious. Milton Murray thought Marshall was being taken to a "necktie party" down by Duck River. Murray and Popeye Bellanfant took considerable credit for saving him. Walter White felt that Weaver and Looby following the official vehicle in which Marshall was held, instead of going on to Nashville as ordered by the officers, prevented Marshall's lynching.[17]

Were Thurgood Marshall and his future civil rights legal accomplishments truly at risk? Marshall's reaction to the experience is telling. There is no mention of his visit to Maury County in his papers at Columbia University. However, he did discuss this arrest/abduction with Juan

Williams, who was interviewing him for a new biography shortly before the justice's death. Marshall said that of all the threats he faced during his work in the South for the NAACP before and after World War II, he felt the most danger and fear in Columbia, Tennessee![18]

Though details of accounts vary and some have inflated their roles in it, there is no doubt this ridiculous apprehension occurred. It is uncertain whether the petulant officers were just doing some harmless (to them) harassment or whether they had something more sinister in mind. Regardless their motives, the incident only further besmirched Columbia's reputation, something peaceable locals did not need. Citizenry response was best expressed by Horace Frierson, who said, "Practically everyone in Columbia is convinced that the arrest of Marshall was a very stupid thing, and everyone seems to be very much pleased that Mr. Pogue handled the matter in the way he did."[19]

FINIS

Their admirers gave Weaver and Looby fetes in Chattanooga and Nashville. In response to an appreciative address extolling his support of constitutional rights, Looby said civil rights lawyers must work as Americans, not colored defenders.[20]

Kennedy's appeal ended in the Tennessee Supreme Court in June 1947. Justice Alan Prewitt denied that Negroes had a constitutional right to trial by a mixed jury. Rather, all the Constitution guaranteed was that there be no racial discrimination in the selection of grand or *petit* juries. Papa Kennedy presented himself to the state penitentiary in April 1948, becoming the only man to serve time of the more than one hundred arrested after the Mink Slide riot.

Governor McCord received some pressure to commute Kennedy's sentence. Carey Eldridge wrote from Chattanooga "that all of us Tennesseans are somewhat guilty in the tragic events at Columbia and that justice would be served in closing this case for once and all." After obtaining the blessings of Judge Ingram and General Bumpus, he commuted the sentence to one year for "Attempt to Commit a Felony." With good behavior credit, Kennedy left the prison in January 1949, having served nine months.[21]

CHAPTER NINE

A Hemi-Century Perspective

THE TIMES

Professor Charles Lawrence Jr. of Fisk University called the February 1946, civil disturbance in Columbia, Tennessee, "the first major inter-racial violence after V-Day."[1] It was not the last such event though. The year was characterized by the consequences of the massive, expensive, and dislocating war—labor unrest, inflation, jobless-ness, shortages, and reorientation from military to civilian life. In the first full year after the war, nearly five million workers struck, shutting down the automobile, steel, and coal industries for long periods. Retained servicemen fomented "wanna-go-home" riots in Manila, Paris, and Germany. Joseph Stalin slammed down the Iron Curtain. The country reacted with disdain toward the unfamiliar president who had succeeded Franklin Roosevelt, whom they had followed and trusted. The United States and the fabric of World War II victory seemed to be unravelling.[2]

The regional violence that precipitated from this boiling social cauldron often had racial overtones. Late in 1946, the NAACP recorded eighteen murders (including those of William Gordon and James Johnson) and one blinding, all perpetrated by whites against blacks in the South. The most notorious of these were the daylight assassinations of two black couples in Monroe, Georgia. The blinding of veteran Issac Woodard by lawmen occurred in South Carolina on February 12, thirteen days before the Mink Slide riot.[3]

115

Racial violence had been prevalent throughout World War II, both in the military and on the home front. Because of lower educational achievement, most black servicemen usually tested in the bottom quartile of recruits. The military tended to assign them to support units. The few in combat units usually had white, southern officers. The idea was that these usually reluctant whites could best manage Negro troops. Whatever their assignment, Negro servicemen's morale and efficiency were usually low.

Off duty, black soldiers had little access to recreational facilities in and around the large number of southern training bases. This was particularly hard to take for northern Negroes. Military police allegedly did not protect these men when they got into trouble with local constabularies. The services maintained strict segregation even on posts. On-base disruptions occurred at Fort Dix, Camp Stewart, and Fort Bliss; others probably were not reported.

Worse riots occurred in U.S. cities throughout the war, peaking during 1943. Troops were necessary to squelch outbreaks that year in Harlem, Los Angeles, Mobile, Philadelphia, Beaumont, and Detroit. There was a gradual diminution of such disturbances during 1944 and 1945.[4] Still, towns and cities throughout the country dreaded racial riots. Columbia Tennesseans knew about these events and surely were anxious about the possibility of such social-municipal disruptions in their town.

VETERANS

If the military experience was not as it could have been, it helped many black servicemen, instilling discipline, broadening horizons, and enhancing confidence. These men were more sophisticated and tougher than when they had left home. They had heard of opportunities not available to those of their race back in the South. They had lived, played, and fought with men of all colors from other parts of the country. For instance, blacks had constituted 25 percent of James Stephenson's boxing team. Such experiences made the return to the segregated South very uncomfortable, if not intolerable.

Negro soldiers recognized the incongruity of fighting against totalitarianism and then coming back to it. In general, these military men returned militant in their desire for social equality. As much as any of the more heralded civil rights eras that followed, World War II was a major turning point in Negroes' attitudes toward the United States and their rights within their nation.[5]

Southerners had feared the returning black servicemen would cause trouble and realize a "double victory" from the war, i.e., military triumph abroad and the end of segregation at home. They remembered the precedent riots after World War I and believed the returning Negro servicemen were bound to be dangerous in two special regards. First, they might have developed the courage to finally insist on their rights. Second, after military experience they would be more dangerous fighters for this goal. Maury County home folks, therefore, perceived the returning veterans as a new social unit of uncertain sociopolitical potential. Outside journalists framed their concern about the riot by wondering just how Columbia Negro *veterans* might react as a group.

As the riot unfolded, white Columbians, for all these reasons, feared what their town's more than one hundred Negro veterans would do. Their perspective was perhaps exemplified in the extreme by the comments of a supposedly sympathetic Georgian commenting on one of the victims at Monroe. "Up until George went in the army, he was a good nigger. But when he came out, they thought they were as good as any white people."[6]

It is unlikely Columbia Negroes saw themselves as a unit. As individuals though, they and their families certainly felt different about their old status as second-class citizens. They expected respect and intended an end to Jim Crow laws. The threat to the Stephensons coalesced them into action with all their recently acquired martial skills. Sheriff Underwood heard more than one resolute comment from the hostile crowd around him on Mink Slide the evening of February 25 about the necessity to continue the fight for democracy at home. V. K. Ryan was a black mortician who got along with both races. As commander of the newly instituted Post No. One of the Global War Veterans, he called for an end to the troubles but pointed out various civil problems that blacks wanted corrected. Herbert Johnson recalled that the black men decided that those who had just fought for their country could just as well defend East Eighth and its patrons. His wife, Irena, said the war had made some of the Negro veterans bitter. They wanted to be recognized as *men* after having fought for their country.[7]

LYNCHING

From the Columbia colored-community viewpoint, there was no doubt about the unifying fear that fueled the end they sought in the Mink Slide riot. There would be "no more social lynchings."

Columbia Colored Division, led by V. K. Ryan, "snappy marchers" who were "bringing up the rear" of the V-J Day parade. (Courtesy—*DH*)

Most lynchings occurred in the South or border states, and more than 90 percent were whites hanging blacks. Before 1930, Tennessee had the third-lowest incidence of lynching among the Confederate States, .32 per ten thousand population, an obscure statistic doubtless of little comfort to the state's Negroes. The average number of U.S. lynchings had decreased from 187.5 per year before 1900 to 16.8 before 1930. The typical southern town in which a lynching was more likely to occur was rural, below the state average in income and education, and predominantly Baptist and Methodist. Although only one-sixth of lynchings were done after alleged sex crimes, the romantic myth prevailed that most were necessary to avenge despoliation of innocent southern women.

The act was usually consummated by young men of a lower socio-economic stratum. However, studies repeatedly showed that they could not have lynched without the tacit approval of community leaders. As in Columbia, witnesses developed selective blindness, and perpetrators were rarely identified, much less punished. Collusion among local officials was common in order to prevent prosecution. Between 1900 and 1930, less than 1 percent of lynchers in the United States were convicted for the crime.[8]

Such data, however, were irrelevant to the personal experiences of Columbia colored people. As recorded at the time and reiterated in numerous interviews of surviving participants, the horrible and ignominious memories of Henry Choate and Cordie Cheek remained sore in the hearts of Maury County Negroes. Whites either did not know of these murders or recalled them as minor, perhaps occasionally necessary, social glitches. They, therefore, did not expect or understand the spontaneous reaction of Maury County blacks to rumors of lynching after the Stephensons' arrests. Julius Blair, Calvin Lockridge, and all of Mink Slide intended this would not happen again. Ed Kimes said, "This has got to stop!" Irena Johnson concluded that lynching was "the bottom line of the story."[9]

RUMOR

If this demonstration of collective Negro anathema to the ultimate contemporaneous degradation of murder by lynching was the primary cause of their reaction to the episode at Columbia, then the motor that perpetuated, perhaps instituted, the unfolding events was rumor. The story of rope purchased by a white mob from a hardware store on the town square was retold with certitude within hours of the Stephensons' arrests. Whites also heard but paid little attention to it. After all, there was no regional history of blacks lynching whites.

After this action-instigating rumor, others arose and have been endowed with legitimacy over years of retelling. The rumors were not extremely original, and some qualified as cliches. Most fit snugly into racial categories that had been well defined by the early 1940s.

Analogous to the blacks' fear of lynching, many whites were convinced a Negro revolution was imminent. Because of racial unrest during World War II, this perception was more prevalent than anytime since before the Civil War, when rumors of slave uprisings abounded. There was said to be a mysterious Negro leader, a modern Nat Turner, who would marshall forces throughout the South when the white population was most vulnerable. Rumors spread that Negroes had bought up ice picks, knives, and even guns in certain communities across the South to prepare for offensive action. All would be mobilized by an efficient signal. Sheriff Underwood's daughter said Maury County Negroes were called to Mink Slide by the ringing of church bells in the country. This has not been substantiated by any Columbia Negro and was never presented at any legal hearing.[10]

Many southerners feared Negro rebellion instigated by "outside agitation." In support of this, Columbia authorities made much of mysterious calls to Negro leaders, particularly to James Morton's home, within twelve hours of the policemen shootings. Despite repeated referral to phone calls in authorities' trial testimonies, nothing more conspiratorial than concerned calls from relatives and friends or offers of help from interested social agencies could be documented.

The emerging specter of international communism piqued both national and regional paranoia in 1946. Uncle Joe Stalin had become an apparently much greater United States domestic threat than Hitler ever had been. Although the espionage hysteria created by Alger Hiss, the Rosenbergs, and Joe McCarthy were in the future, apprehension about Communist fifth columnists was everywhere, even in Columbia, Tennessee. Attorney General Bumpus and Commissioner Bomar repeatedly expressed their fears of "communistic" destruction led by angry Negroes. Jimmy Underwood Jr. told of finding boxes of Communist literature in Mink Slide that told of plans to take over Columbia office buildings. His sister said similar inflammatory materials were found in William Gordon's house. Horace Gordon said his brother did not finish high school, read very little, and, except for weekend carousing, only worked on the farm.[11] In spite of obsession with the critical tracts that flooded Columbia after the riot, no one ever introduced any Communist propaganda as trial exhibits. Apparently, no such material was preserved.

It was perhaps unrealistic for Tennessee politicians to appreciate the subtle struggle for power among groups wanting to lead mid-century Negroes. The southern politician perspective was figuratively and literally still black and white. However, plenty of contemporaneous evidence of the antipathy between U.S. Communists and mainstream black leadership, especially within the NAACP, existed. These two organizations had fought mightily for preeminence in defending the Scottsboro boys during the 1930s.[12] In those depression-era cases, the Communist Party had seen opportunities for both social redress and disruption. The propaganda value of the party's involvement was immeasurable. Its lawyers had aggressively usurped the cautious NAACP, winning the favor of defendants and their families and leading management of their cases during several trials.

That competition had continued through the Columbia matter as both sought the loyalty of what they saw as their natural constituencies in Maury County and the nation. In subsequent decades of red scare, political rivals of the NAACP tried to smear the organization as being communistic. Walter White, Thurgood Marshall, and others tried just as hard to sanitize the association of the dreaded odor of communism. All of this had little to do with political philosophy and everything to do with consolidating control.[13]

Much publicity transpired concerning the arsenal on Mink Slide. Newspapers ran pictures of huge stacks of weapons. The assertion that Negroes had been storing them for some time reinforced the prevalent white theory of black insurrection. V. K. Ryan, however, testified that the call for arms only went out the night of the February 25. Vigorous questioning of Digger Johnson by Bumpus's interrogation board and the FBI about conspirational activities at the black American Legion lodge came a cropper.

The rumor of guns brought in by caskets was another notion not coined in Columbia. However, alleged insiders contended for years that rifles were smuggled into town in caskets and delivered to Morton Funeral Home. Milton Murray pointed out that the parlor only had six caskets. Bernard Stofel said it was beyond comprehension that such a scheme could get past constant police scrutiny in this small town and that no one could afford any expensive weapons at the time. He considered the story to be "baloney."[14]

An even more colorful story about Morton's caskets dealt with their use as beds. Thurgood Marshall was said to have spent some nights in Columbia and, reasonably, to have feared for his safety. In order for him to get some secure rest, his hosts supposedly had him sleep in one of the caskets in the funeral parlor. Morton's daughter, Cemora, said she remembered all the lawyers traveling to Nashville at night and that the story was bunk.[15]

The jailhouse killings of Digger Johnson and William Gordon have remained a source of debate since 1946. In retrospect, all interested black persons said they believed the men were set up. John Morgan thought rifle shells may have been slipped to Gordon on top of a sack of cigars brought in by a deputy. The angry Gordon and the luckless Johnson had bragged of being among the police shooters, and the THP, including Chief Griffin's son, were just too conveniently nearby when the supposed trap was sprung.

To believe this conspiracy theory though requires some imagination. How could the deputy and constable be lounging so casually in harm's way if they had been aware of such a plot? Were they just excellent thespians? Were their law-enforcement cohorts ready to subject them to a shoot-out in a little room? Just how did Gordon get the correct ammunition for one of the many guns lying about? Jim Squires noted that Napoleon Stewart survived the gunfight, and Squires's grandfather, Sgt. Dave White, would never have missed an intended victim at such a close range.[16] Though the full truth about these avoidable fatalities will never be known, they likely resulted from inadequate security work by overworked and casual, trusting law officers.

If these killings were not tragic and sensational enough, rumors of scores of deaths were prevalent then and remain certain to some now who recall the riot. Victor Wilson insisted that jailers killed *nine* prisoners. In response to an alleged *Time* article depicting many bodies floating in the Duck River, Sheriff Underwood offered a reward to anyone who could prove the rumored occurrence. No one claimed any reward. Similarly, workers said bodies were buried in the mining excavations at Monsanto. Herbert Johnson believed that black marksmen killed five whites who attempted to invade Mink Slide by car before the police came. V. K. Ryan was supposed to have cooperated with white morticians in preparing bodies. White shame required that their obituaries announce they had died of unexplained causes. No such epidemic occurred, according to local obituaries after the riot. These tales were examples of inflated casualty reports. Stofel again assigned the rumors to the porcine repository of "baloney."[17]

OFFICIAL RESPONSE TO RIOT

Officials' reactions to the Mink Slide riot only compounded those factors that caused it. Sheriff Underwood had been somewhat disappointed with the general lack of civil discipline since the return of veterans and his own soft response to their behavior. Other local officials did not seem troubled by new socioeconomic currents swirling about them. None questioned the necessity and legal justification for segregation or the effect of this caste clarification on restive, former Negro servicemen. Neither did any recognize the electric effect a rumor of lynching might have on a black community who had tolerated such a killing thirteen years prior. They all had tunnel vision as events of February 25 progressed, recognizing a black mob on Mink Slide but assigning only merit to armed whites roaming through the town's center.

If they could imagine a black offensive was coming out of the Bottom, why could they not believe the blacks down there might feel the same way about the good ole boys on the square?

The Columbia riot was one of the worst things any local official could conjure for his town. None foresaw it. Only Underwood worked throughout the evening to contain chaos. The office of mayor in Columbia provided little executive muscle, and Mayor Denham's meager action on February 25 proved as much. He was essentially missing in action and confused matters by not coordinating with the sheriff in calling for state help. After finally admitting late in the evening there just might be a problem and calling the chief back to duty, the police department stumbled right into history and out of jurisdictional authority. Chief Griffin's impromptu walk was presumptuous of his control over his fellow colored citizens. The huddled, armed, partially inebriated, scared, and angry mob on the darkened street was much different from the fellows which he and his force usually related to with comfortable but condescending authority. The chief made a bad choice.

Then there was the state. Governor McCord had no choice but to quickly respond to Sheriff Underwood's plea for help. He may have chosen the highway patrol because of their ability to quickly mobilize or his faith in Bomar's capability. His subsequent inspection of the scene and Ernest Smith's summary later in the week resulted only in officially exonerating memoranda, one-sided and intended for political cover as much as real communication. His office issued little further information except his assertion that, once again, outsiders were trying to run Tennessee's affairs. Though black journalists continually chided him through the next election for his handling of the Mink Slide matter, the issue never seemed important to most voters; he was reelected.

The short-lived Tennessee State Guard was perhaps flawed in concept and certainly deficient in manpower. Many guard enlistees were boys who probably joined in patriotic fervor and envisioned nothing exceedingly dangerous, perhaps just glorified camping trips glamorized with weapons. There was great interest in signing up after the riot if enlistees could be guaranteed a trip to Columbia. Sam Kennedy was a nineteen-year-old army noncommissioned officer on leave in February 1946. Even to this teenager, the state guardsmen looked infantile. When Sgt. Kennedy upbraided one of the lads about his careless handling of a rifle, the chastised soldier assured him the gun was not loaded; Sam had to show him it was. After hearing of her son's hysteria over the dangerous circumstances in Columbia, one Nashville mother expressed her alarm to the governor, who said such youngsters would be withdrawn as soon as possible.[18]

Though it is unknown what the guard would have done if faced with an actual riot, it performed with discipline during the Columbia episode. General Dickinson was justified in defending his boys before the federal grand jury. Their training had been adequate to stand firm in a civil disturbance. There were few accidental gun firings, no deaths, and a good record for controlling traffic and dispersing crowds. There was also no evidence they participated in vandalism or were overtly racist in actions.

John Morgan spoke for many when he observed that the state guard was effectively "nearly nil" and that the THP was the only unit that could have stopped the riot.[19] Whatever the judgment on their results, the patrol performed like a loose cannon at Columbia. They broadly interpreted their charge by Governor McCord and went far beyond their defined limits of authority and expertise. Their questionable, if not illegal, actions included the attempted purloining of weapons from the armory for distribution to white loiterers, the unilateral rejection of the joint plan with the state guard for an orderly opening of East Eighth, the destruction of property on the street (probably including the horrendous vandalism), and the surreptitious pummeling of prisoners. All this was followed by Bomar's participation in the investigation board. The submission of that board's deliberations and Bomar's bellicose behavior on the witness stand were huge weaknesses for the prosecution at Lawrenceburg.

The patrol's motives could not have been as bad as their actions. They doubtlessly saw their conduct as justifiable means to the end of preserving peace. This was a one-sided peace though, tinged with racism and bad judgment. Whether from executive incompetence or clever oversight, the patrol's leaders left no paper trail of their performance at Columbia. Neither did they try to refute the continual panning of their actions by outside journalists. That was one spitting contest they were bound to lose.

It is impossible to quantify the effect of the ubiquitous participation of Billy Fleming's family in the the whole affair. His father certainly ratcheted up the stakes when he got the Stephensons' warrants raised to attempted murder from charges usually associated with a street brawl. Though Sheriff Underwood still held office, there seemed a tacit passing of the guard to the Democrat nominee, Flo Fleming. That officer, who was universally distrusted by blacks, was present during most key events and personally arrested Julius Blair.

Perhaps Mr. Blair's assertion at the Lawrenceburg trial is correct: local officials could have controlled matters long before they came unglued. An amazingly similar race riot occurred that summer in Athens, Alabama, a nearby town less than half the size of Columbia. It had a very different ending.

That riot began when two drunk white servicemen attempted to beat up a black man on a hot Saturday afternoon. When the victim fought back and escaped, whites, mostly servicemen, went on a rampage. They beat or ran out of town scores of Negroes and harassed store owners to replace Negro employees with white veterans. The police had the audaciousness to arrest the white perpetrators, which only inflamed the mob. Though attempting to stand firm, the mayor was forced to release the prisoners.

He maintained control, however. As in Columbia, the state patrol and a local unit of U.S. National Guard were called to Athens. Unlike in Columbia, these forces immediately restored order in a systematic, non-controversial fashion. The mayor quickly opened dialogue with the black community, asking for a biracial committee to address the disorder. His goal was two fold, to keep the peace and *prevent outsiders from taking advantage of the situation.* No Negroes were arrested, a grand jury indicted several whites, and fines were levied.[20]

Athens officials had probably not learned from the riot in Columbia six months prior to their own. Communication was not that comprehensive, and matters were still proceeding in Maury County. It is also uncertain that their response would have been so balanced if the Alabama riot had been started by Negroes. Athens leaders succeeded because they adhered to the law, recognized there were two races in their community and in the riot, and kept things in perspective, correctly identifying a racial squabble arising from uncertain times and nothing more grandiose.

BARRISTERS

The performances of lawyers on both sides of the Columbia 1946 dispute were interesting, occasionally misguided, and sometimes groundbreaking. For some the trial seemed a watershed. Before it, their futures were uncertain. After it, they went on to distinguished careers or professional obscurity.

Defense attorneys and journalists from afar continually criticized Judge Joe Ingram or classified him as a rube. In large part this sprang

from their perception of his unfairness to their cause, either by pushing
proceedings along or refusing certain lines of questioning. These observations may have been accurate. This case was early in his judgeship, and
Ingram probably never had one so difficult. The barrage of defense objections, the prickly personalities of the advocates, and the glare of
unfriendly national publicity apparently strained him close to the limits
of his skill and decorum.

Paul Bumpus took seriously his job of district attorney. He had
always been diligent and successful. As the world left the brief sunlight
of World War victory and began its descent into the dark and uncertain
times of the cold war, his vision of danger to the United States, especially
Tennessee, by evil, outside forces was not unique. It was in many
respects correct. His extrapolation of macroscopic anxiety onto the
microscopic case of a rural race conflict was, however, dead wrong. The
ragtag bunch of Negroes were not minions of world communism. They
were a scared mob who reacted in an almost organic manner to
perceived threat and saw the only colored business street in Columbia
destroyed by the state.

Some of that mob shot four Columbia policemen, and Bumpus
would have been wrong not to seek the guilty parties. However, he
never had a case—no identification, ballistics, or confession. Trying a
bunch of the "usual suspects" was a dog that would not hunt even in
Lawrence County. The presentation of a conspiracy against Columbia
was based more on imaginative geopolitics than proof. Bumpus also
compromised that dubious strategy with the tactics of denying counsel
to the accused while interrogating them in front of intimidating local
authority figures.

In the absence of anything else, it probably seemed reasonable to use
this method of painting with a broad, conspirational brush. It had
worked before and might have succeeded again, except that the scores of
defendants had professional help of their own. In addition to the novelty
of facing a biracial defense team, the state also had to contend with
competent and dedicated lawyers.

Negro lawyers were extremely rare in the South during the first half
of the twentieth century. The few practicing in that clime so inhospitable
to their talents were often poorly trained and rarely accepted major cases.
From its beginning in 1909, the NAACP turned to white lawyers, especially in the South. From the early 1930s, that gradually changed as more
black lawyers graduated from an improved Howard Law School and a
few Ivy League institutions. Racial pride was the main impetus to

increased reliance on these now more-competent black graduates. At age thirty-one in 1939, Thurgood Marshall was NAACP chief counsel.

Columbia blacks in 1946 had no experience with black lawyers. None were in the Maury County Bar Association. Ed Kimes said he vaguely remembered some black "property lawyers" but none who did defense work. Raymond Lockridge said, "Black folks didn't have opportunity for black lawyer[s] to stand up for them." After the riot, several arrested Negroes tried unsuccessfully to reach white lawyers who had defended them before. Julius Blair may have first contacted Alexander Looby. After the NAACP committed its resources to the Columbia matter, Ransom and, sporadically, Marshall were on the scene. Neither contributed as much to the cases as Looby; but their presence, especially Marshall's, lent more expertise and were symbolic of the importance the NAACP and other national liberal organizations assigned to the case. Both Ransom and Looby had earned doctorates in jurisprudence. Thus, on hand were a plethora of competent and prestigious Negro civil rights lawyers, who would after the 1946 trials become heroes to Maury County blacks.[21]

Maurice Weaver's type of dedicated firebrand was probably more common than competent black civil rights lawyers. Such "cause" lawyers used their intelligence and energy to redress society through legal advocacy. He was stereotypically brave, brash, and indefatigable. He was also clever. In Weaver's absence, the Columbia defendants still might have won acquittal. Their cases would not, however, have been nearly so interesting.

DEFENDANTS

The defendants whose actions, alleged or actual, toward whom all this legal moxie was directed were an unlikely gang of murderers. Ten of the twenty-five men accused in the Lawrenceburg trial were supposedly veterans, and their new attitudes toward racial discrimination probably lured them to Mink Slide the night of the Stephensons' arrests and rope rumors. Yet this was not, as many sympathetic journalists breathlessly suggested, a band of stalwart heroes standing at the ramparts to push back the invading forces of injustice. Most of the large mob with awareness and ingenuity had easily escaped entrapment in Mink Slide the night of the Stephensons' arrest. Those captured that morning were either unlucky, unaware, or unfacile. The shooters of the policemen were perhaps long gone when Bomar made his sweep.

Local lawmen well knew many of the fellows, as their names were frequently on police blotters or court dockets for minor offenses such as drunkenness or illegal liquor sales. Many were young, carefree, and prone to trouble. Yet, most were employed in 1946, and most of the others soon were. A couple joined the postwar Negro migration to the North. Some became farm owners or laborers; others were odd jobbers. At least a half-dozen worked in Maury County chemical plants. Calvin and Raymond Lockridge continued to preach, though Calvin put bread on the table as a mechanic, Raymond as a carpenter. The Blairs, Morton, and Meade Johnson were the only independent businessmen among them.[22]

Whatever their backgrounds, defendants comported themselves well at the Lawrenceburg trial. Virginia Weaver thought Julius Blair was effectively dignified.[23] His appearance enhanced his reputation and belied the alleged role of guerrilla-leader intent on reversing the racial hierarchy in Columbia, site of his own little cell of a purported international megalith. In whisking the Stephensons away from potential lynching, he had acted as a true leader for Negroes. Mainly though, he had just been Julius, a successful businessman who wanted to go along with people in order to get along.

DENOUEMENT

Were relations between the two races different in Columbia after the riot? Whites did not think so; blacks did. Milton Murray felt nobody won, both blacks and whites losing self-respect. Other blacks noticed a subtle but immediate difference in attitudes of many whites. Though Jim Crow laws persisted and some law officers were as racist as ever, stores were more receptive, whites had a greater readiness to converse with blacks, and blacks had less fear. Mary Morton thought that after the trials a greater racial awareness and a general community realization of the necessity to correct problems existed in order to prevent a recurrence of the Mink Slide riot. A "friend" of the SRC exulted that race relations were improved after the Lawrenceburg trial but they would likely regress unless preventive measures were taken.[24]

Several suggestions were made regarding such measures. The ideas were prototypes of those that would be heard during the next several decades of racial strife in the United States. In May 1946, Agnes Meyer, wife of the publisher of the *Washington Post*, had written articles about the riot that were thoughtful, partly inaccurate, and roundly despised in Maury County.[25] In a harbinger of imminently prevalent *Post* editorial policy, she suggested the solution to racial problems throughout the nation was to improve housing and economic conditions for Negroes by increased federal expenditures via Health, Education and Security, a new cabinet post that had just been proposed by President Truman.

Early on, the SRC had sent a field secretary, M. E. Tilly, to investigate the riot. Her comprehensive, though hodgepodge, report had included a recommendation for a community interracial committee. She said the committee should include representatives of the local ministry, a societal segment prominent in the South that had been missing in action during the tribulation. Mrs. W. A. Dale, whose father-in-law had fought with General Nathan B. Forrest during the Civil War, was a prominent civic and Presbyterian leader in Columbia. As a local director for the SRC, she asked that organization to send one of its experts to advise local leaders on preventive measures. No evidence has surfaced that they ever favored such a request.

Such reluctance of white leaders to seek outside help was based on both parochial pride and some common sense deriving from a century and a half of living cheek by jowl with blacks. That relationship was based on dominance and subservience but, in the majority, was also characterized by subtle understanding and compassion that were often absent in other parts of the nation because of different history. Most Columbians still firmly believed in segregation and the native superiority of whites. An emerging minority of thoughtful white leaders and intelligentsia recognized these premises and conditions were untrue and unsustainable.

One of the very few things that reporter Vincent Sheean agreed with Paul Bumpus about was that the South would have to solve its own problems and would always resist outside interference. Sheean had come to admire several unbiased southerners whose energy and will, he believed, would overcome their "inherited problems." Whatever the value of the many suggestions raining on frustrated and distraught Maury Countians of both races, they themselves would also have to solve their problems.[26]

Doubtless to the relief if its citizens, Columbia was only transiently a national focal point of racial strife. Traumatic and revolutionary national events associated with a few major leaders would lead the dance of ethnological rapprochement for the next half-century. These would include *Brown* v. *Board of Education of Topeka* (largely deriving from the work of Thurgood Marshall), Malcom X, sit-ins, boycotts, riots, George Wallace, the Great Society, Martin Luther King Jr.,

Vietnam, Jackie Robinson (and Branch Rickey), television, Timothy Leary, and busing. These influences would not be universally salutary, and society in Columbia and the nation would not approximate nirvana as the millennium approached.

Columbia had survived an initial shocking introduction to an inevitable social upheaval. Its racial history was more brutal than most communities'. Perhaps for that reason its people required a bitter dose of racial salts to begin dismantling racial barriers and to hopefully live together in peace and without fear. Maury County had other more benign and much more prevalent features to its history and people than the riot. Despite some denial and resistance, Columbians matured from the racial reveille and were capable of moving along with southern equanimity, fatalism, sensibility, and (yes, indeed) grace.

Epilogue

MAURY COUNTY TODAY

By the mid-1980s, Monsanto and other companies could not profitably mine phosphate or produce its products in Maury County. For environmental reasons, the products were less marketable. The cost of TVA power had become more expensive. Union pressures in other local plants had pushed wages higher. It was estimated in 1985 that Monsanto had paid five hundred million dollars in wages over its fifty years in Maury County. Though perhaps not a pacesetter in race relations, Monsanto had responded to the times and easily adjusted to social liberalization and civil rights legislation.[1] Now the area's bell-cow industry decided to pull out.

As the chemical industry wound down, Maury County citizens enjoyed cleaner air but suffered a sluggish economy. From 1982 to 1987, wholesale trade from the county decreased 19.6 percent. The economic breach was quickly filled by the erection in 1986 of the new Saturn plant outside Spring Hill, a five-billion-dollar investment by General Motors. Cars began rolling off the line in the summer of 1990. Though production jobs were not immediately available for local workers at the plant because of union agreements with displaced General Motors employees, a substantial economic ripple effect occurred. Service and supply industries sprang up, new roads and schools were built, and workers moved to the area. With other auto plants in the region, Saturn enhanced Middle

Tennessee's growing reputation as "Detroit South." Between 1990 and 1994, Maury County's population increased 10.4 percent.

The Saturn effect has not been entirely good. Executives from the old manufacturing industries lived in Maury County, providing leadership in cultural, civic, and religious matters. Saturn executives mostly settled in Williamson or Davidson County. Blue collar, line workers live near the plant. These well-paid employees have provided obvious economic impetus. They may have also brought with them unfamiliar, sometimes threatening inner-city mores and practices. Expeditious zoning has permitted the quick construction of numerous cheap housing developments all over the county. Beautiful rolling hills once so profitably devoted to agriculture now resemble one big trailer park.

By 1992, per capita income in Maury County was $18,188. Though this was a little less than the national mean, Maury was the fifth most prosperous county in Tennessee. In 1994, the county population was 63,888, 58 percent greater than in 1940—not exactly a booming statistic but still representing solid growth. Actually two thousand fewer blacks were living in Maury County in 1994 than in 1940, a 20 percent reduction. Blacks now represented approximately 15 percent of the population, down from 25 percent in 1940. Negroes had left the area, and the emigres were apparently predominantly white.

Saturn was by far the largest employer in the county in 1996. The county's unemployment rate was 5.2 percent. The Columbia Chamber of Commerce proudly touted new small industries, strong beef production, Columbia's status as a regional medical center, a fine airport, and superb baseball teams, including amateur squads at all levels and the Columbia Mules, the new professional team. Mule Day festivals were very healthy, attracting more than three hundred thousand fans annually. Though he was from a different social stratum than James K. Polk, the county had a new hero in the NASCAR driver Sterling Marlin.

There were six, totally integrated, public high schools in the county in 1996. Columbia Military Academy was defunct, going the way of most such institutions in the South. It had been replaced by a Church of Christ private school. There were three other Christian secondary high schools in the county, another reflection of national educational trends. Founded in 1966, Columbia State University was Tennessee's first junior college. Lyndon Johnson had come to dedicate it. It had prospered and enhanced the county's education and intellectual environments.

Maurians remained cognizant of the county's history and were proud of its many, well-preserved, old homes. The Majestic Middle Tennessee Fall Tour was popular and well attended; and the county contributed significantly to the Antebellum Trail, the highest concentration of ante-bellum homes in the South.[2]

What about Maury County's darker side? Was this still an unseen but ever dangerous cancer within an apparently healthy civic body? Without entering the swamp of the ever-popular question regarding the persis-tence of racism, the answer must be yes and no.

Yes, certain segments of society seeking succor or revenge for perceived injustices ostensibly responsible for their own failures were capable of violent acts against the opposite race. Three Maury County white men, led by a Culleokan, contributed their share to the alleged 1994–1996 national epidemic of bombing rural black churches.[3] They fire-bombed a tavern owned by a black man and two small, black churches. Their destructiveness was exceeded only by their clumsiness, and they were quickly implicated. In addition to local publicity, their escapade received a tad of national notoriety, though not on the scale of the Mink Slide riot a half-century before.

Both the justice system and southern society had also changed since 1946. For violating federal civil rights statutes, all three were fined and sentenced to jail terms. Though retaining some persistent fear of danger based on racism, the pastor of one of the churches expressed gratitude for the financial, physical, and moral support provided by white Maury Countians, including a chapter of the Sons of Confederate Veterans.[4]

No, Maury County was not still segregated, and racism did not influ-ence every waking decision by its citizens. There were still "black" and "white" parts of town. There were also some middle-class neighborhoods that were gradually and peacefully being integrated, often influenced by the influx of middle-level executives. The black bourgeois, a nonexistent class in 1946, lived easily in these subdivisions. Mixed marriages were rare but increasing. Because of a labor shortage, some Mexicans had also migrated to Maury County. Ease of travel, television, and economics had made the area almost cosmopolitan. Racial dividing lines seemed less clear or necessary.

Not many blacks were represented among Maury County professionals. Though there had been some black physicians in recent years, there were none in 1996. *Still* no black lawyers worked in the entire Twenty-second Tennessee State Judicial District, a professional opportunity unfulfilled. Eight percent of current Maury County teachers were black. The county education department has had difficulty recruiting black teachers, and those who entered the system when integration occurred are retiring.[5]

A current stroll around the four blocks surrounding the courthouse reveals changes inherent in modern urban economics. The square no longer bustles, on Saturday or any other day. Most retail businesses have fled to suburban strip malls now surrounding the town. Most of the stores that purveyed hardware, drugs, groceries, dry goods, and fun (although one pool hall remains) have vanished. Still the area is clean and useful. Professional and government offices fill tastefully restored buildings. Ingenious realtors seek uses, including downtown residences, for other old but sound structures formerly used for retail business.

Mink Slide is a shell of its former self. Black mom-and-pop stores have dispersed throughout the town. A few social establishments have moved across Woodland further east on Eighth Street. Many buildings have been razed. On the north side of the street, only the First Baptist Church is functional. Morton Funeral Home is defunct. On the south side, another church, a new funeral establishment, a restaurant, and one barbershop are active. Of fifteen identified real estate parcels on East Eighth, ten are owned by six black families and five properties are owned by four whites. Eighth is just another under-utilized downtown street.[6]

THE MAIN ACTORS' LIVES

A glance at the remaining lives of some of the key participants in the Mink Slide riot shows that for most of them life went on without discernable effect from it. Whether due to journalistic decorum or because the event had been largely forgotten, their obituaries rarely included any mention of the 1946 riot.

J. Walter Griffin
Chief Griffin retired in 1950. Mr. Griffin died in 1952 at age seventy-seven. Editorialists deemed him a good, wise, and respected man.[7]

Jacob McGavock Dickinson
After the demise of the Tennessee State Guard in 1946, General Dickinson continued to work in various state executive positions. When he died in 1963 at age seventy-two, he was director of the Franchise and Excise Tax Division of the Tennessee Department of Finance and Taxation. In recalling his distinguished heritage and interesting life, editorialists lauded his personality and sense of duty.[8]

Joe Ingram
Judge Joe Ingram served on the circuit court bench for forty years. His closest election call was against Paul Bumpus in 1949, which Ingram won

56 percent to 43 percent. His career was deemed honorable, and he never had any trial so profound as the one following the Mink Slide riot. He became known as a plaintiff's attorney, sometimes to the chagrin of appeal courts. Never after the Lawrenceburg trial was he accused of racism. The majority regional professional opinion was that he was fair and sensible. Like most conscientious judges, he seemed to improve with age. He died in 1986 at age seventy-four.[9]

Julius W. Blair

The senior black "leader" ran an unsuccessful campaign for city council in 1953, finishing last in a field of eleven candidates. At that time, candidates represented one ward but ran at large, a system that neutralized a Negro's chances of winning in a segregated society. Blair's historic electoral effort was marred when the Maury County Election Commission found him distributing marked ballots at the predominantly black third precinct.

He died in 1962 at age ninety-two. A front-page obituary recalled his long life as a barber and businessman. Blair was not mentioned among several laudatory eulogies on the *Herald* editorial page that day.[10]

Saul Blair

Julius's businessman son died in 1965 at age seventy-three. In his obituary, the World War I veteran was said to have been "active in political and civic matters."[11]

James J. Underwood

Much to the pleasure of his family, who had been worried about his health, the sheriff did not run as an independent against Flo Fleming in 1946. Rather, he retired to farm until he died in 1966 at age seventy-nine. His son J. J. Jr. felt his father's health improved remarkably after he left public life.[12]

Lynn Bomar

Bomar became the warden at the state prison in Nashville after leaving the Tennessee Department of Safety in 1949. His tenure there was marked by controversy in 1960 when the *Tennessean* published a series of articles depicting crime in the prison and brutality against inmates. A Davidson County Grand Jury did not recommend indictments but commented on "an arrogant attitude" of the institution's authorities.

Bomar died at age sixty-three of a heart attack on June 11, 1964. He was fondly remembered on the Nashville sports pages. Regarding his law-enforcement career, a *Banner* editorialist noted, without specifics, he had served Tennessee well during "some troublous times."[13]

Vincent Sheean

The journalist and author died at his home in Italy in 1975 at age seventy-five. In its obituaries, the *New York Times* prominently mentioned his coverage of the Lawrenceburg trial. The *Washington Post* discussed his leftist, anti-capitalist leanings and closed by saying he wrote most passionately against organized injustice, the subversion of many by the few.[14]

Z. Alexander Looby

Looby remained active in civil rights law. He and his partner, Avon Williams, spearheaded numerous civil rights changes across the state and argued important local school desegregation cases before and after *Brown v. Board*. In 1950, Looby and Robert Lillard became the first blacks elected to the Nashville City Council. He served on the Charter Commission, which organized Nashville Metropolitan government in the early 1960s.

Not everyone appreciated his civil rights work. Looby's home was fire-bombed in 1960. Nashville blacks and all important civic leaders rallied around him. He was respected as an excellent city councilman and a calm, consistent leader for his people. He said his aim was for them to hold their heads up. He was a popular man who played a good hand of poker and never conspicuously created controversy as he pursued his ends.

Looby died in March 1972 at age seventy-two. The Nashville Bar Association, which many years previously had rejected his application, posthumously awarded him membership in 1982.[15]

Maurice Weaver

Vincent Sheean uncannily predicted the effects of Maurice Weaver's successful and controversial defense efforts in the Mink Slide matter. "Mr. Weaver has kicked over the traces of the society in which he lives, and, like a character in an Ibsen drama, will be living out the consequences for the rest of his life."[16] Other features of his tortured personality would also influence the duration of his colorful and tragic existence.

Sheean was wrong in predicting to Virginia Weaver that Maurice's actions would ruin his career in the South. He immediately developed a large plaintiff's law practice. According to Mrs. Weaver, the rednecks believed that if he could "get them niggers off he's the guy I need to defend me."[17] He developed a large black clientele and, though not obsessed with politics, could deliver some black vote at election time. A cross burned in the Weaver's yard after Maurice got some blacks put on juries in Chattanooga.

He remained brilliant, witty, acerbic in the courtroom but unprepared and erratic out of it. He became addicted to alcohol and prescription drugs. Among his sociopathic and unethical actions were stealing from his firm to run off with a newly hired teenage secretary and sleeping with another teenager who, prior to that, had been prepared to testify against her father.[18] He was married several times, twice to Virginia.

The Chattanooga Bar Association instituted disbarment proceedings against Weaver in 1965. Among the charges were failure to pay federal income tax, having an affair with a client's wife, representing opposing parties in a case, absconding with a client's money, and threatening attorneys.[19] Despite his vigorous resistance, the Eastern Section of the Tennessee Court of Appeals upheld his disbarment in May 1968. Maurice Weaver died of cirrhosis and emphysema in Chattanooga on October 30, 1983, at age seventy-two.

James Morton

Morton's mortuary business continued to thrive after 1946. He remained prominent in his community and profession. He died in 1965 at age fifty-five. The business did well under his widow's leadership. After her death in 1990, it failed badly and was sold at public auction.

Thurgood Marshall had a personal influence on Morton's daughter, Cemora Newsome. In 1946, he expressed interest in the fifteen-year-old girl's education plans and influenced her to go to Howard University. She loved Washington, D.C., and spent the majority of her professional and married life there, where she is now retired.[20]

Paul Bumpus

After losing the election to Joe Ingram, Bumpus felt he would never be successful pleading cases before the judge. He moved to Nashville and worked on the staff of the U.S. Attorney for most of the 1950s. Subsequently he did some private practice and worked for the Nashville Metropolitan Attorney's office before retiring in 1972. He now lives in Murfreesboro, Tennessee.

Bumpus denied that his efforts as district attorney were ever motivated by ambition for higher office as opposing attorneys and critical journalists averred. Some attorneys did not admire Bumpus's work as district attorney. Defense lawyers at Lawrenceburg believed he was way over his head. Many others admired him. No one questioned his honesty, morality, or tenacity. The Mink Slide murder case was the apogee of his career.[21]

Leon Ransom

Lawrenceburg was not the first southern town Ransom had visited to defend Negro clients. He participated with Thurgood Marshall in attaining admission to the University of Missouri Law School for Lloyd Gaines in the late 1930s. In 1940, he had argued in Knoxville for the admission of five Negroes to the University of Tennessee. In 1942, a deputy sheriff assaulted him in a courthouse corridor in Nashville where he had been pleading for a client just convicted by a white jury.

Though he enjoyed prestige and was active in Washington, D.C., civic affairs, his life was somewhat chaotic after 1946. He resigned in controversy from the Howard University faculty in the spring of that year. While in a hectic private practice, he went missing from his home due to "amnesia" in 1949.[22] He died in New Jersey while on a fishing trip in 1954 at age fifty-seven.

Thurgood Marshall

Before and after 1946, Marshall achieved unparalleled legal success, especially for a black attorney. He had already won a major voting-rights case, *Smith* v. *Allwright*, in 1944. Laboring tirelessly and prodigiously as NAACP chief counsel, he achieved major triumphs in real estate restrictive covenant suits and in university-admissions policies for Negroes in various states. His most important victory was the 1954 *Brown* v. *Board of Education of Topeka*.

President Kennedy appointed Marshall to the U.S. Court of Appeals. President Johnson made him the solicitor general, in which role he successfully argued the precedent privacy case *Griswold* v. *Connecticut*. Marshall stood before the Supreme Court thirty-two times in his career and won twenty-nine of those cases. Johnson appointed him the first black associate justice of the U.S. Supreme Court in 1967, saying Marshall and the court were "the right man and the right place." On that bench, he was a predictable liberal, heartily joining the majority in *Roe* v. *Wade* and other decisions of the Warren and Burger courts. His later years on the more conservative Rehnquist court were ideologically frustrating. This solitary, angry man was no consensus builder and, therefore, wrote few significant majority opinions. Because of poor health, Marshall retired in 1991. He died in 1993 at age eighty-four. Perhaps one of the most ironic honors bestowed on Marshall was the naming of the law library at the University of Maryland after him. He had been denied admission to that graduate school.

Marshall never pretended to be sophisticated or subtle. He used lots of profanity, smoked, and drank whiskey prodigiously.[23] He loved playing cards and was a great raconteur. Justice Brennan said that one of Marshall's favorite stories was about the sobriety test given him in Columbia. When the tall Marshall had grasped the shoulders of the very short Squire Pogue and, as requested, breathed close and hard into the magistrate's face, Marshall had very promptly won his freedom.

His career was devoted to the protection and improvement of minorities, particularly blacks. He was not considered a balanced jurist but led huge sociopolitical gains for Negroes, often braving hostile and apparently dangerous environments such as Columbia, Tennessee.[24]

James Stephenson

The original, unwilling combatant in the Columbia riot happily lived his adult life in Detroit, never even considering returning to the South. He worked in an automobile plant and as a shipping clerk for a graphic arts company. He raised a family and continued to enjoy athletics—baseball, bowling, and, most recently, golf. He remained unconcerned about danger in Maury County, and his visits to Middle Tennessee, particularly Spring Hill where he had many relatives, were never surreptitious. He never considered he had done anything except participate in a fight that he won. Unfortunately that fight had been with a white man.

June Pie's relatives who were with him at the beginning of the Columbia troubles also enjoyed long, pleasant lives in Detroit. Gladys died in March 1987, age seventy-seven. His grandmother, Hannah Peppers, outlived her daughter, dying four months later at age one hundred.[25]

THEIR TOWN

Columbians can best speak for themselves and their town and county. A short, thoroughly unscientific amalgamation of their observations serves as coda to this book on their place and history.

Segregation is gone. A block from where this soda jerk could not allow a black person to drink a Coke at the drugstore fountain, I recently sat beside an old, black man enjoying a cup of coffee at a sandwich shop. His white peers treated him with comfortable conviviality.

Still, there is a subtle, lingering suspicion between the races. Some blacks suspect they are treated differently than whites. Examples include the perception of preferential treatment of whites at checkout counters or quick white presumption of black guilt in legal matters. Whites generally believe blacks are preferred in job selections because of government mandates and that blacks are responsible for an unacceptably high crime rate. Parents of both black and white youngsters condemn interracial dating, which is sometimes done to challenge authority as much as for attractiveness. Jim Crow no longer saturates southern statutes, however, and differences are usually resolved on bases of merit and reason, not civil disturbance or intimidation.

Columbia blacks and whites generally worry about the same problems, most of which are not race related and mirror concerns of people around the nation. These include housing, medical care, education, and drugs. The public school system is overcrowded and faces the currently prevalent charge of educational inadequacy. In addition to white flight from public schools, there is some wealth flight; so Maury County has the dilemma of potentially becoming educationally two tiered again—public schools for poor children and private for those who can afford it. Twenty-one percent of Maury County public school students are black, 6 percent more than their race's proportion of the population.[26]

Some claim drugs are a bigger problem in the county because of Saturn, the northern city youngsters having allegedly imported their more sophisticated and ravenous habits. Because of the higher prevalence of drug use in the black community, some apologists indulge in the rationalization that once again whites are trying to bring down blacks by habituating them.

Lifelong Columbians regret its recent growth and its societal homogenization. They recall former days when Columbia was known as a town of "old families." Now there are no old families, and people are liable to visit their favorite restaurant or hardware store without recognizing anyone they know. There is no regret though among blacks who have recognized changed times and opportunity and seized it. For example, there is no evidence of real estate covenants in Columbia.

The Mink Slide riot was the opening act of several events after World War II that broke down rigid racial barriers in Columbia. Those Negroes who constructively led the way did so by the example of their accomplishments and civility and with the gradual acceptance of an increasingly tolerant white community.

George Newburn was two years into his career as the Negro county agent when the riot occurred. His work was frustrating. Local blacks had such little faith in themselves or anyone of their color that they would go to the white agent to substantiate agricultural advice given them by Newburn. He had to work out of his car, usually parked on East Eighth, for years until the state finally found the money to rent an office for him. He had great difficulty getting blacks to stand on their own feet instead of remaining tenant farmers and reliant on white contractors. Gradually, he taught many of them to buy and register property, vote, build their own homes, and educate themselves. He had backbone and taught determination to his clients. All the while, he raised and educated his own family, built his own home (despite lack of local banking help), and supported his church.[27]

A second generation Columbia barrier breaker was Rose Ogilvie McClain. As a third grader working in her mother's restaurant, she heard Carver-Smith students describe the limited job opportunities they antici-pated after graduation from their admittedly inferior school. Rose, herself, decided to attend a more challenging and better equipped school, i.e., a white one. She became the first black to attend McDowell School in 1964, suffering isolation, taunting, and playground danger before attaining trust and friendship from her fellow students. Belying its latter-day reputation for racism, the town seemed to view her attendance at McDowell as a nonevent.[28]

As she anticipated before her school transfer, she was behind her white peers and had to be held back. "We were counting apples out of a basket, while at McDowell they were multiplying." That was the last time

James Stephenson family on occasion of his grandmother's ninety-first birthday. Left to right—Front row: James's granddaughter Shalonda Sanders; Mrs. Peppers; James's mother, Gladys Harris. Back row: James Stephenson, James's daughter Theresa Sanders. (Courtesy— *Michigan Chronicle*)

though, as she succeeded at Central High, earned degrees from Middle Tennessee State University, and became a teacher in the Columbia system. While teaching, she also learned mortuary science and, with her mother, entered that business in Columbia and Mt. Pleasant. She is now assistant principal at Columbia Central High School.[29]

The blacks who "rioted" on Mink Slide in 1946 and their defenders are just as responsible as later, more famous civil rights leaders for the opportunities afforded Rose and others. They had no plan but recognized change was afoot and seized the moment to symbolically, as well as actually, have no more social lynchings. The great majority of whites they faced still believed in segregation. However, there were fewer unrepentant crackers among those whites than the fearful, distrusting blacks imagined. From experience and study, I know that Maury Countians, black and white, were and are mostly nonviolent, decent, realistic people. They recognized the need for change and, occasionally kicking and screaming, did it.

There is no guarantee against riot recurrence in the Dimple of the Universe, but the likelihood seems remote. Four decades after the 1946 debacle that put Columbia so disastrously in the national limelight, Rufus Black, a local Negro, assessed the possibility, "It won't happen no more—never in this world."[30]

Abbreviations

C of C	Maury County Chamber of Commerce pamphlet, TSLA
CNFP	*Chattanooga News Free-Press*
DH	Columbia (Tennessee) *Daily Herald*
DWNY	*Daily Worker of New York*
GJ	Proceeding Before the United States District Grand Jury for the Middle District of Tennessee in the Matter of Columbia, Tennessee, Investigation
LDU	*Lawrenceburg* (Tennessee) *Democrat-Union*
LL	*Louisville* (Kentucky) *Leader*
LT	Transcript of *State of Tennessee* v. *Sol Blair, et al.*
MD	Columbia (Tennessee) *Maury Democrat*
NB	*Nashville Banner*
NG	*Nashville Globe*
NT	*Nashville Tennessean*
NYHT	*New York Herald Tribune*
NYT	*New York Times*
TSLA	Tennessee State Library and Archives
WP	*Washington Post*
WSJ	*Wall Street Journal*
WAA	*Washington Afro-American*

Notes

Preface

1. I also recall no discussions of Maury County lynchings, one of which occurred approximately four years before my birth.

2. "Looking Backward through the *Herald*," *DH*, 25 February 1966, 2.

3. In an editorial fifty years ago, a Nashville black newspaper, *NG*, "Time Marches to and Fro," 18 October 1946, 4, suggested a book should be written about the trial that followed the riot. That has heretofore not been done.

Chapter One

1. William Bruce Turner, *History of Maury County, Tennessee* (Nashville: The Parthenon Press, 1955), 11; D. P. Robbins, ed., *Century Review of Maury County, Tennessee, 1805–1905* (Columbia, Tenn.: Auspices of the Board of Mayor and Aldermen of Columbia, 1905), 6; Jill Garrett, *'Hither and Yon' the Best of the Writings of Jill K. Garrett* (Columbia, Tenn.: The Maury County Tennessee Homecoming '86 Committee, 1988), 245; *Columbia, Maury County Tennessee, Her Progress and Importance* (Enterprise Publishing Company, 1885), 6, TSLA; C of C, 1946.

2. Turner, *Maury County*, 12–13, 44, 59; Garrett, *'Hither and Yon,'* 245; *A Historical Sketch of Maury County* (Columbia, Tenn.: Excelsior Printing Office, 1877), 32. General Nathanael Greene received an especially large grant of 25,000 acres.

3. Jill Garrett, *'Hither and Yon' II: More of the Writings of Jill Garrett* (Columbia, Tenn.: Polk Memorial Association, 1992), 5–8, 114, 192

4. Blanche Henry Clark, "The Agricultural Population in Tennessee, 1840–1860: With Special Reference to the Non-slaveholders" (Ph.D. diss., Vanderbilt University, 1938), 16, 200–2; 1850 Maury County Slave Census, microfilm, TSLA;

Reid Smith, *Majestic Middle Tennessee* (Pratville, Ala.: Paddle Wheel Publications, 1975), 8–62. Local charities today use many of these striking, well-preserved antebellum homes for pilgrimages.

5. Clark, "Agricultural Population," 16, 58; Chase C. Mooney, *Slavery in Tennessee* (Bloomington: Indiana University Press, 1957), 5, 123.

6. Turner, *Maury County*, 207–33; Lew Wallace, "The Capture of Fort Donelson" in *Battles and Leaders of the Civil War, Vol. 1* (Secaucus, N.J.: Castle), 422; James M. McPherson, *Battle Cry of Freedom* (New York: Oxford University Press, 1988), 400–1; Sam R. Watkins, *"CO. AYTCH," Maury Grays, First Tennessee Regiment* (Dayton, Ohio: Morningside Bookshop, 1982). On West Seventh Street in Columbia is a beautiful, little park with an impressive obelisk honoring General Pillow.

7. *A Historical Sketch*, 64–65.

8. Robbins, *Century Review*, 7, 103; Turner, *Maury County*, 319; Needham Coppedge and John L. Christian, "A History of Phosphates in Maury County," in Turner, *Maury County*, 331–38.

9. *MD*, 9 March 1956, 3.

10. C of C, circa 1939.

11. Ibid. Rogers's remarks were taken from a McNaught syndicated article of 3 March 1935.

12. Garrett, *'Hither and Yon,'* 214–5; Columbia Tennessee City Directory Supplement 1942 (Gulfport, Miss.: State Directory Company, 1942), 3. After James K. Polk, Mule Day has provided Columbia its main fame.

13. Reminiscent of Columbia's antebellum history, a popular summer course on female etiquette, dress, and lifestyle circa 1861 is still taught at the rectory, the Athenaeum's only preserved building; Stuart Maddux, "Oh to Be a Southern Belle," *Southern Living* (May 1997): 60–100.

14. Turner, *Maury County*, 127–41; C of C, 1946; Colene Anderson, "Ruins of College at Spring Hill Stand; Columbia's Athenaeum, Institute Gone," *DH*, 13 November 1965, 6, 9.

15. C of C, 1946; United States Department of Commerce, *Sixteenth Census of the United States: 1940* (United States Government Printing Office, 1943), vol. 1, 1014; *U.S. Census, 1940*, vol. 2, 593.

16. Robbins, *Century Review*, 103; C of C, circa 1939. Whether the term *nigger* was then contemporary jargon or an expression of contempt depended of course on one's perspective.

17. *U.S. Census*, 1940, vol. 1.

18. Turner, *Maury County*, 367; John Cimprich, *Slavery's End in Tennessee, 1861–1865* (University, Ala.: University of Alabama Press, 1985), 10, 44, 119.

19. Allen W. Trelease, *White Terror: The Ku Klux Klan Conspiracy and Southern Reconstruction* (Westport, Connecticut: Greenwood Press, 1971).

20. Trelease, *White Tenor*, 23, 25–6, 28–31, 40, 178; Turner, *Maury County* 357–8.

21. "Negro Believed Guilty Attempted Assault Held—Wiley Pleads with Posse," *DH*, 11 November 1927, 1, 3; "Candidates at Wire Ready to Race Tomorrow," *DH*, 11 November 1927, 1.

22. "Negro Rapist Is Hanged by Mob Last Night from Balcony at Court House," *DH*, 12 November 1926, 1, 2; "All of Society Shares Guilt of Mob Violence," *DH*, 14

November 1927, 1; "Turner Raps Mob Violence Jury Charge" *DH*, 14 November 1927, 1; "No Indictment Lynching Case Jury Reports," *DH*, 29 November 1927, 1, 3.

23. Robert Minor, a Communist and labor journalist who covered the Mink Slide riot, claimed to have identified the stump of this tree, which was apparently cut down after the lynching; Robert Minor, *Lynching and Frame-up in Tennessee*, (New York: New Century Publishers, 1946), 42.

24. *DH*, 17 November 1933, 1; *DH*, 18 November 1933, 1; *DH*, 19 December 1933, 1, 2; *DH*, 20 December 1933, 1; *NYT*, 16 December 1933, 1; *NYT*, 17 December 1933, 35; Thomas Jones, summary of findings, Cordie Cheek Folder, Fisk Special Collections, Fisk University, Nashville, Tennessee.

25. Harold Hinton, "NY Times Notes No Negro Repression Here" *DH*, 8 July 1946, 1, 3.

26. Wade Hall, *The Rest of the Dream* (Lexington: The University of Kentucky Press, 1988), 59; *U.S. Census, 1940*, vol. 2, 593.

Chapter Two

1. Argument over a "small debt" is how the *Nashville Tennessean* described the precipitating event. *NT*, 27 February 1946, 1.

2. Mr. and Mrs. Herbert Johnson, interview by author, tape recording, Columbia, Tenn., 14 June 1995; LT, testimony of Julius Blair, 27 September 1946.

3. W. D. Hastings, "The Rambler," *DH*, 25 February 1946, 2.

4. GJ, vols. 1, 2, testimonies of William M. Fleming and Gladys Stephenson, 8 April 1946.

5. GJ, vol. 1, testimony of William Fleming, 8 April 1946; GJ, vol. 3, testimony of J. J. Underwood, 10 April 1946; GJ, vol. 10, testimony of Ira Latimer, 27 May 1946; *DH*, 25 October 1945, 1; Margarete Campbell and J. J. Underwood Jr., interview by author, Columbia, Tenn., 28 December 1996. The *Herald* considered the election's closeness an upset. Returning servicemen candidates were generally electoral shoo-ins; "Election Results," *DH*, 26 October 1945, 2. Flo Fleming currently works as a bailiff in Columbia. He rejected several entreaties for an interview.

6. James Stephenson, interview by author, Detroit, Mich., 18 July 1995, 14 February 1996; Harry Raymond, "Negro Woman Victim Tells How It Started," *DWNY*, 12 March 1946, 1, 2; "Negro Vet's Own Story," *DWNY*, 15 March 1946, 1, 12.

7. GJ, vols. 1, 2, testimonies of Lavala LaPointe and Gladys Stephenson, 8 April 1946.

8. GJ, vols. 1, 2, testimonies of William Fleming, Lavala LaPointe, and Gladys and James Stephenson, 8 April 1946; Stephenson, interview, 18 July 1995. Events were to show that the Fleming family had somewhat traditional regional ideas about racial hierarchy and deferential behavior.

9. Harry Raymond, *DWNY*, 15 March 1946, 1.

10. GJ, vols. 1, 2, testimonies of Gladys and James Stephenson and William Fleming; Bernard Stofel, interview by author, tape recording, Columbia, Tenn., 8 August 1995; Stephenson, interview, 18 July 1994. In his testimony, Billy said James delivered the first blow. In repeated questioning by me, Stephenson insisted that Fleming hit him first in the back of the head. No relation existed between Stephenson's Drug Store and Gladys and James Stephenson.

11. GJ, vol. 1, testimony of Lavala LaPointe, 8 April 1946, 9 April 1946. GJ, vol. 2, testimonies of Gladys and James Stephenson and Walter Griffin, 8 April 1946, 9 April 1946.

12. GJ, vol. 7, testimony of Saul Blair, 16 April 1946. This was generally accepted throughout the black community and continually arose as an issue, particularly later at the Lawrenceburg trial. Albert Barnett had investigated the Cordie Cheek lynching and asserted in a letter to Governor McCord that Denton's car was used; "Dr. Albert E. Barnett Urges Columbia Probe," *NG,* 29 March 1946, 4. Blacks were leery of any politician from Denton's district, thinking it one of the more racist and dangerous in the county; GJ, vol. 7, testimony of Julius Blair, 16 April 1946.

13. Gladys told Harry Raymond of the *Daily Worker* that she fought back because she was afraid "they were going to kill my boy"; "Negro Woman Victim Tells How It Started," *DWNY,* 12 March 1946, 2.

14. GJ, vol. 2, testimonies of Gladys and James Stephenson and Hayes Denton, 9 April 1946; GJ, vol. 1, testimony of William Fleming, 8 April 1946; LT, testimony of Hayes Denton, 25 September 1946.

15. GJ, vol. 2, testimony of Gladys Stephenson, 9 April 1946; Stephenson, interview, 18 July 1995, 17 October 1996. Nepotism was rampant in the local law establishment. While Flo was waiting for his election to sheriff, he served as a driver's-license examiner for the Tennessee Highway Patrol (THP). Chief Griffin's son, Billy, served in the same capacity.

16. The seriousness of Billy Fleming's injury was amplified with each telling; his life supposedly hung in the balance.

17. The street allegedly got its name from the (now extinct) minks that *slid* into the creek between East Eighth and Ninth Streets; Johnson, interview, 14 June 1995. However, "Mink Slide" may be a designation (of uncertain but probably southern origin) for black urban areas. There was contemporaneously a street with the same moniker on the public square in Murfreesboro, Tennessee. South Maple (its official designation) also had black businesses on it. The name supposedly derived from mink trading which took place on a vacant lot in earlier times and a slick, sloping sidewalk which caused many falls. See Charles Byron Arnette, *From Mink Slide to Main Street* (Nashville: Williams Printing Co., 1992), 3.

18. LT, testimony of Hannah Peppers, 30 September 1946.

19. LT, testimony of Julius Blair, 27 September 1946; "J. W. Blair Longtime Local Barber Dies," *DH,* 17 January 1962, 1; *DH,* 15 February 1965; Maury County Trustee's Office Tax Books, microfilm, Roll 509, TSLA. In addition to his home in another district, Julius Blair owned seven lots, one with Saul, on East Eighth. Sheriff Underwood resented the Blair's frequent bailing of too many rough types.

20. GJ, vol. 6, testimony of James Morton, 15 April 1946.

21. LT, testimony of Julius Blair, 27 September 1946; LT, testimony of Hannah Peppers, 30 September 1946; GJ, vol. 6, testimony of James Morton, 15 April 1946; GJ, vol. 7, testimony of Saul Blair, 16 April 1946.

22. LT, testimony of Julius Blair, 27 September 1946; GJ, vol. 7, testimony of Saul Blair, 16 April 1946.

23. GJ, vol. 3, testimony of Eldridge Denham. J. Mike Blair described Eldridge Denham as "an old bachelor who loved everybody"; J. Mile Blair, telephone interview by author, Columbia, Tenn., 20 June 1995.

24. GJ, vol. 2, testimony of Walter Griffin, 9 April 1946; LT, testimony of Walter Griffin, 21 September 1946.

25. GJ, vol. 7, testimony of Beasley Thompson, 16 April 1946. Thompson was a *Nashville Tennessean* reporter. He had interviewed numerous blacks and Chief Griffin about this. John Fleming had been a deputy and was said to be "tough on Negroes." Flo Fleming's Uncle Gene had allegedly been killed by a black who was then killed before the opportunity of trial.

26. GJ, vols. 2, 3, testimony of J. J. Underwood, 9 April 1946, 10 April 1946; LT, testimony of J. J. Underwood, 21 September 1946.

27. GJ, vol. 1, testimony of W. E. Hopton, 8 April 1946; GJ, vol. 3, testimony of J. J. Underwood, 10 April 1946.

28. GJ, vol. 7, testimony of Saul Blair, 16 April 1946; LT, testimony of J. J. Underwood, 21 September 1946.

29. GJ, vol. 3, testimony of J. J. Underwood, 10 April 1946; GJ, vol. 2, testimony of James Stephenson, 9 April 1946.

30. GJ, vol. 1, testimony of W. E. Hopton, 8 April 1946; GJ, vol. 3, testimony of Eldridge Denham, 10 April 1946; GJ, vol. 6, testimony of James Morton, 15 April 1946; GJ, vol. 7, testimony of Saul Blair, 16 April 1946; *NT,* 27 February 1946, 1; *MD,* 27 February 1946, 1; Johnson, interview. I found a man who was a clerk working at Porter-Walker the day of the lynching rumor. He denied selling any rope or knowledge of anyone else who did. Russell Church, telephone interview by author, Columbia, Tenn., 26 June 1995.

31. GJ, vol. 2, testimony of Walter Griffin, 9 April 1946; LT, testimony of Walter Griffin, 20 September 1946; Stofel, interview, 8 July 1995.

32. GJ, vol. 2, testimony of James Stephenson, 9 April 1946; LT, testimony of Julius Blair, 27 September 1946.

33. GJ, vol. 11, testimonies of James Bellanfant, John Snipes, Andrew Snipes, George Watkins, and Audrey Claiborne, 29 May 1946.

34. *A Historical Sketch*, 36; Johnson, interview, 14 June 1995. Blacks bought their popcorn on the street, entered through an alley, and sat in the movie theater balcony. I never recall seeing a black person in the Princess before it burned in the late 1940s. Herbert Johnson said trouble started only when a full theater forced Columbia Military Academy boys into the balcony with the usual occupants. Saul Blair supposedly never went to the movies because he could not enter from the front; Ernest Smith, assistant attorney general of Tennessee, report to Gov. Jim Nance McCord, McCord Papers, Box 18, No. 7, TSLA.

35. LT, testimony of Lee and Early [*sic*] Shyers, 23 September 1946. The Royal Dukes Club was a social club for young black men. It had been organized before World War II. The meeting that evening of February 25 was to be hosted by the Shyers' future brother-in-law, Herbert Johnson.

36. GJ, vol. 6, testimony of John Finney, 15 April 1946.

37. GJ, vol. 4, testimonies of James Beard and Borgie Claude, 11 April 1946.

38. GJ, vol. 7, testimony of Calvin Lockridge, 16 April 1946; Raymond Lockridge, interview.

39. GJ, vol. 3, testimony of J. J. Underwood, 10 April 1946; LT, testimony of Meade Johnson, 28 September 1946; LT, testimony of Rufus Kennedy, 30 September 1946.

40. Though their offices were a block apart, subsequent lack of communication, much less coordination, between the county and city law officials seemed total.

41. GJ, vol. 2, testimony of J. J. Underwood, 9 April 1946; GJ, vol. 7, testimony of Roy Scribner, 16 April 1946; GJ, vol. 10, testimony of Ira Latimer, 27 May 1946; LT, testimony of J. J. Underwood, 21 September 1946.

42. LT, testimony of J. J. Underwood, 21 September 1946; GJ, vol. 7, testimonies of Saul Blair, Julius Blair, Calvin Lockridge, 16 April 1946; Raymond Lockridge, interview by author, tape recording, Columbia, Tenn., 8 July 1995.

43. LT, testimony of J. J. Underwood, 21 September 1946; GJ, vol. 7, testimonies of Saul Blair, Julius Blair, Calvin Lockridge, 16 April 1946; Raymond Lockridge, telephone interview by author, 20 April 1996.

44. LT, testimonies of Bernard Stofel and Sam Richardson, 20 September 1946; Stofel, interview, 8 July 1995.

45. GJ, vol. 2, testimony of J. J. Underwood, 9 April 1946; GJ, vol. 7, testimonies of Saul Blair and James Morton, 16 April 1946; LT, testimony of J. C. Goad, 1 October 1946.

46. GJ, vol. 2, testimony of J. J. Underwood, 9 April 1946; LT, testimony of J. J. Underwood, 21 September 1946.

47. GJ, vol. 2, testimony of James Stephenson, 9 April 1946; GJ, vol. 7, testimony of Saul Blair, 16 April 1946; LT, testimony of Julius Blair, 27 September 1946.

48. While waiting in the dark in front of Haynes Haven, James Stephenson saw several THP cars race with sirens blaring south toward Columbia. He was unaware of events in Columbia that had prompted their mobilization; Stephenson, interview, 17 October 1996.

49. GJ, vol. 2, testimony of James Stephenson, 9 April 1946; GJ, vol. 8, testimony of James Bellanfant, 17 April 1946; LT, testimony of Saul Blair, 27 September 1946; LT, testimonies of Thomas Neely and George Nicholson, 30 September 1946.

50. LT, testimony of Julius Blair, 27 September 1946; LT, testimony of J. J. Underwood Jr., 2 October 1946.

51. LT, testimonies of S. E. Jones, Johnnie Fulton, G. A. Newburn, and Andrew Armstrong, 28 September 1946; LT, testimony of Joseph Blade and Mary Morton, 30 September 1946; GJ, vol. 6, testimony of James Morton, 15 April 1946.

52. Johnson, interview, 14 June 1995; Ed Kimes, interview by author, tape recording, Columbia, Tenn., 12 July 1995; Milton Murray, interview by author, tape recording, Columbia, Tenn., 28 June 1995.

53. Ibid. These assertions are repeatedly made by blacks who were there. They are otherwise difficult to substantiate. There certainly was no organized invasion of Mink Slide.

54. See note 53 above.

55. LT, testimonies of Johnnie Fulton and S. E. Jones, 28 September 1946; GJ, vol. 6, testimony of James Morton, 15 April 1946. Noles was another lawman

whom the blacks feared. James Beasley testified he was "supposed to go for bad"; LT, 24 September 1946.

56. GJ, vol. 11, testimony of John Lockridge, 29 May 1946.

57. LT, testimony of Alldie Sharpgon, 21 September 1946.

58. GJ, vol. 2, testimony of Walter Griffin, 9 April 1946; LT, testimonies of Bernard Stofel, Sam Richardson, and J. Walter Griffin, 20 September 1946; LT, testimony of T. F. Collins, 25 September 1946.

Chapter Three

1. GJ, vol. 2, testimony of Walter Griffin, 9 April 1946; LT, testimony of Will Wilsford, 19 September 1946; LT, testimonies of Bernard Stofel, Will Wilsford Walter Griffin, and Sam Richardson, 20 September 1946; Stofel, interview, 8 July 1995.

2. Wilsford's son, Billy Wilsford, said his father was hit "only" with bird shot, not buckshot, and that they periodically picked pieces out of his face for years; Billy Wilsford, telephone interview with author, Columbia, Tenn., 12 June 1995.

3. GJ, vol. 3, testimonies of J. J. Underwood and Eldridge Denham, 10 April 1946; W. D. Hastings, "The Rambler," DH, 28 August 1952, 2.

4. Fred W. Schott Jr, "Servants . . . Not Lords," A History of the Tennessee Highway Patrol (Paducah, Ky.: Taylor Publishing Co., 1981), 6. Schott wrote this history to commemorate the fiftieth anniversary of the patrol. Both he and I were amazed at the paucity of records kept by the patrol during its first twenty-five years. There essentially are none—neither orders, notes, budgets, mission statements or summaries. Schott could not prove it but wondered if all records were destroyed whenever administrations changed. This lack of documentation obviously hampers research on the patrol. Fred W. Schott Jr., telephone interview by author, Springfield, Tenn., 11 June 1996.

5. Schott, THP, 8, 11, 13.

6. Joe Hatcher, "Politics," NT, 2 August 1944, 1, 2; "'Gestapo' Tactics by State Police Used at Polls Here," NT, 4 August 1944, 1, 6; Schott, interview, 15 July 1996; James D. Squires, The Secrets of the Hopewell Box, (New York: Times Books, 1996), 57, 61.

7. LT, testimony of Lynn Bomar, 26 September 1946.

8. Ibid., 27, 29, 44, 45; Fred Russell, "Lynn Bomar," NB, 12 June 1964, 14; John Bibb, "Lynn Was Great Player in a Great Vandy Era," NT, 12 June 1964, 32.

9. Dickinson papers; "State Official Dickinson Dies," NB, 15 March 1963, 1, 6. Dickinson was an expert on Arabian horses, allegedly one of the group that established Tennessee Walking Horses as a distinctive breed.

10. GJ, vol. 3, testimony of Lynn Bomar, 10 April 1946.

11. Col. J. W. Barker, Report of Armory Incident, 15 April 1946, in Dickinson papers; Myron Peck, telephone interview by author, tape recording, Columbia, Tenn., 12 July 1995.

12. Report on Tour of Active Duty, 2nd Brigade Took Force to the Adjutant General of Tennessee, Dickinson papers; GJ, vol. 5, testimony of Jacob McGavock Dickinson, 12 April 1946.

13. GJ, vol. 4, testimony of Lynn Bomar, 11 April 1946; GJ, vol. 5, testimony of Jacob McGavock Dickinson, 12 April 1946; Report of Active Duty, Dickinson papers.

14. GJ, vol. 4, testimonies of James Beard and Borgie Claude, 11 April 1946; GJ, vol. 7, testimony of Beasley Thompson, 16 April 1946.

15. Raymond Lockridge, interview, 14 December 1996; GJ, vol. 7, testimony of Calvin Lockridge, 16 April 1946; GJ, vol. 11 testimony of Horace Gordon, 17 April 1946; GJ, vol. 9, testimonies of Charlie Edwards, Luther Edwards, Raymond Lockridge, Charlie Smith, Elmer Dooley, and Hollis Reynolds, 29 May 1946. In describing their actions before the grand jury, some of these men were vague. It is hard to tell whether they were protecting themselves or were simply unaware.

16. Raymond Lockridge, interview, 8 July 1995; Kimes, interview, 12 July 1995. Blacks on Mink Slide had been notified by callers from Spring Hill who had seen both patrol and guard vehicles racing through their town.

17. Report of Active Duty, Dickinson papers. Bomar thought the conference took place before midnight. He was imprecise about details such as times in all his testimonies. GJ, vol. 4, testimony of Lynn Bomar, 11 April 1946.

18. GJ, vols. 3, 4, testimony of Lynn Bomar, 10 April 1946, 11 April 1946; GJ, vol. 6, testimony of James Morton, 15 April 1946; GJ, vol. 7, testimonies of Saul Blair, John Thompson, Beasley Thompson, and George Nicholson, 16 April 1946; LT, testimonies of Lynn Bomar and J. A. Kingcaid, 26 September 1946; LT, testimonies of Mattie Smith and Marcia Mayes, 28 September 1946; LT, testimony of Mary Morton, 30 September 1946.

19. See note 18 above.

Chapter Four

1. Headquarters were established in the City Hall. Though Chief Griffin had given over control of Columbia's streets to the state, he still imposed his standards of abstemiousness on the intruders by insisting the state guard remove the cases of beer they had brought. Stofel, interview, 13 November 1996.

2. GJ, vol. 5, testimony of Jacob McGavock Dickinson, 12 April 1946; LT, testimony of J. J. Underwood, 21 September 1946; Dickinson Papers.

3. GJ, vols. 3, 4, testimonies of J. J. Underwood and Lynn Bomar; 9 April 1946, 10 April 1946; GJ, vol. 5, testimony of Jacob McGavock Dickinson, 12 April 1946; GJ, vol. 6, testimonies of W. Edward Clark and Henry Schofield, 15 April 1946; GJ, vol. 7, testimonies of John Thompson and John Malone, 16 April 1946; GJ, vol. 8, testimony of J. J. Jackson, 17 April 1946; GJ, vol. 11, testimonies of Charlie Edwards, Luther Edwards, Charlie Smith, Elmer Dooley, John Porter, John Blackwell, Hollis Reynolds, Leonard Evans, and Henry Edwards, 29 May 1946; LT, testimony of J. J. Underwood, 21 September 1946; LT, testimony of Lee Shyers, 23 September 1946; LT, testimony of Lynn Bomar, 26 September 1946.

4. See note 3 above.

5. As he lost control of proceedings, Underwood must have felt ambivalence and sadness. His allegiance to all Maury Countians was shown by a story told by Irena (Shyers) Johnson. She and her mother walked to Columbia early on February 26 to retrieve the family auto left by her now incarcerated brothers. When Underwood saw them, he hugged Irena, said he was glad they came, and helped them get the car off East Eighth; Irena Johnson, interview by author, Columbia, Tenn., 12 October 1996.

6. "How Hitler-Like Police Looted Columbia Businesses," *WAA*, 16 March 1946, 16; GJ, vol. 6, testimony of James Morton, 15 April 1946; GJ, vol. 7, testimony of Saul Blair, 16 April 1946; Guy B. Johnson, "What Happened at Columbia," *New South* 1 (May 1996): 1–8. The "KKK casket" picture was first run in the March 17, 1946, issue of the *Daily Worker of New York*. It was later used by the *Washington Post* on May 19. A photographer named Robert Martin, hired by Harry Raymond, allegedly took the picture. No regional photographer or reporter saw the besmirched casket, and the guilty vandal has never been identified. Some have suggested the blacks did it to gain sympathy. If the picture is a fraud, it is more likely that someone from a publication perpetrated it.

7. Ed Clark quoted the patrolman, "God damn you, I ought to blow your God damn black brains out. I hope you die"; GJ, vol. 6, testimony of Ed Clark, 29 May 1946.

8. *DH*, 26 February 1946, 1; *NB*, 26 February 1946, 1; *NT*, 26 February 1946, 27 February 1946, 1; GJ, vol. 7, testimony of John Thompson, 16 April 1946.

9. GJ, vol. 4, testimony of Lynn Bomar, 11 April 1946; GJ, vol. 6, testimony of Edward Clark and John Schofield, 15 April 1946; GJ, vol. 11, testimonies of Charlie Edwards, Luther Edwards, Leonard Evans, and Henry Edwards, 29 May 1946.

10. GJ, vol. 8, testimony of J. J. Jackson, 17 April 1946. The woman never showed up with the allegedly proffered weapons. Jackson was identified by Ed Clark and Henry Schofield as the officer who originally broke out Morton's parlor window; GJ, vol. 6, testimonies of Ed Clark and Henry Schofield, 15 April 1946. Jackson and the *Tennessean* were at political odds. He saw Clark and Schofield in cahoots with that paper.

11. GJ, vol. 3, testimony of Lynn Bomar, 11 April 1946; GJ, vol. 5, testimony of Jacob McGavock Dickinson, 12 April 1946; GJ, vol. 9, testimony of Roy Beeler, 18 April 1946; GJ, vol. 10, testimonies of H. H. Wall and Thomas Potter, 28 May 1996; Report to Adjutant General, Dickinson papers; *DH*, 27 February 1946, 4; Kimes, interview, 12 July 1995; Murray, interview, 28 June 1995.

12. See note 11 above. Milton Murray claimed he retained a Thompson submachine gun and a "burp" gun.

13. GJ, vol. 3, testimony of J. J. Underwood, 9 April 1946, 10 April 1946; GJ, vol. 6, testimony of Edward Clark, 15 April 1946; GJ, vol. 7, testimony of Julius Blair, 20 April 1946; GJ, vol. 9, testimony of John Dudley, 9 April 1946; GJ, vol. 11, testimonies of James Martin, Alexander Bullock, Hiawatha Leftrick, and Joe Calloway, 29 May 1946; LT, testimony of Alexander Bullock, 24 September 1946; LT, testimony of Julius Blair, 27 September 1946.

14. See note 13 above. Not all Tennesseans jumped on the bandwagon to praise the THP. A guard company commander told of patrolmen stealing cigarettes, destroying windows, and freeing a white who had shot at a black man and was arrested by guardsmen; W. W. Hogan, letter to Jacob McGavock Dickinson, 21 April 1946, Dickinson papers.

15. GJ, vol. 5, testimony of Jacob McGavock Dickinson, 12 April 1946; "Order Restored in Columbia," *NB*, 26 February 1946, 2; "Order Restored after Race Riot," *MD*, 27 February 1946, 1; *DH*, 28 February 1946, 1.

16. A jail that was "meant to hold 20 now held 120"; J. J. Underwood Jr., interview by author, Columbia, Tenn., 28 December 1996.

17. Ibid.; GJ, vol. 7, testimonies of Saul Blair and Calvin Lockridge, 16 April 1946; GJ, vol. 11, testimonies of Raymond Lockridge, Charlie Smith, and Elmer Dooley, 29 May 1946.

18. This will be further addressed in a later section.

19. GJ, vols. 2, 3, testimony of J. J. Underwood, 9 April 1946, 10 April 1946; GJ, vol. 7, testimony of Julius Blair, 20 April 1946; GJ, vol. 9, testimony of Paul Bumpus, 18 April 1946.

20. GJ, vols. 2, 3, testimony of J. J. Underwood, 9 April 1946, 10 April 1946; GJ, vol. 7, testimony of Calvin Lockridge, 16 April 1946; GJ, vol. 8, testimony of Horace Gordon, 17 April 1946; Raymond Lockridge, interview, 8 July 1995.

21. Napoleon Stewart said Fleming grabbed his hat, threw it on the floor, looked to see if other officers were watching him, and then hauled off and hit him. Stewart seems not to have had a death wish, and this explanation seems plausible. GJ, vol. 9, testimony of Napoleon Stewart, 18 April 1946.

22. GJ, vol. 3, testimony of J. J. Underwood, 10 April 1946; GJ, vol. 4, testimony of Lynn Bomar, 11 April 1946; GJ, vol. 8, testimonies of John Morgan and J. J. Jackson, 17 April 1946; GJ, vol. 9, testimony of Napoleon Stewart, 18 April 1946; Ernest Smith, report; John E. Morgan, telephone interview by author, Nashville, Tenn., 25 July 1995; "Columbia 'Riot' Case Ideal, Southern Conference Told," *WAA*, 30 March 1946, 2; James Underwood Jr., interview by author, Columbia, Tenn., 28 December 1996. The shoot-out was a near thing for the Underwood family. Some of the shots from the patrolmen went through a wall into a bed to which Underwood Jr.'s wife had been confined for a tenuous pregnancy. She had been moved from there after the riot. Mrs. Underwood Sr. was conversing in the hallway with Billy Griffin, which took her out of a line of fire into the living quarters.

23. GJ, vol. 9, testimony of Paul Bumpus, 18 April 1946; Raymond Lockridge, interview, 8 July 1995.

24. Ernest Smith, report; *DH*, 28 February 1946, 1; *DH*, 1 March 1946, 1; *DH*, 4 March 1946, 1, 2; *DH*, 7 March 1946, 1.

25. *DH*, 28 February 1946, 1; *DH*, 5 March 1946, 1.

Chapter Five

1. Walter Francis White, *A Man Called White* (New York: Arno Press, 1969), 309–10. Much of White's account of the Columbia riot is inaccurate. I use his version of NAACP organizational actions, which I presume are correct. Jack Lusk, telephone interview by author, Chattanooga, Tenn., 22 January 1996; Sam Plummer, telephone interview by author, Chattanooga, Tenn., 22 January 1996; Virginia Weaver, interview by author, Chattanooga, Tenn., 24 January 1996. Lusk and Plummer are Chattanooga lawyers. Plummer briefly practiced with Weaver. Virginia Weaver is one of several Weaver widows. She was candid, helpful, polite, and generous.

2. GJ, vol. 8, testimony of Maurice Weaver, 17 April 1946; *DH*, 11 November 1946, 6. District Attorney Bumpus had recommended preventing Weaver access to the prisoners because he felt the lawyer represented the NAACP and not them; GJ, vol. 9, testimony of Paul Bumpus, 18 April 1946.

3. See note 2 above.

4. See note 2 above.

5. See note 2 above. *DH,* "City Nears Normal As Restrictions End," 4 March 46, 1; "13 Negroes Freed on Local Bonds. . . ," *DH,* 7 March 1946, 1; "Habeas Corpus Hearing Slated in Circuit Court for 2 Negroes," *DH,* 12 March 46, 1; "Bond Is Quickly Made after Judge Denies Writ of Habeas Corpus," *DH,* 13 March 46, 1; Harry Raymond, "Tenn. Negroes Bail Out 12 Heroes," *DWNY,* 9 March 1946, 4; GJ, Maurice Weaver, memorandum to grand jury.

6. Minutes of NAACP Board of Directors, New York, N.Y., 8 April 1946; "What the Branches Are Doing," the *Crisis* 53 (June 1946): 184; Ibid., (October 1946): 312.

7. Clark H. Foreman, *The Truth about Columbia Tennessee Cases,* Southern Conference for Human Welfare, Nashville, Tenn., 1946; Johnson, "What Happened at Columbia" *New South* 1 (May 46): 1–8; Harry Raymond, "NAACP Demands Release of 34 Facing Tennessee 'Lynch Justice,'" *DWNY,* 3 March 46, 2. *The Truth* was not nearly as inaccurate or inflammatory as some others; it was just the earliest and most widely disseminated. For a thorough description of roles played by the SCHW and SRC during the peri-war civil rights struggle, consult John Egerton, *Speak Now Against the Day* (New York: Alfred A. Knopf, 1994).

8. "Cowards in Columbia," *LL,* 23 March 1946, 1; "The Tennessee 'Uprising,'" *LL,* 27 April 1946, 1; "America's Year of Decision," *Ebony,* (May 1946): 5–9.

9. "Pogrom in Tennessee," the *New Republic,* 114 (1 April 1946): 429.

10. Virginia Weaver said Raymond, of all visiting correspondents, got along best with the natives, who had no idea what paper or ideology he represented; Virginia Weaver, interview, 24 January 1996.

11. Robert Minor, "There Was to Be a Lynching," *DWNY,* 2 March 46, 2; Harry Raymond, "Columbia Arrests Continue As Negroes Dig Out of Rubble," *DWNY,* 11 March 1946, 3; Harry Raymond, "White Union Men Toured Columbia, Held Back Civilian Mob," *DWNY,* 13 March 47, 5; Robert Minor, *Lynching and Frame-up in Tennessee* (New York: New Century Publishers, 1946).

12. "Group Protests Columbia Action," *NT,* 14 March 46, 1, 2; "Party Votes Nation Drive to Defend Tennessee Victims," *DWNY,* 14 March 46, 12; "Chattanooga Group of Ministers Gets 'Off on Columbia,'" *NG,* 22 March 46, 1; "Cleric, Victim of Columbia Riot, to Address NNC Rally," *WAA,* 6 April 1946, 15; "Negroes to Go on Tour to Raise Funds to Finance Legal Defense," *DH,* 16 April 1946, 1; Minutes, Chicago Civil Liberties Committee, 5 March 1946, Chicago Historical Society Archives and Manuscripts Department; ibid., Report of Chicago Delegation to March 13, Washington, D.C., Emergency National Conference on Columbia, Tenn., Lynch Terror; "Report on the Columbia Case," the *Crisis,* (June 1946): 180; "Annual Conference," the *Crisis* (August 1946): 249; Raymond Lockridge, interview, 8 July 1995; Stephenson, interview, 17 October 1996. Raymond Lockridge enjoyed his Minnesota visit so much that he later worked there many years. He was also a lifelong NAACP activist.

13. Among the several minor inaccuracies in this propagandistic screed were the stories that Billy Fleming hit Gladys instead of James Stephenson and that Cordie Cheek instead of Henry Choate was hanged from the courthouse. Among the false and inflammatory depictions were discriptions of both the guard and patrol invading Mink Slide with massive arsenal, including machine guns, and the application of the same methods to urban Negro homes as they searched for

weapons on February 26. Harrington correlated the THP and state guard with the Klan and Nazis. Oliver Harrington, "Terror in Tennessee," The National Committee for Justice in Columbia, Tenn., 1946.

14. Various papers, Franklin D. Roosevelt Library, Hyde Park, N.Y.; Harold W. Odum, "The First Lady's Heritage to the Folk Story" in *Race and Rumors of Race* (Chapel Hill: University of North Carolina Press, 1943), 81–89.

15. White, *A Man Called White*, 312–13.

16. Harry Raymond, "NAACP Demands Release of 34 Facing Tennessee 'Lynch Justice,'" *DWNY,* 4 March 1946, 2; "FBI Making Careful Probe at Columbia," *NG,* 15 March 1946, 2; *NG,* 22 March 1946, 4.

17. *NT,* 5 March 1947, 4; "To the Bottom," *NT,* 17 March 1946, 28A; *NG,* 8 March 46, 1; *NG,* 15 March 46, 1, 2; "'Tennessean' Breaks with South's Tradition on Federal Authority" *NG,* 22 March 1946, 1.

18. Harry Raymond, "Lynch Probe on, Clark States," *DWNY,* 7 March 46; *DH,* 29 March 46, 1; "U.S. Jury Probe Ordered in Tenn.," *WAA,* 30 March 1946, 1; *NT,* 30 March 1946, 2; "Federal Grand Jury Begins Probe," *NG,* 12 April 1946, 1.

19. Notes from the state minutes, Maury County Circuit Court, 22 March 1946.

20. "Columbia 'Riot' Case Ideal, Southern Conference Told," *WAA,* 30 March 1946, 1, 2.

21. *DH,* 29 March 1946, 1; "'New Day' Dawns For Columbians," *NG,* 6 June 1946, 1, 2; "Maury Negroes Summoned for Jury Duty, Three Testify," *NT,* 18 June 1946, 1, 4; "Maury Case Indictments Upheld; Ask Venue Change," *NB,* 19 June 1946, 1, 2.

22. "Thinking" Columbians actually doubted guilt could be proved against the multiple defendants and were irritated at the accusation that a fair trial could not be had in their town; Harold Hinton, *DH,* 8 July 1946, 1, 3.

23. Virginia Weaver, interviews, 24 January 1996, 1 April 1997. Mrs. Weaver is fairly certain she saw the sign. Roy Wilkins likely did not, but he also described it in his autobiography: Roy Wilkins with Tom Mathews, *Standing Fast: The Autobiography of Roy Wilkins* (New York: The Viking Press, 1982), 218.

24. "State Attacks Misnomer Plea in Maury Case," *NB,* 17 June 1946, 1, 2; Minutes, Maury County Circuit Court, 23 July 1946; "Big City More Likely to Give Fair Trial, NAACP Attorneys Declare," *DH,* 11 July 1946, 1, 6; "NAACP Lawyers Fight against 'Hurry' Trials," *NG,* 31 May 1946, 1; "Want Trials Moved to Nashville," *NG,* 28 June 1946, 1; "Columbia Is Worried over Its Mass Trials," *NG,* 12 July 1946, 1; *MD,* 4 August 1946, 1; *U.S. Census: 1940,* vol. 2; John Wagster advised me on legal terms.

Chapter Six

1. Young Tommy Osborn was a rising star on the Tennessee legal/political scene after World War II. He was a major force behind the precedent *Baker v. Carr* reapportionment suit in 1962. His star fell from the skies though when he was convicted of jury tampering in 1964. This charge stemmed from his defense of Jimmy Hoffa in a 1962 Nashville trial. After serving time in federal prison, Osborn committed suicide in 1970. See Squires, *The Secrets of the Hopewell Box,* 205–35, 279–80.

2. Correspondence in U.S. Department of Justice file No.144–71–4; Charles R. Lawrence Jr., "Race Riots in the United States, 1942–1946," in *Negro Year Book: A Review of Events Affecting Negro Life, 1941–1946,* 10th ed., edited by Jessie Parkhurst Guzman (Tuskegee: Tuskegee Institute, 1947), 251.

3. "U.S. Grand Jury Hears Five Witnesses in Maury Probe," *NT,* 10 April 1946, 2; GJ, vols. 1, 10, 14, testimony of W. E. Hopton, 8 April 1946, 27 May 1946, 14 June 1946. GJ, 13 June 1946. This material is stored in Federal Archives Building in Atlanta. Three of fourteen volumes (vols. 11, 12, and 13) are missing.

4. GJ, vol. 1, testimony of Lavala LaPointe and William Fleming, 8 April 1946; GJ, vol. 2, testimonies of Gladys and James Stephens, 9 April 1946. Columbia blacks did not know much about the NAACP and certainly did not know its lead counsel. James's malapropism of Marshall's name was inadvertently accurate. "Thoroughgood" was his Christian name until, as a teenager, he persuaded his mother to change it.

5. GJ, vol. 2, testimony of Walter Griffin, 9 April 1946; GJ, vols. 2, 3, testimony of J. J. Underwood, 9 April 1946, 10 April 1946. In a very paternal way, Underwood said race relations in Maury County were excellent.

6. GJ, vols. 3, 4, testimony of Lynn Bomar, 10 April 1946, 11 April 1946. As noted before, the dearth of patrol documents on this action is peculiar. It was at least unprofessional, at most, devious.

7. GJ, vol. 4, testimony of Ernest Smith, 11 April 1946.

8. GJ, vol. 4, testimony of Ernest Smith, 11 April 1946; GJ, vol. 9, testimony of Roy Beeler, 18 April 1946.

9. GJ, vol. 9, testimony of Paul Bumpus, 18 April 1946.

10. GJ, vol. 5, testimony of Jacob McGavock Dickinson, 12 April 1946. General Dickinson was much more outspoken about the potential danger of independent action such as Bomar's in a "confidential," "urgent" report to the adjutant general on March 8. He strongly urged the governor to issue a directive in the event of future disturbances that, until law and order was restored, all troops be placed under one authority, whether military officer, safety commissioner, or local law officer. Nothing about this critical uncertainty of command and its obvious consequences in Columbia ever got into the press. See "Report on Tour of Active Duty," Dickinson papers, TSLA.

11. GJ, vol. 10, testimonies of T. V. Woodring, Aubrey Ottarson Jr., Victor Wilson, Thomas J. Potter, H. H. Hall, and Arthur R. Green, 27 May 1946.

12. GJ, vol. 6, testimonies of J. A. Kingcaid, M. Edward Clark, and Henry J. Schofield, 15 April 1946; GJ, vol. 7, testimonies of John Thompson, Beasley Thompson, and John Malone, 16 April 1946; GJ, vol. 8, testimonies of John Malone and John Morgan, 17 April 1946; GJ, vol. 9, testimony of Charles Lambert, 18 April 1946; "Jury Summons Local Newsmen," *NT,* 11 April 1946, 1, 2.

13. GJ, vol. 4, testimonies of James Beard and Borgie Claude, 11 April 1946; GJ, vol. 7, testimony of Roy Scribner, 16 April 1946.

14. GJ, vol. 7, testimonies of Saul Blair, Julius Blair, and Calvin Lockridge, 16 April 1946.

15. GJ, vol. 8, testimony of James Bellanfant, 17 April 1946; GJ, vol. 11, testimonies of Charlie Edwards, Luther Edwards, Raymond Lockridge, J. C. Smith, John Lockridge, James Bellanfant, John Snipes, Andrew Snipes, George Watkins, Audrey Claiborne, James Martin, John Porter, John Blackwell, Joe Daniel Calloway, Hollis Reynolds, Leonard Evans, Henry Edwards, Hasting Edwards, and Robert Edwards, 27 May 1946.

16. GJ, vols. 8, 9, testimony of Maurice Weaver, 17 April 1946, 18 April 1946.

17. GJ, vol. 6, testimony of A. O. Denning (assistant U.S. district attorney), 15 April 1946; Theron Caudle, memo to Attorney General Tom Clark, DJ file, 144–71–1, 11 June 1946. Newspapers reported on Judge Davies' orienting the jury's attention to the inflammatory literature in the middle of proceedings. See NG, 3 May 1946, 1, 4. I could find no transcript of that instruction.

18. GJ, vol. 10, testimony of Ira Latimer, 27 May 1946. Frequently mentioned in newspaper and court records, the Committee of 100 was apparently a group of liberal activists (e.g., Norman Thomas, Harry Emerson Fosdick) who, after the riot, sought justice and retribution for Columbia blacks. Headed by Columbia University professor Carl Van Doren, its writings on the situation were especially offensive in Middle Tennessee. Though it probably had similar agendas and constituencies as the National Committee for Justice in Columbia, Tennessee, the committee was not as influential. I have been unable to find any residual records of the organization. See "Many and Varied Race Riot Stories Are Told," DH, 30 April 1946, 1, 3; "Heresay . . .," NB, 18 June 1946, 6.

19. DJ file, 144–71–4, April 1946. This is a long, rough copy of a memo to the department. The precise date and author are uncertain.

20. Theron Caudle, letter to Horace Frierson, DJ file, 144–71–4, 16 April 1946 (it is uncertain this letter was mailed); Theron Caudle, memo to U.S. attorney general, DJ file, 144–71–4, 6 May 1946.

21. See note 20 above. Turner Smith, memorandum to John Kelley Jr., DJ file, 144–71–4, 17 May 1946.

22. Theron Caudle, memo to the attorney general, DJ file, 144–71–4, 11 June 1946.

23. GJ, jury summary; "Grand Jury Puts Blame Where It Belongs," NB, 15 June 1946, 4.

24. See note 23 above.

25. See note 23 above.

26. "U.S. Jury Praises Officers in Race Riot," DH, 14 June 1946, 1, 4; "The Truth about the Columbia Cases—The Grand Jury Report," DH, 14 June 1946, 3; "South Can Handle Its Own Affairs," NB, 17 June 46, 4; "Grand Jury Puts Blame Where It Belongs," NB, 15 June 46, 4; "No Civil Rights in Maury Abused, U.S. Jury Reports," NT, 15 June 46, 1, 2. Fellow travelers were those sympathetic to communism.

27. "Unpopular Report Is Made by Federal Jury," NG, 21 June 1946, 1, 4; "Too Late, Your Honor," NG, 21 June 1946, 4. In urging Negroes to join the Communist party, Robert Minor had stressed Davies' Klan membership and asked, "Isn't the political party denounced by such a man as Davies the kind of party you ought to belong to?" Robert Minor, Lynching and Frame-up in Tennessee, 87, 95. Davies

had voluntarily told the Senate Judiciary Committee the story of his joining the Klan in his hometown of Arcadia, Louisiana, when he was in college. A couple of years later when he was a law student at Vanderbilt, he had attended one meeting in Nashville. He never paid any dues and had no further association with the Klan. This revelation briefly stalled his Senate confirmation as federal judge for the Middle Tennessee District. See *NT*, "Davies Facing Further Delay on Bench Post," 8 July 39, 1, 2; *NT*, Bascom N. Timmons, "Confirmation Given Davies Is Recalled from White House," 13 July 39, 1, 2; *NT* "Davies Expected to Get U.S. Bench Commission This Week," 14 July 39, 2 *NB*, Jesse S. Cottrell, "Davies Tells of Joining Klan; OK Indicated," 6 July 39, 1, 2; *NB*, "Davies Commissioned by President." 13 July 39, 1.

28. Tom C. Clark, Washington, D.C., to Mrs. Eleanor Roosevelt, Hyde Park, N.Y., 8 October 1946, Holdings at the Franklin D. Roosevelt Library; ibid., Thurgood Marshall, New York, N.Y., to Eleanor Roosevelt, 28 October 1946; ibid., Tom Clark to Eleanor Roosevelt, 26 November 1946; ibid., Thurgood Marshall to Tom Clark, 27 December 1946.

29. Theron Caudle, memo to Timothy McInery, DJ file, 144–71–4, 23 April 1946.

30. Theron Caudle, letter to Albert Barnett, DJ file, 144–71–4, 24 June 1946; Tom Clark, letter to Eleanor Roosevelt, DJ file, 144–71–4, 9 July 1946; Theron Caudle, letter to Charles Mackey, DJ file, 144–71–4, 25 July 1946; Tom Clark, letter to Eleanor Roosevelt, DJ file, 144–71–4, 8 October 1946.

31. "We Expect Nothing," *NG*, 2 August 1946, 4.

Chapter Seven

1 This was a designation repeatedly used by the *Daily Worker of New York*.

2. *DH*, "Lawrence Mayor Hits Bumpus, Trial Rule," 9 July 1946, 1, 4.

3. R. W., "Tennessee Trial," the *Crisis* (November 1946): 329; "Attempt to Quash Panel of Jurymen," *LDU*, 16 August 1946, 1; ibid., "Let's Make the Best of It," 6; *DH*, "Race Trial Meet Ends in Harmony with No Results Given Reporters," 9 July 1946, 1, 6; ibid., "Bumpus States Stand on Site for Big Trial," 1, 2.

4. Virginia Weaver, interviews, 24 January 1996, 1 April 1997. Mrs. Weaver observed that blacks could buy sandwiches in back of the local bus station. Thurgood Marshall was not present at the Lawrenceburg trial because of pneumonia, which kept him mostly bedridden in New York. He made several trips to Tennessee and continually advised on the case; *LDU*, "Negro Trial Definitely Is Set Here," 9 August 1946, 1.

5. "Bumpus Pledges to Spring Big Surprise," *NG*, 30 August 1946, 1.

6. Danny Bingham, "Negro Lawyer Flays State on Jury System," *NB*, 14 August 1946, 1, 8; Harry Raymond, "Charge Tennessee Jury Fraud," *DWNY*, 15 August 1946, 12; *DWNY*, 17 August 1946, 12; *DWNY*, 20 August 1946; "Tradition Abandoned at Lawrenceburg Trials," *NG*, 16 August 1946, 1; *LDU*, 16 August 1946, 1.

7. *DWNY*, 16 August 1946, 12; *DWNY*, 17 August 1946, 12; *DWNY*, 23 August 1946, 12; *DWNY*, 19 September 1946, 12; *NG*, 23 August 1946, 1; *NG*, 18 October 1946, 1, 4; *MD*, 25 August 1946, 1; *LDU*, 23 August 1946, 1; *LDU*, 6 September

1946, 1; *LDU,* 13 September 1946, 1; *LDU,* 20 September 1946, 1; *DH,* 17 August 1946, 1; *DH,* 28 August 1946, 1; *DH,* 2 September 1946, 1; "Mink Slide: The Aftermath," *Time* (14 October 1946): 29; Marjorie Smith, "Racial Confrontation in Columbia, Tennessee: 1946," (Master's thesis, Atlanta University, 1974), 29, 47; James Weatherford, telephone interview by author, Lawrenceburg, Tenn., 19 March 1996. Judge Weatherford served with Judge Ingram on the circuit bench.

8. See note 7 above.

9. See note 7 above.

10. *DH,* 29 August 1946, 1; *DH,* 30 August 1946, 1; *DH,* 15 September 1946, 1; *DWNY,* 28 August 1946, 12; *DWNY,* 31 August 1946, 12; *DWNY,* 3 September 1946, 12; *DWNY,* 12 September 1946, 3; *DWNY,* 14 September 1946, 12; *LDU,* 30 August 1946, 2.

11. *LDU,* 20 September 1946, 1; *LDU,* 27 September 1946, 1; *DH,* 2 September 1946, 1; *NG,* 13 September 1946, 1, 4; *NG,* 20 September 1946, 1, 4; Weaver, interview, 24 January 1946. The jurors were W. E. Staggs, Wash King, Segal Davis, John Pigg, J. R. Bradley, A. J. Jordan, Herbert Patterson, J. J. Cleveland, Arthur Pollack, Frank Kersteins, and Howard Vandiford.

12. Tommy Baxter died before the trial. Thus, there were only twenty-five defendants.

13. LT, testimony of Charley McKissick, 19 September 1946.

14. LT, testimony of Will Wilsford, 19 September 1946, 20 September 1946; LT, testimonies of Bernard Stofel, Sam Richardson, and Walter Griffin, 20 September 1946; *NB,* 20 September 1946, 1, 6. In previous text, I have told in detail the sequence of events and, therefore, here present them only in general terms.

15. LT, testimonies of J. J. Underwood and Alldie Sharpgon, 21 September 1946.

16. LT, testimonies of Leonard Evans, Lee Shyers, Early [*sic*] Shyers, William Pillow, and James Alderson, 23 September 1946.

17. LT, testimonies of Mamie Fisher and Alexander Bullock, 24 September 1946.

18. *DWNY,* 25 September 1946, 3; *LDU,* 27 September 1946, 1. At another moment in the trial, Bumpus allegedly threatened to wrap a chair around Ransom's head; *Time* (14 October 1946): 29.

19. LT, testimonies of George Watkins, Audrey Claiborn, James Beasley, and Horace Snipes, 24 September 1946.

20. LT, testimony of J. J. Underwood, 25 September 1946.

21. Ibid., testimonies of C. H. Denton, G. I. Reeves, T. F. Collins.

22. LT, testimony of Lynn Bomar, 26 September 1946; *DWNY,* 27 September 1946, 12; Vincent Sheean, *NYHT,* 1 October 1946, 26.

23. See note 22 above.

24. LT, testimony of J. A. Kingcaid, 26 September 1946.

25. LT, testimony of Theo Fite, 26 September 1946.

26. LT, testimonies of Clydell Castleman, E. L. Davidson, Will Wilsford, Roy Staggs, and Greg O'Rear, 26 September 1946.

27. *DWNY,* 2 October 1946, 12. The Communist paper also called the circuit court a "Jimcrow institution."

28. LT, testimonies of Julius and Saul Blair, 27 September 1946.

29. LT, testimonies of Meade Johnson, S. E. Jones, Johnnie Fulton, G. A. Newburn, Andrew Armstrong, Mrs. Meade Johnson, Jennie Arnell, Mattie Smith, Marcia Mayes, and Rosa Calloway, 28 September 1946.

30. See note 30 above. LT, testimonies of Mary Morton, Rufus Kennedy, and Joseph Blade, 30 September 1946. Maurice Weaver cutely played off the emphasis the prosecution had made on the athletic careers of Bomar and Castleman by pointing out that George Newburn had played football for *five* years at Tennessee A & I College.

31. LT, testimonies of Gillespie Beasley, Church Watkins, Thomas Neely, Bernard Stephenson, George Nicholson, William Bills, George Bills, and J. W. Bills, 30 September 1946; LT, testimony of Henry Sellers, 1 October 1946.

32. LT, testimonies of J. C. Goad and Lewis Hargrove, 1 October 1946; LT, testimonies of S. W. Underwood and J. J. Underwood Jr., 2 October 1946.

33. Ibid.

34. "Mink Slide: The Aftermath," *Time* 48 (14 October 46): 29; *DWNY*, 27 September 1946, 12. Bob Cromie of the *Chicago Tribune* frequently bated Ingram. He told Virginia Weaver not to look at the judge or her baby would look like him, i.e., porcine.

35. Vincent Sheean, "A Social Question Outlaws Law," *NYHT*, 1 October 1946, 26; *DWNY*, 4 October 1946, 12; *NYHT*, 4 October 1946, 10; Paul L. Montgomery, *NYT*, 17 March 1975, 32. Sheean's first major work, the autobiographical *Personal History* was a hit and had several reissues. Other books include biographies of Sinclair Lewis, a close friend, and Mahatmas Ghandi.

36. Vincent Sheean, *NYHT*, 3 October 1946, 24.

37. LT, summation of W. A. Harwell, 2 October 1946.

38. Ibid., summation of Leon A. Ransom.

39. LT, summation of Hugh T. Shelton, 3 October 1946; *NYT*, 4 October 1946, 12.

40. LT, summation of Maurice Weaver, 3 October 1946.

41. Ibid.

42. Ibid.

43. Ibid.

44. LT, summation of Alexander Looby, 3 October 1946.

45. LT, summation of Paul Bumpus.

46. Ibid.

47. Ibid.; *NYT*, 4 October 1946, 12.

48. *LDU*, 4 October 1946, 1; *NG*, 4 October 1946, 1, 8; *NYHT*, 2 October 1946, 30; *NYHT*, 3 October 1946, 24.

49. LT, 4 October 1946; Harry Raymond, *DWNY*, 5 October 1946 1, 3; *NYHT*, 5 October 1946, 1, 12; *MD*, 6 October 1946, 1; *NYT*, 5 October 1946, 1, 18.

50. *NYHT*, 11 October 1946, 11; *DWNY*, 5 October 1946, 1, 3; *LDU*, 11 October 1946, 1, 5; *NG*, 18 October 1946, 4.

51. The Scottsboro boys were nine young Negro transients (ages thirteen to twenty) who were accused of raping two white women (also hobos and later proven to be prostitutes) on a freight train outside Scottsboro, Alabama, in March 1931.

Several guilty verdicts and death sentences came from their trials, which created international outrage and were perceived as exemplars of southern racial injustice. The boys' legal defense became a *cause celebre* for many, including the Communist party and the NAACP. No defendant was executed, and all were eventually released from prison, the last in 1950. See Dan T. Carter, *Scottsboro: A Tragedy of the American South,* 2nd ed., (Baton Rouge: Louisiana State University Press, 1969).

52. "First Round Won," the *Crisis* (November 1946): 328.

53. Virginia Weaver, Chattanooga, Tenn., letter to the author, Nashville, Tenn., 6 March 1996. Mrs. Weaver was three months pregnant and had never tasted brandy. After Sheean shared some of the potable, she promptly vomited.

54. Vincent Sheean, *NYHT,* "Lawrenceburg Verdict Assessed: Reaffirmation of Americanism," 11 October 1946, 11; "Tennessee Trial," the *Crisis* (November 1946): 330.

55. *NG,* 25 October 1946, 1, 4; *NG,* 1 November 1946, 4; R. W., "Tennessee Trial," the *Crisis* (November 1946): 329–30; Dorothy Beeler, "Race Riot in Columbia, Tennessee, February 25–27, 1946," *Tennessee Historical Quarterly* (Spring 1980): 59.

56. Vincent Sheean, *NYHT,* 1 October 1946, 26.

57. Beeler, "Race Riot in Columbia, Tennessee, February 25–27, 1946," *Tennessee Historical Quarterly* (Spring 1980): 50–60; DH, 26 October 1946, 1.

Chapter Eight

1. Minutes of state circuit court; Harold Hinton, *NYT,* 4 November 1946, 22; *DWNY,* 19 November 1946, 12.

2. I could find no transcript of this trial. Its depiction must therefore be less complete than that of the Lawrenceburg trial, reliant on a few primary and mostly tertiary sources.

3. "Pillow-Kennedy Set July 15 As Preliminary Motions denied," *DH,* 5 July 1946, 1, 6.

4. *DH,* 15 November 1946, 1; J. Mike Blair, interviews, 20 June 1995, 3 May 1996; Ed Coker, interview, 14 May 1996.

5. "Change of Venue Is Asked in Negro Case,"*DH,* 11 November 1946, 1, 6; "Change of Venue Denied, Motion to Quash Jury Panel 'Argued,'" *DH,* 12 November 1946, 1, 3; "One Juror Chosen in Negro Trial, Motion to Quash Yet to Be Heard,"*DH,* 13 November 1946, 1, 4; "Negro Trial Starts with State Patrolmen Telling of Shots," *DH,* 15 November 1946, 1.

6. J. Mike Blair, interview, 20 June 1995; Ed Coker, interview, 14 May 1996; Minutes of state circuit court; Danny Bingham, *NB,* 11 November 1946, 1, 8.

7. Harry Raymond, *DWNY,* 18 November 1946, 12; *DWNY,* 19 November 1946, 12; Danny Bingham, "Maury Trial Underway As Motion Denied," *NB,* 15 November 1946, 1; *NB,* 12 November 1946, 1, 2; NB, 18 November 1946, 1, 2; *DH,* 15 November 1946, 1; "Sheriff and Reporter Tell of 'Slide' Raid,"*DH,* 16 November 1946, 1, 2; "Verdict Likely Today in Trial of Negroes," *DH,* 18 November 1946, 1, 6; J. Mike Blair, interview, 20 June 1995, 3 May 1996.

8. *NYT,* 5 October 1946, 1.

9. *DH,* 18 November 1946, 1, 6; "Kennedy Guilty Gets Five Years, New Trial Asked; Pillow Is Freed," *DH,* 19 November 1946, 1, 6.

10. See note 9 above.

11. See note 9 above. Closing argument of Paul Bumpus, pamphlet published by Bumpus and Kelley R. Hix, court reporter. Bumpus graciously provided a copy of this.

12. J. Mike Blair, interviews.

13. Z. Alexander Looby, Nashville, to Leon Ransom, Washington, D.C., 25 November 46, Fisk University special collections, Folder 15, Box 1.

14. Carl T. Rowan, *Dream Makers, Dream Breakers* (Boston: Little, Brown and Company, 1993), 109.

15. Ibid.

16. Ibid., 109–10; Looby, letter; "Intimidation Probe Asked by NAACP," *NB,* 19 November 1946, 1, 8; "NAACP Lawyers' Auto Searched, Weaver Protests," *DH,* 19 November 1946, 1, 3; "Bumpus and Bomar in Limelight Again, *NG,* 22 November 1946, 1, 2; *DWNY,* 20 November 1946, 12; "NAACP Counsel Intimidated," the *Crisis* 54 (January 47): 19–20.

17. Horace Frierson to Theron Caudle, 25 November 1946, DJ file 144–71–4.

18. Rowan, *Dream Makers,* 110; White, *A Man Called White,* 321; Murray, interview, 28 June 1995; Weaver, interview, 24 January 1996; Juan Williams, telephone interview by author, Washington, D.C., 19 September 1996. When Columbia attorney William Leach argued before the U.S. Supreme Court, Marshall called him aside after session to commiserate about his times in Maury County; Robin Courtney, telephone interview by author, Columbia, Tenn., 10 March 1996.

19. See note 18 above.

20. "Notable Tribute Paid to Z. Alexander Looby," *NG,* 20 December 1946, 1, 4.

21. "Negro Conviction Upheld," *NYT,* 27 June 1947, 5; Commutation message, Jim McCord, 29 December 1948, Index to Commutations of Second Term, Gov. Jim McCord, 1947–1949, Book 870, TSLA; Carey D. Eldridge, letter to Gov. McCord, Nashville, Tenn., 27 March 1948, McCord papers, Box 12, Folder 9.

Chapter Nine

1. Guzman, *Negro Year Book,* 246.

2. William R. Manchester, "The Fraying Flags of Triumph," in *The Glory and the Dream* (Boston: Little, Brown and Company, 1973), 392–416.

3. Harold Preece, "Klan 'Murder Inc.,' in Dixie," the *Crisis* 10 (October 1946): 300; Egerton, "Epidemic of Violence," *Speak Now,* 359–75.

4. Harvard Sitkoff, "Racial Militance and Interracial Violence in the Second World War," *The Journal of American History* 43 (December 1971): 661–81; Richard Dalfiume, *Desegregation of the U.S. Armed Forces* (Columbia: University of Missouri Press, 1969), 64–104; Charles Lawrence Jr., "Race Riots in the United States, 1942–1946," in Guzman, *Negro Year Book,* 232–57.

5. Dalfiume, *Desegregation of the U.S. Armed Forces,* 105–31.

6. "Tennessee Race Riot: A Danger Sign," the *Christian Century* 43 (13 March 1946): 325; Egerton, *Speak Now,* 369; Howard W. Odum, *Race and Rumors of Race,*

(Chapel Hill: University of North Carolina Press, 1943), 54–5; Lee E. Williams II, *Post-War Riots in America 1919 and 1946* (Lewiston, N.Y.: Edwin Mellen Press, 1991), 9–111.

7. Johnson, interview, 14 June 1995; M. E. Tilly, the Columbia, Tenn., Tragedy, report to the executive committee of the Jurisdiction Woman's Society of Christian Service—the Conference Presidents and Secretaries of Christian Social Relations, 1946; *DH*, 27 February 1946, 1.

8. *Lynchings and What They Mean*, (Atlanta: The Commission, 1931), 8, 61; *Lynching and the Law* (Chapel Hill: The University of North Carolina Press, 1933), 4, 13, 18–20; Arthur F. Raper, *The Tragedy of Lynching* (Chapel Hill: The University of North Carolina Press, 1933), 483; Egerton, *Speak Now*, 360–61.

9. Kimes, interview, 12 July 1995; Johnson, interview, 14 June 1995.

10. Odum, *Race and Rumors*, 102–04; Margarete Campbell, telephone interview by author, Columbia, Tenn., 7 May 1996.

11. Odum, *Race and Rumors*, 142–55; J. J. Underwood Jr., telephone interview, 18 January 1996; Margarete Campbell, interview; Wallace Gordon, telephone interview, Columbia, Tenn., 7 May 96.

12. Dan T. Carter, *Scottsboro: A Tragedy of the American South* (Baton Rouge: Louisiana State University Press, 1969), 51, 137.

13. White, *A Man Called White*, 69, 129–31, 314–15; Rowan, *Dream Makers*, 122–23, 236. A current controversy is whether Thurgood Marshall did a thing just as racially traitorous as being a Communist by officially cooperating with the despised J. Edgar Hoover to combat communism. There seems little doubt he did cooperate with Hoover to root out communist infiltration of the NAACP. Whatever purpose he had in doing so, Marshall defenders have rushed to erase a perceived smear from his escutcheon. See: "FBI Cooperation Shouldn't Hurt Legacy," *NT*, 4 December 1996, 12A; Carl Rowan, "Marshall, FBI Cozy? No Way," *NT*, 6 December 1996, 13A; Laura Myers, "Odd Pairing Indeed: Thurgood Marshall and Ever Wary FBI," *NT*, 15 December 1996, 2D.

14. Odum, *Race and Rumors*, 101; *NB*, 26 February 1946, 16; *MD*, 1 March 1946, 4; Ernest Smith report to Gov. McCord; Murray, interview; Stofel, interview, 8 July 1995.

15. Cemora Newsome, Washington, D.C., telephone interview by author, 10 January 1997.

16. Jim Squires, telephone interview by author, Versailles, Ky., 9 July 1996.

17. Ibid.; Odum, *Race and Rumors*, 103; Johnson, interview; Murray, interview; Stofel, interview, 13 November 1996; Victor Wilson, telephone interview by author, 27 June 1995. When interviewed, Col. Wilson said he was ninety-eight years old. He hinted darkly about other secrets he knew about this affair but would not be interviewed in person.

18. Sam Kennedy, interview by author, Columbia, Tenn., 25 May 1995; Agnes Meyer, "The Untold Story of the Columbia, Tenn., Riot," *WP*, 19 May 1946, 1B, 2B, 20 May 1946, 9. M. E. Tilly, report on Columbia tragedy, 1946, 7.

19. John Morgan, interview, 25 July 1995.

20. Guzman, *Negro Year Book*, 253–55; Williams, *Post-War Riots*, 113–21.

21. August Meier and Elliot Rudwick, "Attorneys Black and White," in *Along the Color Line* (Urbana: University of Illinois Press, 1976), 128–73; Murray, interview; Kimes, interview; Wade Hall, *The Rest of the Dream*, 203; Wallace Gordon, WSMV television interview, Wallace Gordon, Nashville, Tenn., 1 April 1993; Raymond Lockridge, WKRN television interview, Nashville, Tenn., 1 April 1993; Will Dale, telephone interview by author, Columbia, Tenn., 18 November 1996; Dawson Frierson, telephone interview by author, Columbia, Tenn., 18 November 1996; Robin Courtney, telephone interview by author, Columbia, Tenn., 19 November 1996.

22. Herbert Johnson, telephone interview by author, 14 November 1996; Raymond Lockridge, interview by author, 14 December 1996.

23. Virginia Weaver, interview, 24 January 1996.

24. Milton Murray, interview, 28 June 1995; Irena Johnson, interview, 14 June 1995; Ed Kimes, interview, 12 July 1995; Marjorie Smith thesis, 62; Guy Johnson, "SRC's Work and Plans," *New South* (December 1946): 5.

25. Mrs. Meyer enjoyed her trip to Columbia and a candid conversation with Sheriff Underwood. In her autobiography, she noted his criticism of the patrol and implication that the blacks awaiting trial were innocent. She was presumptuous in depicting the effect of her articles. After their alleged introduction into the Lawrenceburg trial, the case supposedly immediately turned for the defense. Agnes E. Meyer, *Out of These Roots* (Boston: Little, Brown and Company, 1953), 263–66.

26. M. E. Tilly, report on Columbia tragedy, 1946; Agnes Meyer, "Columbia (Tenn.) Riot," *WP*, 20 May 1946; Vincent Sheean, "Lawrenceburg Verdict Assessed: Reaffirmation of Americanism," *NYHT*, 11 October 1946, 11; Harold Hinton, "May Let Off Others in Mink Slide Case," *NYT*, 4 November 1946, 22.

Epilogue

1. Monsanto, Columbia Plant, fiftieth anniversary booklet, 14 June 1986; Hallie Hudson, telephone interview by author, Columbia, Tenn., 16 January 1996.

2. "Almanac," Visions for Maury County, 1996, 4; "Doing Their Part for the Good Earth;" ibid., 7–9; "Education for the 'Real World,'" ibid., 10–11; "Natural Attraction," ibid., 14; "Maury County Schools," ibid., 18–19; "Good Health, Good Business," ibid., 22–23; Larry Woody, "Still the Same Sterling," ibid., 26–28; "Hardball Headquarters," ibid., 29; "Columbia/Maury County Economic Profile," ibid., 32–33; "Road Map to the Past," ibid., 35; "Of Chariots and Mules," ibid., 38–39; *DH*, "1996 Tennessee Bicentennial Majestic Middle Tennessee Tour 1996," insert, 27–29 September 1996, 1–16; R*and McNally 1995 Atlas & Marketing Guide,* (Rand McNally & Co.), 510; 1994 U.S. Department of Commerce population data were supplied by the Maury County Chamber of Commerce.

3. There were good data that suggested there was no such "epidemic." The perception of one was perpetrated mainly by certain special-interest groups and articles in *USA Today*. There followed such a political and journalistic brouhaha that the incidence may have increased by "copycat" arsonists. Michael Fumento, "A Church Arson Epidemic? It's Smoke and Mirrors," *WSJ*, 8 July 1996, A8.

4. Gary Fields and Tom Watson, "Fear Still Shadows Black Congregations," *NT*, 18 March 1996, 1, 2; Deborah Highland, "'I Learned a lot about Racism'. . ." *NT*, 13 March 1996, B1; Dennis Farney, "A Time to Build Up," *WSJ*, 15 July 1996, A1, A7.

5. Billy Jack, telephone interview by author, Columbia, Tenn., 18 November 1996; Frank Dale, telephone interview by author, Columbia, Tenn., 18 November 1996; Tom Dake, telephone interview by author, 6 January 1997; Linda Rivers, Maury County Department of Education, telephone interview by author, 8 January 1997, 9 January 1997. The Twenty-second Tennessee State Judicial District (formerly the eleventh) contained Maury, Giles, Lawrence, and Wayne Counties.

6. JaDonna Cummins, personal interview by author, Columbia, Tenn., 8 August 1996; Jim Dooley, telephone interview by author, 21 November 1996; Maury County, Tennessee Assessment Roll. Reflecting the continuing major role of organized religion in blacks' lives, there are seven churches in the two and one-half blocks of Eighth Street extending east from South Main.

7. "Griffin, Wilsford Retire from City Police Force," *DH*, 1 July 1950, 1, 3; W. A. Hastings, "The Rambler," *DH*, 27 August 1952, 1, 5; *DH*, 28 August 1952, 2.

8. *NB*, 15 March 1963, 1, 6; "J. Walter Griffin, Retired Police Chief, Succumbs," *NB*, 16 March 1963, 4.

9. Jerry Colley, telephone interview by author, Columbia, Tenn., 1 March 1996, John Hollins Sr., telephone interview by author, Nashville, Tenn., 3 March 1996, Robin Courtney, telephone interview by author, Columbia, Tenn., 10 March 1996, Sam Kennedy, telephone interview by author, Columbia, Tenn., 11 March 1996, James Weatherford, telephone interview by author, Lawrenceburg, Tenn., 19 March 1996; "Joe Ingram, Longtime Maury Judge, Dies," *DH*, 29 October 1986; *DH*, 30 October 1986.

10. *DH*, 17 January 1962, 1.

11. "Saul Blair, 73, Dies Sunday; Rites Wednesday," *DH*, 15 February 1965, 1.

12. "J. J. Underwood Dies; Was Former Sheriff in Maury," *DH*, 21 September 1966, 1, 2; J. J. Underwood Jr. telephone interview by author, Columbia, Tenn., 18 January 1996; J. J. Underwood Jr., personal interview, Columbia, Tenn., 28 December 1996.

13. David Halberstam, *NT*, 2 September 1960, 1, 6; *NT*, 3 September 1960, 1, 5; *NT*, 4 September 1960, 1, 2; Steve Horpan, *NT*, 5 September 1960, 1, 6; *NT*, 9 September 1960, 5; *NT*, 12 June 1964, 1, 10; John Bibb, *NT*, 12 June 1964, 32; *NB*, 12 June 1964, 8; ibid., Fred Russell, 14.

14. Paul L. Montgomery, "Vincent Sheean, Journalist, Dies at 75," *NYT*, 17 March 1975, 32; Jean R. Hailey, "Vincent Sheean Dies,"*WP*, 17 March 1975, C10.

15. Linda T. Wynn, "Leaders of Afro-American Nashville," pamphlet prepared for 1984 department of history conference, Tennessee State University; George Barker, "Man Behind the Move," the *Nashville Tennessean Magazine* 16 (April 1961): 12–14.

16. Vincent Sheean, *NYHT*, 3 October 1946, 24.

17. Virginia Weaver, interview.

18. Ibid.; Jack Lusk, interview; Sam Plummer, interview; "Weaver Case Judge Named," *CNFP*, 6 August 1965, 5; "Court Takes Fined Action," *CNFP*, 20 July 1968, 5; "Maurice M. Weaver Dies at 72, District Attorney," *CNFP*, 31 October 1983, B6; *Chattanooga Bar Association v. Maurice Weaver*, 14 May 1968; Virginia Weaver, Chattanooga, Tenn., letter to author, Nashville, Tenn., 6 March 1996.

19. See note 18 above.

20. "James Morton, Mortician, Dies Thursday," *DH*, 10 March 1965, 1; Cemora Newsome, telephone interview by author, Washington, D.C., 20 December 1996.

21. Jerry Colley, interview by author, 1 March 1996; John Hollins Sr., interview by author, 3 March 1996; Pauline Wehby, interview by author, Nashville, Tenn., 10 March 1996; Sam Kennedy, interview by author, Columbia, Tenn., 11 March 1996; Paul Bumpus, interview by author, Murfreesboro, Tenn., 22 February 1996.

22. *Knoxville Journal*, 8 June 1940, 1; *WAA*, 18 April 1942, 1, 2; *WAA*, 13 April 1946, 1; *Washington Evening Star*, 26 August 1954.

23. Linda Greenhouse, The *New York Times* Biographical Service, vol. 24, January 1993, 126–31; Joan Biskupic, "Thurgood Marshall, Retired Justice, Dies," WP, 25 January 1993, A1, A10; Juan Williams is working on a Thurgood Marshall biography, and others will follow. Some of this personal information on Marshall is from the previously noted *Dream Makers* by Carl Rowan. That book is sycophantic.

24. See note 23 above.

25. James Stephenson, interview, 17 October 1996, 29 December 1996; burial programs of New Liberty Baptist Church, Detroit, Mich., March 1987 and July 1987.

26. Data provided by the Maury County Department of Education.

27. George Newbern, interview by author, Columbia, Tenn., 14 February 1996. Worshippers of the Mt. Lebanon Missionary Baptist Church dedicated their new education building to Newbern in 1995.

28. Carver-Smith replaced College Hill as the Columbia black high school in 1949. It was unneeded as a school when comprehensive integration occurred in 1969. "Negro Pupil Enters McDowell, First in Maury," *DH*, 31 August 1964, 1, 4. The author is proud to recognize McDowell as his grammar school alma mater. John Trotwood Moore was a principal at the school in the late nineteenth century.

29. Margarete Campbell, interview, 28 December 1996, Sam Kennedy, interview, 26 December 1996, Christa Martin, interview by author, Columbia, Tenn., 28 December 1996, Rose McClain, interview by author, Columbia, Tenn., 28 December 1996; John Porter, interview by author, Columbia, Tenn., 18 December 1996, Mary Sowell, interview by author, 13 November 1996, J. J. Underwood Jr., interview, 28 December 1996. The undertaking business remains extremely segregated in Columbia. It remains, therefore, a traditionally lucrative one for enterprising blacks.

30. Marchelle Cannon, "1946 Race Riot in Columbia Left a Tragic Mark," *NT*, 26 February 1986, 8A.

Bibliography

Books

A Historical Sketch of Maury County. Columbia, Tenn.: Excelsior Printing Office, 1876; reissued in 1976 by The Book Store, Columbia, Tenn.

Arnette, Charles Byron, *From Mink Slide to Main Street.* Nashville: Williams Printing Co., 1992 (2nd printing).

Brandt, Nat. *Harlem at War, The Black Experience in WWII.* Syracuse University Press: 1996.

Carter, Dan F. *Scottsboro, A Tragedy of the American South.* Baton Rouge: Louisiana State University Press, 1969 (2nd printing).

Chadbourn, James Harmon. *Lynching and the Law.* Chapel Hill: The University of North Carolina Press, 1933.

Cimprich, John. *Slavery's End in Tennessee, 1861–1865.* University, Ala.: The University of Alabama Press, 1985.

Dalfiume, Richard M. *Desegregation of the U.S. Armed Forces—Fighting on Two Fronts, 1939–1953.* Columbia, Mo.: University of Missouri Press, 1969.

Dollard, John. *Caste and Class in a Southern Town,* 3rd ed. Garden City, N.Y.: Doubleday Anchor Books, 1949.

Doyle, Bertram Wilbur. *The Etiquette of Race Relations in the South,* 2nd ed. Chicago, 1971.

Egerton, John. *Speak Now Against the Day.* New York: Alfred A. Knopf, 1994.

Fadool, Cynthia R., ed. *Contemporary Authors.* Detroit: Gale Research Company, 1976.

Garrett, Jill K. *'Hither and Yon'—The Best of the Writings of Jill K. Garrett.* Columbia, Tenn.: The Maury County, Tennessee Homecoming '86 Committee, 1986.

Garrett, Jill K. *'Hither and Yon' II—More of the Writings of Jill K. Garrett.* Columbia, Tenn.: The Polk Memorial Association, 1992.

General Finding of the Southern Commission on the Study of Lynching. *Lynchings and What They Mean.* Atlanta: The Commission, 1931.

Grimshaw, Allen Day. *Racial Violence in the United States.* Chicago: Aldine Publishing Company, 1969.

Guzman, Jessie Parkhurst, ed. *Negro Year Book: A Review of Events Affecting Negro Life, 1941–1946.* Tuskegee: The Department of Records and Research Tuskegee Institute, 1947.

Hall, Wade H. *The Rest of the Dream.* Lexington: The University of Kentucky Press, 1988.

Lawrence, Charles R., Jr. Race Riots in the United States 1942–1946. In *Negro Year Book: A Review of Events Affecting Negro Life, 1941–1946,* edited by Jessie Parkhurst Guzman. Tuskegee: The Department of Records and Research the Tuskegee Institute, 1947.

Manchester, William Raymond. *The Glory and the Dream: A Narrative History of America, 1932–1972.* Boston: Little, Brown and Company, 1973.

McPherson, James M. *Battle Cry of Freedom.* New York: Oxford University Press, 1988.

Meier, August, and Elliot Rudwick. *Along the Color Line: Explorations in the Black Experience.* Urbana: University of Illinois Press, 1976.

Meyer, Agnes E. *Out of These Roots—The Autobiography of an American Woman.* Boston: Little, Brown and Company, 1953.

Mooney, Chase C. *Slavery in Tennessee.* Bloomington: Indiana University Press, 1957.

Odum, Howard W. *Race and Rumors of Race.* Chapel Hill: The University of North Carolina Press, 1943.

Rand McNally 1995 *Commercial Atlas & Marketing Guide,* 126th ed. Rand McNally & Company, 1995.

Raper, Arthur F. *The Tragedy of Lynching.* Chapel Hill: The University of North Carolina Press, 1933.

Robbins, D. P., ed. *Century Review of Maury County, Tennessee, 1805–1905.* Auspices of the Board of Mayor and Aldermen of Columbia, 1905.

Rowan, Carl T. *Dream Makers, Dream Breakers.* Boston: Little, Brown and Company, 1993.

Schott, Fred W. Jr. *"Servants . . . Not Lords,"* A History of the Tennessee Highway Patrol. Paducah, Ky.: Taylor Publishing Co., 1981.

Sheean, Vincent. *Personal History.* New York: Random House, 1935; reprint, 1940.

Smith, Reid. *Majestic Middle Tennessee.* Pratville, Ala.: Paddle Wheel Publications, 1975.

Squires, James D. *The Secrets of the Hopewell Box.* New York: Times Books, 1996.

Trelease, Allen W. White Terror: *The Ku Klux Klan Conspiracy and Southern Reconstruction.* Westport, Connecticut: Greenwood Press, 1971.

Turner, William Bruce. *History of Maury County, Tennessee.* Nashville: The Parthenon Press, 1955.

Wallace, Lew. "The Capture of Fort Donelson" in *Battles and Leaders of the Civil War, Vol. 1.* Secaucus, N. J.: Castle.

Watkins, Sam R. *"CO. AYTCH,"* Maury County Grays, First Tennessee Regiment. Dayton, Ohio: Morningside Bookshop, 1982.

White, Walter Francis. *A Man Called White.* New York: Arno Press and The New York Times, 1969.

Wilkins, Roy, with Tom Mathews. *Standing Fast: The Autobiography of Roy Wilkins.* New York: The Viking Press, 1982.

Williams, Lee E., II. *Post-War Riots in America, 1919 and 1946.* Lewiston: Edwin Mellen Press, 1991.

Graduate Works

Clark, Blanche Henry. "The Agricultural Population in Tennessee, 1840–1860: With Special Reference to the Non-Slaveholders," Ph.D. diss., Vanderbilt University, 1938.

Smith, Marjorie. "Racial Confrontation in Columbia, Tennessee: 1946." Master of arts thesis, Atlanta University, 1971.

Interviews

Virginia Alexander (Nashville)
Addie Lou Blair (Columbia, Tennessee)
J. Mike Blair (Columbia)
Sam Bone (Lebanon, Tennessee)
Cornelia Braden (Columbia)
Paul Brown (Columbia)
Paul Bumpus (Murfreesboro, Tennessee)
Margarete Campbell (Columbia)
Paul Campbell (Chattanooga, Tennessee)
Paige Chamberlain (Columbia)
Russell Church (Columbia)
Kim Cline (Washington, D.C.)
Ed Coker (Columbia)
Jerry Colley (Columbia)
Robin Courtney (Columbia)
JaDonna Cummins (Columbia)
Tom Dake (Columbia)
Frank Dale (Columbia)
Will Dale (Columbia)
Jim Dooley (Columbia)
Irene Dugger (Columbia and Mt. Pleasant, Tennessee)
James Dugger (Mt. Pleasant)
Leonard Evans (Detroit)
Peggy Fleming (Columbia)
J. Dawson Frierson (Columbia)
Franklin Fulton (Columbia)
Jill Garrett (Columbia)
Wallace Gordon (Columbia)
David Halberstam (New York)
George Harding (Lebanon)
John Hollins Sr. (Nashville)

C. D. Hopkins Jr. (Columbia)
Cam Hales (Columbia)
Hallie Hudson (Columbia)
Bill Jack (Columbia)
John Jewell (Columbia)
Herbert Johnson (Columbia)
Irena Johnson (Columbia)
Mildred Johnson (Columbia)
Sam Kennedy (Columbia)
Ed Kimes (Columbia)
D. L. Lansden (Nashville)
Marise Lightfoot (Mt. Pleasant)
Raymond Lockridge (Columbia)
Charles W. (Jack) Lusk (Chattanooga)
Christa S. Martin (Columbia)
Jimmy Matthews (Columbia)
Rose Ogilvie McClain (Columbia)
Mary McKissack (Columbia)
Betty Modrall (Columbia)
John E. Morgan (Goodlettsville, Tennessee)
Milton Murray (Columbia)
George A. Newbern (Columbia)
Cemora Morton Newsome (Washington, D.C.)
Charlene Ogilvie (Columbia)
Clifford Parsons (Columbia)
Geneva Patrick (Columbia)
Myron Peck (Columbia)
Sam W. Plummer (Chattanooga)
Thomas Potter (Nashville)
John C. Porter (Columbia)
Linda Rivers (Columbia)
Ronald Ryan (Columbia)
Fred Schott (Springfield, Tennessee)
Jerry Scott (Nashville)
Evelyn Small (Washington, D.C.)
Frank Sowell (Columbia)
Mary Sowell (Columbia)
James Squires (Versailles, Kentucky)
James Stephenson (Detroit)
Bernard Stofel (Columbia)
Frank Thomas (Columbia)
J. J. Underwood Jr. (Columbia)
John Wagster (Nashville)
James Weatherford (Lawrenceburg, Tennessee)
Virginia Weaver (Chattanooga)
Pauline Wehby (Nashville)

J. L. Whiteside (Columbia)
Juan Williams (Washington, D.C.)
Bill Wilsford (Columbia)
Victor Wilson (Nashville)

Manuscripts, Pamphlets, and Other Sources
1850 Maury County Slave Census, microfilm, TSLA
Burial programs of New Liberty Baptist Church, Detroit, Mich.
Chattanooga Bar Association v. *Maurice Weaver*
City Directory, 1933–1934, Columbia, Tennessee.
Closing argument of Paul Bumpus. Published by Paul Bumpus and Kelley R. Hix, court reporter.
Columbia, Maury County, Tennessee, Her Progress and Importance. Enterprise Publishing Company, 1885.
Dickinson, Jacob McGavock. Papers, 1851–1955, microfilm accession No. 836, Box 62. Tennessee State Library and Archives, Nashville, Tenn.
Foreman, Clark H. *The Truth about Columbia Tennessee Cases.* Southern Conference for Human Welfare, Nashville, Tenn., 1946.
Greenhouse, Linda. The *New York Times* Biographical Service, vol., 24.
Jones, Thomas. Cordie Cheek Folder. Fisk University Special Collections. Nashville, Tenn.
Latimer, Ira. Papers, Chicago Historical Society, Archives and Manuscripts Department.
Liberties Committee minutes, reports. Chicago Historical Society Archives and Manuscripts Department.
Looby, Zephariah Alexander. 1899–1972, Papers, 1922–1981. Fisk University Special Collections. Nashville, Tennessee.
Lynchings and the Law. Chapel Hill: The University of North Carolina Press, 1933.
Lynchings and What They Mean. Atlanta: The Commission. 1931.
Maury County Chamber of Commerce pamphlet, TSLA.
Maury County Tennessee Assessment Roll.
Maury County Trustee's Office Tax Books, microfilm, Roll 509, TSLA.
McCord, Jim. Papers, 1947–1949, Book 870. TSLA; Box 12, Folder 9, TSLA.
Minor, Robert. *Lynching and Frame-up in Tennessee.* New York: New Century Publishers, 1946.
Monsanto, Columbia Plant, fiftieth anniversary booklet, 14 June 1986.
Proceeding before the United States District Grand Jury for the Middle District of Tennessee in the Matter of Columbia, Tennessee, Investigation. Vols. 11, 12, 13 are missing.
Smith, Ernest F. "Report on Investigation Made on February 27–28, 1946, at Columbia, Tennessee." Jim Nance McCord MSS, Box 18, No. 7. Tennessee State Library and Archives, Nashville, Tenn.
The Tragedy of Lynching. Chapel Hill: The University of North Carolina Press, 1933.
Tilly, M. E. Special report to the executive committee of the Jurisdiction Woman's Society of Christian Service—The Conference Presidents and Secretaries of Christian Social Relations, 1946.

Transcript of *State of Tennessee* v. *Sol Blair, et al.*

United States Department of Commerce, *Sixteenth Census of the United States, 1940.*
    United States government printing office, 1943.

United States Department of Commerce, *Religious Bodies: 1936,* vol. 1. Bureau of
    the Census, United States government printing office, Washington D.C.: 1941.

Various papers, Franklin D. Roosevelt Library, Hyde Park, N.Y.

Visions for Maury County, 1996.

Wynn, Linda T. "Leaders of Afro-American Nashville," Tennessee State
    University, 1984.

Newspapers

Chattanooga News Fress-Press

Columbia (Tennessee) *Daily Herald*

Columbia (Tennessee) *Maury Democrat*

Daily Worker of New York

Knoxville (Tennessee) *Journal*

Lawrenceburg (Tennessee) *Democrat Union*

Louisville (Kentucky) *Leader*

Michigan Chronicle

Nashville Banner

Nashville Globe

In mid-1946, the name of this newspaper was changed to the *Nashville Globe-Independent.* To maintain consistency, I have throughout used *NG* for abbreviation.

Nashville Tennessean

In 1972, the name of this newspaper was changed to the *Tennessean.* To maintain consistency, I have throughout used *NT* for abbreviation.

New York Herald Tribune

New York Times

Washington Evening Star

Washington Post

Wall Street Journal

Washington Afro-American

Periodicals

Christian Century

The *Crisis*

Ebony

The *Journal of American History*

Nashville Tennessean Magazine

New Republic

New South

Tennessee Historical Quarterly

Time

Southern Living

Index

Page numbers in bold type indicate photo captions.

A

Agronsky, Martin, 103
Akron, Ohio, 57
Alderson, James, 88
American Legion, 121
American Missionary
    Association, 54
Anderson, Dabney, 107
Andrew Jackson Hotel, 80
Antebellum Trail, 133
Antigua, British West Indies, 51
Arkansas, 18
Armour plant, 56
Armstrong, Andrew J., 15, 95
Arnell, Jennie, 95
Associated Press, 71, 84
Athens, Alabama, 125
Austin, Ray, 60, 105, 108–10

B

Baltimore, Maryland, 56, 109
B & O Railroad, 56; Civil
    Liberites Car, 56
Barmore, Seymour, 6–7
Baxter, Tommy, 85
Bear Creek Pike, 20, 24
Beard, James, 21, 32–33, 71

Beasley, James, 89
Beaumont, Texas, 116
Bedford County, 1
Beeler, Roy H., 42, 68
Bellanfant, James "Popeye," 20,
    24, **46**, 60, 72, 85, 89, 92, 98, 112
Bells of St. Mary's, The, 20
Bethune, Mary, 58
Bigby Grays, 2
Bills, William "Moot," 60, 85, 95
Black, Rufus, 142
Blackwell, John, 34, 38, **39**,
    40–41, **41**, 60, 72, 86, 110
Blade, Joseph, 25, 95
Blair, Addie Lou Flippen, **16**
Blair, J. Mike, 108
Blair, Julius, 16, **16**, 17–20, 22–25,
    40, 45, 50, 52–53, 60, 67,
    72–73, 85–87, 90, 93–100, 106,
    109, 119, 124–25, 127–28, 135
Blair, Saul "Sol," 16, 18–20,
    22–24, 28, 36, 38–40, **41**, 45,
    48, 50, 52, 56, 60, 65, **66**, 67,
    70, 72–73, 85–88, 90, 93–95,
    97–98, 100, 105, 128, 135
Bomar, Lynn, 29–30, **30**, 31–32,
    34–37, 39, 41–42, 47, 52, 55,

67–68, 70–77, 85, 90–92,
    95–96, 99–100, 102, 108–09,
    112, 120, 123–24, 127, 135–36
Bontecou, Eleanor, 64, 74
Bottom, the. *See* Mink Slide
Branham and Hughes Military
    Academy, 5
Brennan, William Joseph, Jr., 139
Brown, Clarence, 34, **44**, 83, 85
Brownlow, William "Parson,"
    6–7, 28
Brownlow's Band. *See*
    Metropolitan Police District
    of Memphis
Brown's Cafe, 34
Brown v. *Board of Education of
    Topeka*, 129, 136, 138
Bryant, Mark, 107
Bullock, Alexander, 42, 88–90,
    101
Bumpus, Paul, 45, 47–48, 52–53,
    53, 55, 59, **61**, 63, 65, 68–69,
    79–82, 85–91, 93–94, 96,
    100–103, 107–10, **110**, 113,
    120–21, 126, 129, 134
Burger, Warren Earl, 138
Butts, A. M., 112

C

Calcutta, India, 99
Caldwell, A. B., 64, 74
Caldwell, Erskine, 9
California, 25
Calloway, Joe, 42, **44**
Calloway, Rosa Lee, 95
Camp Stewart, 116
Carlton, Jack, 109
Carlton, Wayne, 28
Carolinas, 1
Cartwright, C. A., 60
Carver-Smith School, 141
Castleman, Clydell "Clyde," 33, 92
Castner-Knott appliance store, 11–12, 14, **46**
Caudle, Theron, 75
Century Review, 5
Charter Commission, 136
Chattanooga, 51–52, 56, 113, 137
Chattanooga Bar Association, 137
Cheek, Cordie, 8–9, 15, 21, 56, 86, 90, 119
Cheek, Tenny, 8
Chicago, Illinois, 24, 42, 56–57
Chicago Civil Liberties Committee, 54, 56, 73, 74; *Civil Liberty News*, 74
Chicago Civil Liberties Union, 58
Chicago Defender, 54
Chicago Tribune, 84
Choate, Henry, 7–8, 56, 119
Christian, John, 108
Circuit Court of Lawrence County. *See* Lawrence County Circuit Court
Civil War, 2–4, 6, 20, 120, 129
Claiborn, Audrey, 89
Clark, Ed, 70–71
Clark, Tom C., 54, 58–59, 63–64, 74, 76–78, 112
Clark Training High School, 5
Claude, Borgie, 21, 32–33, 71
Cleveland, Ohio, 57
"CO. AYTCH," Maury Grays, First Tennessee Regiment, 3
Coker, Ed, 108
College Hill High School, 5, 9, 13, 20, 89, 95
Collins, T. Frank, 22, 28, **41**, 90, 94

Columbia Athenaeum, 5
Columbia Central High School, 142
Columbia Chamber of Commerce, 5, 132
Columbia City Hall, 23, 38, 42
Columbia Colored Division, **118**
Columbia Female Institute, 5
Columbia Military Academy, 5, 88, 132
Columbia State University, 132
Columbia University, 112
Columbus, Georgia, 42
Committee of 100, 74
Communist Party, 54, 56, 120
Confederate(s), 2–3, 6
Confederate States, 118
Congress of Industrial Organizations, 51, 56; Mine, Mill, and Smelter CIO, 56
Cooper, Prentice, 4
Copeland, Constable, **41**, **44**
Cotham, William, 32
Crisis, the, **40–41**, **55**, **82**, **94**, **102**, **104**
Crockett, Davy, 104
Crump, Edward "Boss," 29, 59, 77
Culleoka, 12–13, 15, 95
Culleoka Highway, 8
Cumberland Mountains, 75
Cumberland River, 1

D

Daily Herald, 8–9, 11, 20, 50, 77, 84, 107–08, **118**, 135
Daily Worker of New York, 55, 93, 96, 105–06
Dale, W. A., 129
Dallas Eat Shop, 24
Darnell, Tom R., 48, **49**
Davidson County, 2–3, 8, 61–62, 132
Davidson County Grand Jury, 9, 135
Davies, Elmer D., 59, 64, 74–77, 85
Davis, Bette, 58
Dawson, William, 60, 85
Denham, Eldridge, 17, 23, 28, 50, 123
Denning, A. O., 64, 74
Denton, Hayes, 15, 17, 19, 52, 72, 90, 99

Detroit, Michigan, 11, 56, 57, 116, 139
Dickinson, Jacob McGavock, 30–31, **31**, 32, 34, 37, **38**, 39, 41–42, 69, 76, 91, 124, 134
Dixie Manufacturing Company, 25
Dombrowski, James, 67–68, 72–73
Dooley, Elmer, 34, 38
Dowell, J. F., 107
Downey, R. O., 79
Duck River, 1–2, 7, 111–12, 122
Dudley, John, 17–18, 42, 45

E

Eastern Section of the Tennessee Court of Appeals, 137
East Tennessee, 98
Ebony, 41, 55, 86
Edwards, Charlie, 34
Edwards, Clifford, 85
Edwards, Henry, 34
Edwards, Luther, 34, 60, 85
Eighth Street, 16–18, 20–23, 25–28, 31–34, 36–37, 39, 41, 72, 85–88, 92–93, 109, 117, 124, 134, 140. *See also* Mink Slide
Einstein, Albert, 58
Eldridge, Carey, 113
Eleanor Clubs, 58
Eleventh Circuit Court Grand Jury, 60, 61
Eleventh Judicial Circuit, 11
Europe, 13, 20
Evans, Leonard, 38, **43**, 88, 99

F

Farley, Jim, 4
Faulkner, William, 58
Federal Bureau of Investigation, 50, 59, 64–65, 74–75, 77, 88, 121
Federal Grand Jury for the Middle District of Tennessee, 63, 64–66, 69, 72–78, **78**, 81, 84–85, 88, 90, 101, 106
Federal Grand Jury for the Middle District of Tennessee files, **33–36**, **38–39**, **41**, **43–44**, **46**, **49**, **66**, **70**, **92**
Finney, John, 20–21, 108
First Baptist Church, Columbia, 134

Fisher, Mamie Lee, 88–89, 99–101
Fisk University, 8, 115
Fite, Theo G., 92
Fleming, Flo, 12–13, 16, 18, 31,
    39, 45, 48, 55, 65, 73, **92**, 112,
    124, 135
Fleming, John, 13, 15, 124
Fleming, Peggy Dickinson, **31**
Fleming, Will, 65
Fleming, William, 90
Fleming, William "Billy"
    "Willie," 12–16, 18, 50, 65,
    76, 124
Fleming family, 12, 16, 124
Flippin, Sadie, 47
Foreman, Clark, 54, 58, 69, 73
Forrest, Nathan B., 129
Fort Bliss, 116
Fort Dix, 116
Fort Donelson, 3
4-H Club, 34
Fox, Eulus, 107
Frazier, W. C., 15
Freedmen's Bureau, 6
Frierson, Horace, 50, 59, 64,
    74–75, 78, 113
Frierson, Robert, 24
Fulton, Johnnie Belle, 24, 95

G
Garner, Joe, 52
General Motors, 131
Gentry, Robert "Bob," 53, 60, 85,
    88, 93, 101–04
Germany, 115
Giles County, 1, 6, 11
Gilmer, Henry, 107
Glendale, 8
Goad, J. C., 17, 21, 23–24, 86, 95
Godwin, Claude, 8–9
Goering, Hermann, 100
Gordon, Horace, 34, 47, 60, 85, 120
Gordon, William "Willie," 22,
    43, **46**, 47–48, **49**, 52, 76, 88,
    115, 120–22
Gray, Malcom, 112
Great Society, 129
Greyhound, 81
Griffin, Billy, 42, **43**, 45, 48, **49**,
    95, 121
Griffin, J. Walter, 15, 17–19,
    21–22, 26–28, 32, **43**, 48, 65,
    86, 112, 121, 123, 134

H
Hammerstein, Oscar, II, 58
Happy Hollow, 19, 42, 92
Hargrove, Lewis, 95
Harlan, Sarah, 7
Harlem, New York, 116
Harrington, Oliver C. "Ollie,"
    73, 80
Harris, Gladys. *See* Stephenson,
    Gladys
Hart, Chester, 8
Harwell, W. A. "Bud," 81, 85,
    97, 107
Hawthorne, Frank L., 40
Haynes, Richard, 108
Haynes Haven mansion, 24
Health, Education and Security,
    129
Helm's Branch, 34
Hickman County, 1
Highlander Folk School, 56, 68
Hiss, Alger, 120
Hitler, Adolph, 120
Hohenwald, 64
Hopkins, C. D., 90
Hopton, W. E., 64–65, 76
Horton, Henry, 29
Howard University, 60, 126, 137–
    38; Howard Law School, 126
Howell, Newt, 107

I
Ickes, Harold, 103
Ingram, Joe, 11, 53, 60–61, **61**, 79,
    82–83, **83**, 86–87, 90–91, 93,
    96–97, 102, 104, 106–10, 113,
    125–26, 134, 137
International News Service, 84
Inter-racial Commission, 9
Iron Bridge Road, 24
Iron Curtain, 115
Italy, 96, 136

J
Jackson, J. J., 37–38, 41–42, 48,
    66, 109
Jackson, Ronald, 107
Jackson College, 5
Johnson, Guy, 54
Johnson, Herbert, 20, 117, 122
Johnson, Irena, 117, 119
Johnson, James "Digger," 21, 47–
    48, 52, 68, 76, 88, 90, 115, 121

Johnson, Lyman, 9
Johnson, Lyndon B., 132, 138
Johnson, Meade, 21, 47, 60, 85,
    94–95, 97–98, 128
Johnson, Milton "Toady," 60, 85
Jones, Samuel E., 25, 95
Jones, Thomas, 8

K
Kelley, John M., Jr., 64, 67, 74
Kelly, Carl, 60
Kelly, Don, **46**
Kennedy, John F., 138
Kennedy, Loyd "Papa"
    "Poppa," 38, 105–06, **106**,
    108–10, **110**, 111, 113
Kennedy, Rufus, 21, 94
Kennedy, Sam, 123
Kimes, Ed, 25, 119, 127
King, Martin Luther, Jr., 129
King, W. B., 107
Kingcaid, John A. "Punjab," 35,
    70, 91–92, 95, 108
Ku Klux Klan, 6–7, 40, 77;
    Maury Klan, 6

L
LaGuardia, Fiorello, 58
Lakeland Problem, 32
LaPointe, Lavala, 13, 15, 65
Latimer, Ira H., 58, 73–74
Lawrence, Charles, Jr., 115
Lawrenceburg, 62, 78, 79–81,
    89–90, 96, 98–99, 101–02, **102**,
    103, **104**, 105, 109, 111–12,
    124–25, 127–28, 135–38
Lawrence County, 1, 11, 62,
    79–82, 97, 126
Lawrence County Circuit Court,
    79, **94**; jury, 81–86, 90–91,
    93–94, 97–102, **102**, 103, 107,
    111
Lawrence County Courthouse,
    80, 83
Leary, Timothy, 130
Lee, Daisy, 38
Leftrick, Hiawatha, 42
Lentz, Curtis, 112
Lewis, Sinclair, 58
Lewisburg Highway, 8
Lewis County, 1
Lexington, Kentucky, 1
Lidice, Czech Republic, 99

Life Magazine, 70
Lillard, Robert, 136
Lion's Club, 108
Lockridge, Albert, 21
Lockridge, Calvin, 21–22, 26, 33, 36, **49**, 56, 67, 72, 85, 89, 98, 119, 128
Lockridge, Johnny "Hewe," 26, 35, 60, 85
Lockridge, Raymond, 21, 26, 33, 36, 50, 56, 60, 72, 85, 127–28
Loftin, Randolph, 108
Looby, Z. (Zebulon) Alexander, 51, 53–54, 56, 58, 61, **61**, 62, 72, 80, **82**, 83, 86, 88–93, 99–101, 103, 106–09, 111–13, 127, 136
Los Angeles, California, 116
Louisville Leader, 54
Lucille's Restaurant, 34
Lynching and Frame-up in Tennessee, 56

M
Macedonia, 20, 22, 42, 92
Main Street, 17–18, 20–21, 25, 27–28, 33, 38–39, 71, 85–87, 91, 93
Majestic Middle Tennessee Fall Tour, 132
Malcom X, 129
Malone, John, 71
Manila, Philippines, 115
Marlin, Sterling, 132
Marshall, Thurgood, 54, **55**, 56, 61, 65, 77–78, 80–81, 105–09, 111–13, 121, 127, 129, 137–38
Marshall County, 1, 54
Martin, James, 42, 53
Mason-Dixon line, 96
Matthews, Webster, 85, 95
Maury, Abram, 2
Maury County Bar Association, 127
Maury County Courthouse, **7,** 27, 42
Maury County Election Commission, 135
Maury County Grand Jury, 8; district jury, 107, 109–10
Maury Democrat, **53**, **83**
Maury Grays, 2
Mayes, Marcia, 35, 95
McAlister, Hill, 8

McCabe, Charles, 29
McCarthy, Joe, 120
McClain, Rose Ogilvie, 141–42
McCord, James, 23, 31, 45, 47, 58, 67, 86, 91, 113, 123–24
McDowell School, 141
McGavock family, 31
McGivens, John, 85, 88, 93, 101–04
McGlothlin, Mr., 112
McKissack, John, 53
Meharry Hospital, 48
Memphis, 12, 29, 59
Metropolitan Police District of Memphis, 29
Meyer, Agnes, 128–29
Michigan Chronicle, **141**
Middle Tennessee, 1–2, 6, 12, 30, 50, 55, 75, 78, 132, 139
Middle Tennessee State University, 142
Miles, Lewis, 85
Miles, Paul, 60, 85
Milwaukee, Wisconsin, 57
Mink Slide, 16–23, 25–28, 31, 33–34, **34,** 36, **36,** 39–41, **43–44,** 46, 48, 53–55, 56, 58, 64, **66,** 67–71, 74–80, 86–92, **92,** 93, **94,** 95, 97–98, 100, 105, 108, 111, 113, 115, 117, 120–23, 127–28, 133–37, 140, 142. *See also* Eighth Street
Minneapolis-St. Paul, Minnesota, 57
Minor, Robert, 56, 58
Mobile, Alabama, 116
Monroe, Georgia, 115, 117
Monsanto, 3, 32, 56, 108, 122, 131
Moore, Henry Carl, 8–9
Moore, John Trotwood, 1
Moore, Joseph, 58
Moore, Lady Ann, 8
Moore (Lauris) family, 8
Morgan, John, 48, 70, 121, 124
Morton, Cemora. *See* Newsome, Cemora
Morton, James, Sr., 16, 18, 22–23, 25–26, 34–36, 41, 45, **46,** 50, 52–53, 60, 65, 67–68, 70–71, 73, 76, 85–86, 89, 91, 93, 95–98, 100, 104, 120–21, 128, 137
Morton, Mary, 25–26, 35–36, 40, 52, 95, 128, 137

Morton children, 26
Morton Funeral Home, 17, 40, **40,** 41, 60, 65, **66,** 67, 71, 121, 134
Mt. Pleasant, 5, 21, 52, 142
Mt. Pleasant Pike, 42
Mule Day, 4, **4,** 5, 9, 45, 132
Murfreesboro, 137
Murphy, Frank, 108
Murray, Milton, 25, 112, 121, 128
Myers, Julian, 34

N
NASCAR, 132
Nashville, 1, 2, 8, 15, 24, 30, 42, 48, **49,** 50, 52–53, 58–59, 62–64, 70, 74–75, 80, 95, 97, 103–04, 107, 111–13, 123, 135–38
Nashville Banner, 8, 35, **46,** 48, **49, 57, 61,** 70–71, 77, **78,** 105, **106,** 136
Nashville Bar Association, 136
Nashville City Council, 136
Nashville Globe, 59, 76, 101, 103
Nashville Grand Jury. *See* Grand Jury for the Middle District of Tennessee
Nashville Metropolitan, 136–37
Nashville Pike, 24
Nashville Tennessean. See Tennessean
Nashville Young Men's Hebrew Association, 72
National Association for the Advancement of Colored People, 9, 51, 53–54, 56, 58, 60, 64–65, 73, 83, 91, 102, 112–13, 115, 120–21, 126–27, 138; National Legal Committee, 51; Thirty-seventh Conference, 56
National Carbon plant, 56
National Committee for Justice in Columbia, Tennessee, 57–58
National Federation for Constitutional Liberties, 56, 58
National Negro Conference, 56
Neely, Tommy, 24
Neuberger, Samuel, 58
Newburn, George, 25, 95, 140–41
New Jersey, 138
New Republic, the, 55
Newsome, Cemora, 121, 137

New York, New York, 51, 109
New York Committee, 54
New York Giants, 92
New York Herald Tribune, 84, 96
New York Times, 136
Nicholson, George, 24, 36
Noles, E. B., 26, 31–32, **44**, 45
Norfolk, Virginia, 56
North Africa, 20, 25
Nuremburg Trials, 99, 101

O

Odd Fellow's Hall, 33, 38, 72, 76
Ohio State Law School, 60
O'Rear, Greg, 92
Osborn, Z. Thomas, Jr.,
    "Tommy," 64, 69, 73–74
Overton family, 31

P

Paris, France, 115
Parsons, Clifford, 109
Peck, Myron, 32
Pennington, Ed, 48
Peppers, Hannah, 16–17, 94, 98,
    139, **141**
Philadelphia, Pennsylvania, 116
Pigg, Willie. *See* Pillow, William
    "Rooster Bill"
Pillow, Gideon, 3
Pillow, William "Rooster Bill,"
    38, 60–61, 85, 88, 105–06, **106**,
    108–10, **110**, 111
Pittsburgh Courier, 54, 80, 84
Pogue, Jim Buck, 111, 113, 139
Polk, James K., 2, 132
Porter-Walker Hardware, 19
Post No. One of the Global War
    Veterans, 117
Powell, Adam C., Jr., 58
Prewitt, Alan, 113
Princess Theater, 20

R

Ransom, Leon A., 56, 60, **61**, 80,
    82, 87, 89, 95–97, 103, 107,
    127, 138
Raymond, Harry, 55, 105–06,
    111–12
Reconstruction, 58
Red Cross, 17
Reeves, George I., 22, 28, 90
Rehnquist, William Hubbs, 138

Republican Party, 112
Revolutionary War, 1
Reynolds, Hollis, 34, 38, **39**,
Richardson, J. F., 64
Richardson, Sam, 22–23, 26–28,
    85
Rickey, Branch, 130
Ritz Cafe, 88
Riverside, 21, 111
Robinson, Jackie, 130
Rochester, New York, 56
Roe v. Wade, 138
Rogers, Will, 4
Roosevelt, Eleanor, 57–58, 77
Roosevelt, Franklin, 115
Rosenberg family, 120
Royal Dukes Club, 20
Russell, J. W., 108
Ryan, V. K., 25, 117, **118**, 121–22

S

Sanders, Shalonda, **141**
Sanders, Theresa, **141**
Saturn, 131–32, 140
Schofield, Henry, 70
Scott, Early, 60, 85
Scottsboro, Alabama, 102, 120
Scribner, James, 21
Scribner, Roy, 19, 60, 71
"Servants . . . Not Lords," 30
Seventh Street, 27
Sharpgon, Alldie, 26, 87
Shaw, T. I., 89, 112
Sheean, Vincent, 96–97, 101–03,
    129, 136
Shelby County, 3
Shelton, Hugh T., 81, 86, 88,
    90–91, 94–95, 98, 100
Shirley, William, 3
Shyers, Earlie, 20, 34, 87–88,
    98–99
Shyers, Irena, 20
Shyers, Lee Andrew, 20, 34,
    87–88, 98–99
Smith, Ernest F., 47, 67–68, 123
Smith, Charlie "Charley," 34, 38,
    85
Smith, Turner, 75
Smith, W. E., 112
Smith v. Allwright, 138
Smitty, Mr., 89
Snipes, Horace, 89
Sons of Confederate Veterans, 133

Southern Conference for Human
    Welfare, 54, 56, 67, 74
Southern Regional Council, 54,
    128–29; *New South*, 54
South Carolina, 115
Spanish-American War, 17
Spring Hill, 24, 95, 100, 131, 139
Squires, Jim, 122
Staggs, W. E., 82, 93
Stalin, Joseph, 115, 120
State of Tennessee (prosecution),
    53, 60, 79, 81, 82, 84–85,
    89–90, 96–100, 105, 109, 126
*State of Tennessee v. Saul Blair, et
    al.*, 60
*State of Tennessee v. Sol Blair, et
    al.*, 79
*State of Tennessee v. William
    Pillow and Loyd Kennedy*, 60
Stephenson, Gladys, 11–12, **12**,
    13–20, 22, 25, 55–56, 60, 65, 68,
    72, 76, 86–87, 90, 94, 97, 100,
    104, 110, 117, 119, 124, 127–28,
    139, **141**
Stephenson, James "Junior"
    Jimmy" "June Pie," 11, **12**,
    13–14, **14**, 15–20, 22–25, 36,
    50, 55–56, 60, 65, 68, 72, 76,
    86–87, 90, 94–97, 100, 104,
    110, 116–17, 119, 124, 127–28,
    139, **141**
Stephenson, John, 12, **12**, 13
Stephenson, Lelia, **12**
Stephenson family, 12–13
Stephenson's Drug Store, 14
Stewart, Napolean, 47–48, 60,
    67, 73, 85, 91, 122
Stofel, Bernard, 19, 22, 27–28, 85,
    121–22
Swann, Ulna, 23

T

Tapley, Bayard, 58
Taylor, Joe, 61
Tellico, 2
Tennessean, 8, 35, 59, 70–71, 105,
    135
Tennessee Department of
    Finance and Taxation,
    Franchise and Excise Tax
    Division, 134
Tennessee Department of Safety,
    135

Tennessee Highway Patrol,
28–30, 32–41, **41**, 42, **44**, 45,
46, 48, **49**, 59, **66**, 67–68, **68**,
69–72, 75–77, 88–89, 91–92,
92, 95, 105, 108, 110–12, 121,
123–24; Middle Tennessee
Division, 37
Tennessee River, 1
Tennessee State Guard, 28, 30,
31, 32, 34, **35–36**, 36–37, 39,
41–42, 45, 50, **66**, 67, 69, **70**,
74, 77, 123–24, 134; Second
Brigade (Middle Tennessee),
30; Second Regiment, 32, 39;
Tenth Regiment, 32
Tennessee State Guard Act of
1941, 30
Tennessee State Legislature, 2
Tennessee Supreme Court, 113
Tennessee Valley Authority, 5,
89, 131
Tenth Machine Gun & Chemical
Company, 32
Thompson, Beasley, 71
Thompson, John, 71
Time, 41, 96, 107, 122
Tilly, M. E., 129
Tobacco Road, 9
Tobias, Channing, 57
Toledo, Ohio, 57
Tomlin, Earl, 21, 60
Turner, Nat, 119
Turner, W. B., 8
Turner, William, 2
Truman, Harry S., 54, 63, 74, 78,
112, 129
Twenty-second Tennessee State
Judicial District, 133

U

U.S. Army, 13, 25, 123; Artillery
Corps, 25; Signal Corps, 13
U.S. Congress, 112

U.S. Constitution, 64, 113;
Fourteenth Amendment, 64
U.S. Court of Appeals, 138
U.S. Department of Justice, 58,
63–64, 67, 74–75, 78, 112
U.S. Marine Corps, 20
U.S. National Guard, 30, 125
U.S. Navy, 12–14, 51
U.S. Supreme Court, 63, 138
Underwood, J. J., 12, 16, 18,
21–25, 28, 34–37, 39, 42,
44–45, 47–48, 52, 65, 68,
71–73, 86–87, 89–91, 94–95,
97–100, 108, 117, 120, 122–24,
135
Underwood, J. J., Jr., "Jimmy,"
48, 96, 120, 135
Underwood, S. W., 95
Union Station, 24
United Press, 35, 70, 84
United States, 2, 106, 115–16,
119, 120, 126, 128
University of Kentucky, 9
University of Maryland, 138
University of Missouri, 138
University of Tennessee, 51, 138;
University of Tennessee Law
School, 51
USS *Prometheus*, 13

V

Vanderbilt University, 30
Veteran's Administration
hospital, 12
Victor plant, 56
Vietnam, 130
Virginia, 1
V-J Day, 79, 115, **118**

W

Wagner, Orville, **92**
Wallace, George, 129
Waltrip, Fred, 31, 108

Warren, Earl, 138
Washington, Booker T., 53
Washington, D.C., 2, 56, 59, 64,
74–75, 137–38
Washington Afro-American, 67, **68**
Washington Post, 128, 136
Watkins, George, 89
Watkins, Sam, 3
Wayne County, 11
Weaver, Maurice Maxwell, 51–54,
56, 60, **61**, 62–63, 70, 72–73, 77,
80, **82**, 83, 86–93, 96–99, 101,
103, 106–09, 112–13, 127, 136–37
Weaver, Virginia, 80–81, 112,
128, 136–37
West End, 19
White, Dave, 44, 48, 108, 122
White, Walter, 51, 54, 58, 60, 112,
121
Wiley, Luther, 7–8,
William, Eugene "Gene," 60, 85, 95
Williams, Avon, 136
Williams, Joe, 19, 60
Williams, Juan, 112–13
Williamson County, 2, 61, 132
Wills, Ridley, II, **4, 7, 80**
Wilsford, Will, 27–28, 60, 85–86,
93, 98, 100, 103–04
Wilson, Victor, 39, 122
WLAC, 50
Woodard, Issac, 115
Woodard Academy, 5
Woodland Street, 17, 27, 33–34,
42, **44**, 92, 134
World War I, 16, 30, 117, 135
World War II, 4–5, 12, 29–30, 79,
99, 109, 113, 115–17, 119, 126,
140
Wright, Albert, 34, 38
Wyoming, 26

Y

Youngstown, Ohio, 57

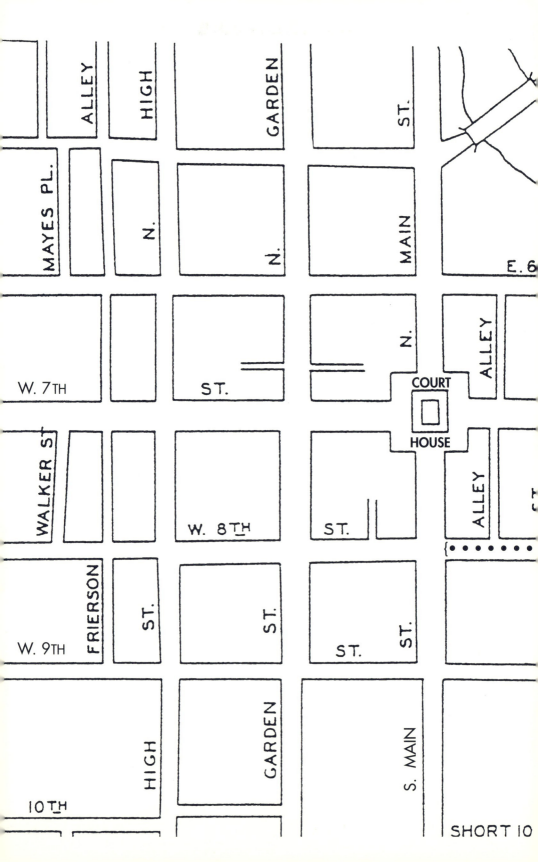